Hunger and Thirst

Food is our marrow. From the ghost pears of an absent father to the left-over custard pudding with raisins served to Wilbur the pig, you'll want to savor this collection slowly, and when you think you might burst, push back from the table and watch the moon rising round as dinner mint, the moon—just as the old poet promised—creeping up over the banquet to the bubbling of bassoons.

Sandra Alcosser
Except by Nature

From percolator to pancake this ambrosial collection nurtures and stirs the senses and cooks up a fine redeemer. Soulfully scrumptious!

Donna Kane
Powell's Books, Portland, OR

The stellar contributions to Hunger and Thirst concern themselves with our collective quest to meet the vital necessities mentioned in the title, but this collection is more than satisfying an appetite or slaking a thirst; in prose and poetry, these writers locate the varied ways we come together to talk, feel, and share in that ineffable quality of being human. These are stories for all of us who hunger and thirst to be part of something greater than ourselves alone, sitting at an empty table. This is a moving and splendidly varied collection.

Dennis G. Wills
D.G. Wills, La Jolla, CA

Hunger and Thirst
food literature

Editor
Nancy Cary

Co-editors
**June Cressy, Ella deCastro Baron,
Alys Masek, and Trissy McGhee**

**SD
CWP**

SAN DIEGO
CITY WORKS
PRESS

ISBN 978-0-9816020-4-2
Library of Congress Control Number: 2008902449

San Diego City Works Press is a non-profit press, funded by local writers and friends of the arts, committed to the publication of fiction, poetry, creative nonfiction, and art by members of the San Diego City College community and the community at large. For more about San Diego City Works Press please visit our website at www.cityworkspress.org.

San Diego City Works Press is extremely indebted to the American Federation of Teachers, Local 1931, without whose generous contribution and commitment to the arts this book would not be possible.

Cover Design: Rondi Vasquez
Production Editor: Will Dalrymple

Published in the United States by San Diego City Works Press, California
Printed in the United States of America

Contents

Eat, Memory

At the Kitchen Table

The Blessings of Dirty Work

Song

My Body Knows

A Little Poison, Along with the Sweetness

Recipes ❧

Acknowledgments

The editor and co-editors thank City Works Press for accepting our proposal. We also would like to thank San Diego City College's Jazz 88 (KSDS 88.3) for helping us promote this work. We appreciate the many amazing writers who submitted their writing and art to *Hunger and Thirst,* and want to give thanks to not only all of those we were able to include in the anthology, but also to all of the rest of you who responded to our call. Your stories, essays, poems, photos and art on themes of hunger and thirst will stay with us.

With five of us working together for a year on the book project, we had the usual life events occur along the way, sometimes bringing us great joy and energy, other times, need for support. Just to share, while we worked through the stages of collecting submissions, then reading and selecting, babies were born — Samaria, a sister for Asa and daughter for Ella and Chris; Trissy earned a contract teaching job at San Diego City College; a good friend to City Works Press and former dean Winston Butler became seriously ill with lung cancer; and the school year began and many of us became busy with our roles there. We met in most every coffee house and also our homes, which reminds me, without the enthusiastic support (most of the time) of our husbands, partners, children, dogs and cats, we wouldn't have this book to show. There are more to thank: City Works Press co-founder Kelly Mayhew for taking many weekend cell phone calls to answer production questions; Eden O'Grady for making copies, bringing coffee, and making me smile; Alys' husband Alan Merriam, who helped us through many eleventh-hour technical difficulties; and Tom Chartrand of www.peripheral-vision.org for helping with artistic improvements on select photographs. In addition, we appreciate the encouragement of our friends throughout the past year. One evening meeting in the Community Room at People's Natural Foods Market, we chanced upon their monthly art show and discovered our cover artist Kathryn Law. We can't imagine a more generous person, who offered her works for our cover and inside sections. She believes paintings and art should be available to people, affordable, so you can own them, trade them in for another. She was an inspiration right when we needed one!

Lastly, as editor, I want to especially thank these superwomen from my writing group, my co-editors: June Cressy—for her careful editor's eye and creative design of our original flyer; Ella deCastro Baron—for her bursts of creative energy and get-down work ethic that resulted in our first mock-ups of the cover, computer synthesis of the manuscript, and enthusiasm for our cover artist; Alys Masek—for her inviting and convincing letters of request to contributors such as to Barbara Kingsolver, for revision help on the introduction, and for her willingness to read through all kinds of food descriptions while faced with early pregnancy queasiness; and Trissy McGhee for hosting meetings, for her ideas about how-to-"grok"-what-we-got, and for her crazy heart that says yes to more than one creative project at a time. Because we all are writers ourselves and also passionate cooks and healthy gourmands, we each added our voice to the anthology. Bon appétit!

Introduction

In reading *Hunger and Thirst* our hope is that you discover pieces of your own story, meet people you already know, welcome new friends, taste again those dishes you remember, and thrill at new flavors. The response to our invitation for writing and art on the themes of hunger and thirst was like a community call for participation in one of our mother's auxiliary cookbooks. Writing poured in from neighbors, far and wide, some with recipes, others with reflections, inventions, and memories. We stood surprised and pleased to hear from so many, to receive their generosity and their urge to share their experiences. Many of the contributors, such as Barbara Kingsolver, Li-Young Lee, Edward Espe Brown, Denise Chavez, Marilyn Chin, and Kim Addonizio, are well-recognized in the writing world, yet their essays, poems, and stories arrived at our doorstep like letters from friends, happy to share their latest tales and familiar dishes.

ॐ

There is comfort in so many aspects of food: cooking, eating, and sharing, but also reading and remembering. When you read about food, you access that deep sensory memory of being back in the kitchen with someone you wiled away the hours with—maybe your grandma teaching you that when money and time are short, simple baking powder biscuits can save the day, or at least the meal. Perhaps it's your mom at your side, elbows deep into canning peaches, juice tickling down your wrists; or maybe dad is frying sweet, smoky sausage from his family's spaghetti recipe.

While food, cooking, and eating with loved ones brings comfort to many, we know discomfort—deep emotional pain—is the experience for others at the kitchen table.

The kitchen table itself is a shifting plane, where sometimes words are shared over food and drink, but just as often, food is chewed in stony silence; where at times eating could be communal, celebrated in praise, song and ode, other times it is cursed. For many, it has been better to excuse oneself from the table.

Many baby boomers of the 50s and 60s came from big families, ones that necessitated the chief cook—probably mom—digging in and cranking out meals. Cooking was labor, not find-the-gourmet-in-you fantasy that *Food Network* and other reality TV chef shows seem to inspire. Women's liberation and rising divorce in the late 60s and 70s sometimes meant a single parent and children eating at a smaller table or even alone. The refrigerator may have been nearly empty.

Many people have taken their ferocious appetite to be accepted and loved away from the table. Some hide in other rooms, while others escape, moving on to the tables of new friends, new lovers, and newly blended families. Some of the women writers in the anthology give voice to young women who deny themselves nourishment through healthy eating in order to have power over their lives. No longer connected to the sensual, eating becomes linked to a distorted perception of body image in the mirror.

For many, food embodies the narrative of loss and exile. Writers of our collection of food literature share images and stories of their ancestors, escaping from their homelands, bread in their pockets, never to return except in dreams or in their descendents' poems and memoirs. Conversely, leaving the familiar sometimes leads writers, their ancestors, their children, and fictional characters to the thrill of travel, to the move across country, to the start of a better life. The table becomes the palm of a hand, a blanket in the sand, a park bench seat. Even food itself becomes shared across new worlds; recipes become reinvented and newly discovered by others. For example, there is hummus—written about and spelled several different ways by writers—a delicacy; a quick-n-easy treat tossed in baskets at *Trader Joe's* or *Whole Foods Market* to serve last-minute guests; or, a nourishing staple—as vital as rice is for Asians—for daily diets or even to break religious fasts.

Whether it is our desire to be loved and accepted or our penchant to deny ourselves that natural want, we recognize the duality in our natures as we read the many ways people write about relationships and food. We may well enter this world at birth alone and leave it, a solitary figure, but in between, we make memories of eating with others. We can hardly speak of the themes of our lives—our families, our bodies, our discovery of sex, our lovers, our work, our art, our illnesses, our losses and death—without speaking of food.

Our connection to food is elemental and thus powerful. However, many of us rightly fear that we are becoming disconnected from our roots—both our food sources and our family histories and cultures. People are searching, looking for a way back to their collective connected source—however we individually or culturally see that path—not a sentimental angst, but a true spiritual quest to recognize our commonality. Co-editor and friend June Cressy recalls a Zen meal chant: "First, seventy-two labors brought us this food; we should know how it comes to us." She says the chant brings her out of a self-centered dream and into the recognition that nothing she does, such as eating what is in front of her, is done apart from the many. Speaking of the collective spirit, I am reminded of Edward Espe Brown's 1999 revised introduction to *The Tassajara Recipe Book,* where he speaks of all that goes on simultaneously around him. While he focuses on the work in front of him, he is mindful of the crew of people preparing food for the guests at his workshops. He says, "When I sit down to eat I feel so blessed and cared for. It seems like such a miracle that there is a place for me at the table and food appears.

"Someone has washed the produce, cut the vegetables, chopped, minced, diced, and sliced. The goodness of the food is also that someone has watched over the sautéing, the baking, the steaming and boiling. Someone has tasted and savored. You can taste it in the food. Someone cares."

૨૬

Barbara Kingsolver and Michael Pollan carry on the works of writers such as Rachel Carson, who in her seminal and lyrically titled *Silent Spring,* written in 1964, exposed the abuse of widespread pesticide use and activist Pete Singer, author of *Animal Liberation,* published in 1975, adopted in many college classrooms and still widely read and quoted by many dedicated people, working for the humane treatment of animals. Like these earlier writers, Kingsolver and Pollan are fiercely dedicated to bringing awareness to the dangers of losing our connection to our food sources—animals and plants—and to the land.

In *Hunger and Thirst* writers research and trace the agribusiness' direction. Once an icon of American society, the family farm has all but disappeared. Any American with Midwest roots probably knows of at least one farming family that has had to declare bankruptcy.

Then there is America's appetite for convenience—the ability to buy anything at any time almost anywhere. Thus we have the strawberry—at one time a welcome call to early summer, luscious, juicy, and sweet—now bred to survive long plane rides across continents, and stacked like blocks year-round at your nearby big-box grocery store. As a reaction to the loss of biodiversity of fruits and vegetables, the industrialization of food production, and the globalization of the food industry, some of our anthology writers turn back to the garden, dig in the dirt, and plant their own seeds. Others will make their weekly trek to the local Farmers' Markets and sing to the onion and the peach.

૨૬

Those of us who like to cook understand that in the doing of it, we find ourselves transported in the moment. We step away from the computer, make the short walk to the garden, and breathe in fresh air as we cut cilantro or thyme from the garden. Maybe we're side-tracked and pull a few weeds, bask in the sun, hope for a bird at the birdbath, watch the cat studying the birdfeeder. Back in the kitchen, we begin the ritual that signifies the end of the work day: we chop and sauté broccoli in olive oil, appreciating the bright green — the magic of heat and oil. Tear leftover French bread into crumbs, toast and sprinkle over the broccoli with shaved parmesan, and a sprinkle of sea salt and ground pepper. Like any performance artist, the cook knows the creation is temporal, what is cooked will soon be eaten and gone, but we cooks are satisfied nonetheless. Of course there will be dishes to clean. Maybe not by the cook.

֍

The five editors of *Hunger and Thirst*, Nancy Cary, June Cressy, Ella deCastro Baron, Alys Masek, and Trissy McGhee, came together as a writing group, some of us published in poetry, others in prose. We met in the usual coffee shops and in our homes, pulling together serendipitous meals from the cupboard and fridge. As we got to know each other, we discovered a shared passion for food and for reading and writing about food. Several of us were devotees of Laurie Colwin's quirky, funny food essays found in her classic collections *Home Cooking* and *More Home Cooking*. To read her essays is to experience the infinite comfort that food writing can offer — the literary equivalent of coming into a warm house on a cold, wet day and finding a grilled cheese sandwich and hot tomato soup.

Over time we experienced and shared the deeper ways in which food has nurtured us in times of crisis and loss: June feeding applesauce, teaspoon by teaspoon to her dying mother; Trissy baking her Gram's shortbread to feed her relatives after the untimely death of a young cousin; Alys sustaining herself through the early weeks of a difficult pregnancy with spicy stir-fried rice noodles; Ella, a long-time vegan, challenged to return to eating meat for the needed protein that would enable her babies to thrive on her breast milk.

In the fall of 2006, I began experimenting with some new assignments in a creative nonfiction course that I teach at San Diego City College. I offered the theme of work as one possible strand or segment for the braided essay. As we explored additional possibilities for up to three to five strands, I encouraged them to bring in the sensory world. I often give them seemingly non-related free writes to spark possible ideas for writing. So, I asked them to write something about cooking. Did they cook for money? Eat in or eat out? Who taught them to cook and what did they remember? I recalled professor and nationally known poet Marilyn Chin of the MFA program at San Diego State University, praising her writing students when they brought food into their poems. Food is family. Food is culture.

One of my students Mike Ferrill took off with that assignment, crafting it into a braided-memoir essay that led him back into the kitchen of his childhood, restaurant and deli work, places where he experienced love and then loss. I would like to say that I helped lead him to some discoveries with that assignment, but truth be told, he, my student, inspired me: I started to think about writing a food book someday.

During that same semester while my students wrote that braided essay, after going in for a routine mammogram, I was diagnosed with breast cancer.

I went to work that week but considered not showing up by Wednesday night to our writing group meeting. Tired from the first few days of keeping up a brave face, I felt my confidence plummet. I wanted to hide under the house like a wounded cat. Instead I climbed the stairs of the old landmark coffee house, and found some of my writing friends already huddled with notebooks and coffee mugs around an oval coffee table. I noticed a couple of them eating dinner. I didn't want to spoil their appetites, but I interrupted the start of the workshop and told them the news. They listened and never turned their eyes away from mine, so I wouldn't feel alone.

And those girls have never let me down. Not to this day. I had surgery near the end of the semester, missing the last three weeks. Once home, not only was my sister there with her homemade chicken matzo ball soup, but each one of my writing group friends came to my door, Ella with her freshly baked vegan banana bread; Trissy with her green dahl; Alys with Vietnamese chicken curry and rice; and June with her package of pfeffernüsse cookies. Oh, and they brought books for me to read. They didn't just show up once either. They and countless other friends kept me company day after day until I grew stronger. They drank tea and took walks with me. They came with me to doctor appointments and wrote notes when I was too frightened to listen. It was like having an old-time church circle, a small town community of dear friends, the ones who show up at your door with a casserole, warm loaf of bread wrapped in a tea towel, a frosted spice cake for your family.

I fantasized about taking them all to brunch, my trusty writer friends, others in my circle, including colleagues, students, other friends, and, of course, family. I pictured us at a sunny, quiet restaurant, where we'd sit at a long table with white cloth napkins, and I'd make a speech about gratitude and all. Instead I got the idea to launch a book proposal, an anthology about food, a literary collection that would be a way to let others experience what I had in having these women bring me their cooking and more. I wanted writers and artists to bring their prose, poems, and art to our doorstep, to our tables. I knew that I wanted food as a metaphor and not just a pretty one. Make it messy like cooking, like life. So I had the theme of hunger. Then when we met, they threw the rest in the pot. So here it is: *Hunger and Thirst*.

Nancy Cary, Editor
March 2008

Eat, Memory

Ivy Warwick
Chocolate Hearts

They could be bought
only in Pomerania;
my cousin sent them to me,
a special food parcel to Warsaw.

I'd eat three at once,
luscious and rich brown,
then begin to ration the supply:
one heart a day, in small bites.

Sometimes I'd moisten
one corner in chamomile tea.
So what if father laughed
that I ate like a grandma.

Ah, and the soft
heart of the heart!
If you have dreams,
you lead a double life.

Now it's another century.
A doctor tells me I shouldn't
eat chocolate. As if it
could ever be the same.

Doctor, I am in danger.
I cannot tell truth from memory.
Everything has changed.
They no longer make

those hearts. Perhaps only I
still remember them,
delirious gingerbread
dipped in dark delight—

Memory can lie. I could say,
"The chocolate was bitter
as tears, the hunger
could not be filled—"

I could recite
schoolbook rhymes.

They smelled of lime-blossom
honey, right through the
cellophane, the stamp
with the price.

Everything is symbolic,
but also it's real. The way I
kiss, slowly, in small bites.
The way I tell my story,

dipping one corner in chamomile,
the other in history—
and the silence
in Pomeranian clouds.

Li-Young Lee

Eating Together

In the steamer is the trout
seasoned with slivers of ginger,
two sprigs of green onion, and sesame oil.
We shall eat it with rice for lunch,
brothers, sister, my mother who will
taste the sweetest meat of the head,
holding it between her fingers
deftly, the way my father did
weeks ago. Then he lay down
to sleep like a snow-covered road
winding through pines older than him,
without any travelers, and lonely for no one.

Li-Young Lee
Eating Alone

I've pulled the last of the year's young onions.
The garden is bare now. The ground is cold,
brown and old. What is left of the day flames
in the maples at the corner of my
eye. I turn, a cardinal vanishes.
By the cellar door, I wash the onions,
then drink from the icy metal spigot.

Once, years back, I walked beside my father
among the windfall pears. I can't recall
our words. We may have strolled in silence. But
I still see him bend that way—left hand braced
on knee, creaky—to lift and hold to my
eye a rotten pear. In it, a hornet
spun crazily, glazed in slow, glistening juice.

It was my father I saw this morning
waving to me from the trees. I almost
called to him, until I came close enough
to see the shovel, leaning where I had
left it, in the flickering, deep green shade.

White rice steaming, almost done. Sweet green peas
fried in onions. Shrimp braised in sesame
oil and garlic. And my own loneliness.
What more could I, a young man, want.

Sharon DeBusk
Pear Tree

Beth Levitan

Cinnamon Twists

The recipe is from Russia, passed from my Bobey's Bobey to her, and from my Bobey to me. New Yorkers call it rugalach, a Yiddish name that is rough in my mouth. My family, assimilated into the hills of New England, but still close to the sea that brought us here, we call them twists. Wrapped in silver foil that is crumpled at the ends, under layers of waxed paper, rows and stacks of cinnamon twists, coils of sugar and love and warmth and memory.

Under a fluorescent light, my mother sits at Bobey's table, the one that folds out by the stove, her cigarette lacing, teasing Bobey that her coffee is strong enough to stand the spoon, and wetting her fingertip for stray sugar on the plate. Overhead a fat plastic chef on the wall counts passing minutes with a red second hand. Outside the foghorn repeats, barely audible through closed windows. The coffee is hot and the milk is cold, and I am the child in the corner, quietly busy.

I eat each one slowly, starting with the pointed end, the one that goes against the pan to hold it all together, uncoiling the dough bit by bit, one quarter turn at a time, until what's left is so small I have to eat half and half again. The smell of salt air mixed with cinnamon, mushrooms, coffee; the rough black planks of the back porch floor; slippery glass doorknobs; how the trunk of wisteria crossed the window by the sink; all this comes to me now, unleashed in my kitchen as I taste the first batch, licking sugar and cinnamon from my fingers, unwinding, moving toward the center where the coil ends, and the last raisin hides.

Yeast is the magic ingredient in these, alive and complex. Bobey used white flour and white sugar; I use whole wheat flour and organic cane sugar. My mother insists that these changes make my cinnamon twists not quite right, but before white flour, brown; before cane sugar, beets. What was baking powder in 1720? Who was that woman who looks a little like us all, who taught her daughter to press out the dough, cut it into triangles, make peace at all costs?

I bake cinnamon twists for winter solstice. "This is a Jewish family recipe," I say, to those who might think they're for Christmas. "From Russia," I say, "Lithuania, from my grandmother." Wedding rings in a cup on the counter, floury hands and apron, tin cookie sheets and cooling racks on every flat surface, my west coast kitchen fills with a fuchsia glow, and the smell of Bobey's Body Satinee.

Each time I move my home, I find myself a few blocks closer to the sea. Remembering Bobey in her kitchen, I invite the salt air into mine. Peeling sugar and butter off my hands, I open the windows and bake and bake until dozens of cinnamon twists cool on the counter and the table and on the shelf over the stove, and the miles between San Francisco and the North Shore of Massachusetts are littered with sand and cinnamon and hot fat raisins. Wrapped first in waxed paper, then aluminum foil, and finally tied with recycled ribbon and jute string, each package holds yards of coiled sweetness ready to spring.

Ray Trautman
Cinnamon Twists

Beth Levitan

❧ Bobey's Cinnamon Twists

1 stick plus 1 T cold butter
2 cups (scant) whole wheat flour (not pastry flour)
1 T dry yeast dissolved in ¼ C warm water until foamy
2 eggs, beaten
cinnamon
white sugar
raisins, chopped walnuts

In a large bowl, cut the butter into the flour to small pieces.
Pour the beaten eggs into a well in the center.
Mix the foaming yeast mixture into eggs, stirring with a fork until blended.
Then stir in larger circles to incorporate the flour.
Mix and then knead the dough to an even consistency.
Form the dough into a ball, wrap it closely in waxed paper and refrigerate for 2 hours or overnight.

Preheat oven to 350 degrees.
In a jar, mix together 1 cup sugar and 3 T ground cinnamon.
With a sharp knife, divide the chilled dough into three or four parts.

Sprinkle some of the sugar and cinnamon mixture over a pastry board or clean counter top.
Form each section into a thick log and roll it in the sugar mixture.
Turn and press several times, lengthening the log and rolling until it is about 2" in diameter and covered with cinnamon and sugar.
Press into a long flat shape about 3-4 inches wide and ¼" thick.

Sprinkle with raisins and chopped nuts.

Press a large knife blade into the dough to cut it into triangles.

Beginning with the wide end of each triangle, roll it toward the pointed end, tucking in raisins and walnuts as you go.

Roll very lightly once more in cinnamon and sugar and place on an ungreased baking sheet, tucking the pointed end underneath. Arrange in rows, filling the cookie sheet.

Bake 20 minutes until brown. Remove immediately to racks to cool.

Scrape the pan with a spatula and fill again.

Makes about 4 dozen.

Denise Chávez

Manteca Vieja

Sylvia Bejarano, a salesperson at the local Hertz Rent A Car at the Hilton Hotel in Las Cruces, sees me fairly often and asks me what I have been working on.

"A book on tacos," I tell her.

"Tacos? Tacos!"

I knew that Sylvia would like the idea. There hasn't been one person who hasn't liked the idea of a book about tacos.

"I have the secret of good tacos," Sylvia said with surety.

"What's that?" I asked curiously.

"Manteca vieja," Sylvia said with delight and consummate understanding.

Manteca vieja? The phrase alone conjured up Mother's tinita, her silver metal grease container she always had on top of her stove. It held her leftover grease, the savory bacon drippings and tasty, congealed hamburger fat, and anything else that constituted re-usable oil.

I hadn't thought of my Mother's silver metal tinita in years. Years! It was always a little bit greasy on the outside, and when I did the dishes I always first wiped down the stove and then the tinita, carefully. I remembered how my Mother re-used her oil and fat. What ever happened to the tinita?

All these thoughts came to me in a sudden flash. Suddenly I was back in the basement of the Hilton filling out car rental information as Sylvia expounded on the merits of manteca vieja.

"If you want a really tasty taco, fry it in manteca vieja."

"Manteca vieja?"

"Tacos taste better cooked in manteca vieja, old oil. I keep it and use it all: bacon grease, taco grease, lard. It's good to use for tamales, you blend in the old oil for flavor. Be sure and skim the top."

I understood what she meant. Our Mothers knew the merit of saving this tasty grease and re-using it to savor our food. This manteca vieja went into the frijoles, the tamales and the stews.

I was a vegetarian for many years, still am in my mind, save for the occasional hot dog, hamburger, taco or the holy albóndigas, sacred meatballs, that our nearby pueblo of Tortugas makes each year and shares with the public for the feast day of Our Lady of Guadalupe.

In addition to these unparalleled meatballs, I will always eat my own tacos. I often eschew a hot dog or hamburger, nearly always avoid chicken and turkey, rarely can eat eggs ("too feather-y") and won't have anything to do with steaks — they have no allure for me — but a good taco is not to be passed up, especially if they are your own family's recipes and you knew the Madrina del Taco, La Mera Mera, the One and Only, and that woman happened to be your own Mother.

I believe Sylvia about the manteca vieja. Sadly, I think few people I know have a tinita of grease on their stove anymore. What happened to that tradition? Is saving manteca vieja a thing of the past? Do certain cultures save more grease and reuse it more than other cultures? I've been taught not to fear grease, and yet I've moved away from manteca vieja to my special health-food store canola oil.

I ponder the unspeakable. I've never saved any kind of grease, ever!

❧

My husband, Daniel, likes to tell the story of one of our dates. It had to be one of our first dates, if not the first. I was living in Santa Fe then, and one night he came over. I reported to him that I had a clogged kitchen drain and I wondered if he could help me out. It never occurred to me that he was virtually a stranger and that I had no business asking for help of such a personal nature. But I did, and maybe this is what endeared me to him.

"Taco grease," I stated with absolute calm as he hunched down in front of the sink and started working on the clogged drainpipe.

"Taco grease? You put taco grease down the sink?" he said, only slightly raising his voice. He seemed relatively calm.

For some reason I had decided to throw the taco grease in the sink. Don't ask me why. I haven't done it since then.

"Yeah, taco grease," I said, apologetically. Cold taco grease converts into a nasty oily white film. No doubt some meat particles were stuck in there as well. I had assigned him an unpleasant task, but he was up to it. I liked that.

I appreciated the fact that the man didn't flinch when I reported the cause of the problem. Most men would have run then, but no, Daniel stayed and has continued to assist me in the many and myriad dramas of domestic life that have ensued over the years: countless mice and birds we've had to chase down in the middle of the groggy night, gifts from our two thoughtful cats; a visiting rat we could never catch that we named Rat-iel, an unwanted adoptee we came to know and love, who lived in our stove for several months and grew to gigantic proportions when I left bananas and nuts out for him "so he wouldn't starve"; an army of insects of all types and sizes that have wandered into our home and have been greeted with my ear-piercing screams: centipedes, worms, flying roaches, bees, and once, a bat that took shelter on the screen door to the back yard. We've had emergency fires and power outages, and once had to vacate our house for four days after a particularly virulent bug spraying rendered the house uninhabitable. I knew when I saw the bug man's hand with several missing fingers and several gnarled remaining claw-like digits that it was a bad omen to have called the exterminators.

❧

We've had taco disasters and grease spillage; we've burned ourselves, but not too badly. My friend and fellow writer Melissa Flores told me about a friend of her mother's who survived a taco grease fire and still lives with badly scarred reddish arms. Consequently, Mrs. Flores rarely makes tacos and when she does, she leans out far and virtually flings the taco into the pan with the oil. I don't blame her.

THINGS THAT HAVE LEFT ME WITH LONGING

The memory of my Mother's arroz
The memory of my Mother's homemade pan
The memory of my Mother's fluffy sopaipillas
My memory of my Granma's Pasta as made by my Mother

UNANSWERED QUESTIONS

The Great Debate: the benefits of lard vs. cooking oil?
Rolled or folded?
Longhorn or Monterey Jack?
Red or green?

FOOD TABOOS

Overly aggressive mashing up of fried eggs
Too much pepper
Too much salt
Being ungracious and not hospitable to guests
Not feeding people when they're hungry
Food snobbery
Choking while eating
Talking while eating
Not having enough food. Food was richness to my Mother. To have a refrigerator full of food and a new dress from the United Department Store was paradise to her, a sign of sure wealth and abundant blessing.

Sonya Huber

The God of Hunger

My grandfather ate out of the garbage; this fact was fixed in my mind's eye well before I understood anything about the Second World War. He fished for curled ribbons of potato peel, green with rot, black with the cloudy furze of mold, angry with the poisoned nubs of purple eyes. He choked them down as he walked northwest through Europe toward home, fleeing the Eastern Front; as a child, I imagined him striding across a map, finding garbage to eat as a sort of Easter Egg hunt along a board-game map with squares blocked out to mark his progress. He and his iron stomach returned. He fathered my mother, and then he died, and then I was born to imagine him eating those curled ribbons, to fear the malignancy of half-turned potatoes.

Before I was born, my mother was a child with my face. She learned to eat: a slice of bread, spread thick with lard, was a delicacy, and even more so if it glistened with dark bits of cooked fat. At this strange table, no one ate until the father picked up his spoon. Bones were grabbed and sucked clean of marrow, and a soup was made of the blood of a goose, stuck in the skull with a knitting needle and drained. The fatty gristle on a piece of meat was chewed like a luscious wad of bubblegum. That was the table where one's value as a kitchen goddess was shown by the skill at wielding a knife, the goal being to slice bread so thin that sunlight showed through its porous surface. In that strange house, my grandfather learned that a jar of rotten pears had been tossed on the trash heap.

Alarmed, compelled, he rescued them, peeled off the mold with a knife, and ate them, risking bacteria and death to appease the god of hunger.

I tasted history first through the way my mother ate: attacking the shiny leavings of meat on our plates, frying every bit of spare egg-and-flour breading after the pork chops were cooked, treasuring the burned *schmaltz* that remained in the frying pan after the meat and potatoes were served. I didn't like rubbery fat. I gagged on the gristle of steak, repulsed at the way tough meat scowled in my mouth, determined to outlast any attack, to rake its fingers inside me, to survive intact. "Why do you *eat* like that?" I asked her, and she invoked the praise-song of meat-ends and discarded bits.

My mother, transplanted from Europe, will drive an hour through the maze of shiny Midwestern strip malls to buy a decent loaf of bread, the kind with a surface lined and creased like a face. When she's paid for a dense loaf, she holds it in her arms as if it were a child, cradling it, feeling the living heft of it. It can't have ever been touched by plastic, she says, because that suffocates the dough.

"Bread is my religion," she says.

Rolf Abrahamson, a Jewish boy from my mother's town, knew this religion. As a teenager, he survived a circuit through the Nazi death camps only to be sent back to Bochum in northwest Germany in the fall of 1944 to work in a grenade factory. After the bombs lit the air, Rolf and the other prisoners were sent to find the un-detonated bombs. He poked through dusty rubble with a broomstick. When he discovered a bomb's metallic hull, he nudged it. If the world did not vanish in a flash of hot light, he was paid with a piece of bread.

Al Zolynas
Bread, In Gratitude

> ...seventy-two labors brought us this food.
> *—from a Zen meal chant*

The parcel on our doorstep has baked
all afternoon in the Southern California sun.
It's from the folks, from their boundless
generosity: two new shirts, two blouses for Arlie,
three towels, two bags of hazelnuts—and
a loaf of dark Lithuanian rye
(bread of my youth, bread of my ancestors!)
wrapped in a paper towel held
by an exhausted rubber band.
The loaf is dry as an adobe brick, and almost as heavy.

We appreciate my mother's endless supply
of clothes and towels and hazelnuts, but
I love this bread, this hard dry loaf,
seemingly stale and beyond saving,
but which I'll resurrect with the old peasant
trick of a sprinkling of water
and ten minutes in a warm oven.

This bread has traveled from Florida and,
before that, from Chicago, from
the Lithuanian Bakery on the Southside, and
before that from fields of rye and wheat
somewhere in the Midwest, and
before that, from a cultural recipe who knows how old.

Miracle bread, never molding,
never too old to rise again,

re-born now on our table among
the cheeses, eggs, jams — and the ghosts of
all the hands that brought them here.

Sue Parman

Eggs a la Goldenrod

"When my mother died last month, she left behind an unopened *Joy of Cooking* (1953 edition) and a well-thumbed *I Hate to Cook Book*. She also left a journal that included a recipe she learned in the fifth grade for Eggs a la Goldenrod.

My sister and I, reading from the journal and stopping frequently to cry and reminisce, knew about Eggs a la Goldenrod, of course. Eggs a la Goldenrod played a central role in narratives about our parents' early marriage when the wealthy debutante (our mother) married the poor but idealistic conscientious objector (our father) and went to live in a Quonset Hut in Iowa City, where the conscientious objector spent seven years trying to justify Herbert of Cherbury as a worthy topic of a doctoral dissertation, only to give up and join the Establishment working for the Atomic Energy Commission in New Mexico. In addition to typing theses and having babies, our mother, as the woman of the house, was expected to cook brilliant meals on a rock-bottom budget. Her solution was to cook Eggs a la Goldenrod.

Again and again.

In my first memories of this story, I imagined Eggs a la Goldenrod to be a complicated French dish requiring ingredients like cream and saffron (she had come, after all, from a wealthy family that managed to keep a cook even during the Depression, and all of the girls spoke French). I did not know she had learned the recipe in the fifth grade. I imagined my heroic mother creating magic in the midst of poverty.

I can't remember when I learned the truth that the dish was nothing but a pretentious name for hard-boiled eggs in white sauce[1], but I remember feeling betrayed. I was initially angry with my mother for perpetuating a lie, and later I became angry with the recipe itself, which I saw as an involuted game to keep women busy even when all they had was an egg. Boil it and be done with it!

She said that Eggs a la Goldenrod was the only recipe she knew how to cook, but I knew that wasn't true. At seventeen she had attended a geology camp in Wyoming, where she must have shared KP; she had marched for civil rights and worked in soup kitchens. Even in her privileged household, she had kitchen duties on Sundays when the cook had her day off. When I asked what she had cooked on these days, she admitted to fudge and popcorn.

I could understand how fudge and popcorn might not make the graduate-student budget, but I expected some remnant of the equation between joy and food to survive. Why base a marriage on the false premises of a fifth-grade recipe that was not only pretentious but bland? Why not admit to the joy, if not of fudge, then at least of peanut butter? As my sister and I discussed Eggs a la Goldenrod, we realized that we had no memory of having actually eaten the stuff. We remembered lots of peanut butter sandwiches, and celery stuffed with peanut butter, and things with cream cheese. We remembered meatloaf. We must have occasionally had baked potatoes because I remember my mother being terrified of them (they exploded when she poked them with a fork).

My sister and I learned to steer clear of the kitchen when meals approached. Somehow, in the culinary politics of marriage, the kitchen became a battleground and food a weapon. My father claimed scientific authority, which always seemed to trump my mother's aesthetic and moral authority. She tried to can green beans and ended up throwing them out because she was afraid of ptomaine poisoning. When my

---

1 Boil eggs and peel, cut in half, and place the yolk in one bowl and the whites in the other. Chop the whites. Make a white sauce from milk, flour, and butter. Mix the white pieces in the white sauce. Pour the white sauce over toast. Grate the yolk on top. Add salt and pepper as desired. Eat.

father and I went out and picked mushrooms, she refused to cook them, and stood holding the phone, ready to call the hospital, as my father and I cooked and ate what we thought might be *Marasmius oreades*. I still have my father's book, *Our Edible toadstools and Mushrooms and How to Distinguish Them* (W. Hamilton Gibson, 1895), the first page of shows a painting of "The Deadly 'Amanita'" that is followed by a "Dedication to the Reader kind, gentle or other, to whom, in the hopes of continued grace and well-being the Frontispiece and the chapter on 'The Deadly Amanita' is herewith particularly referred with the Author's solicitude. 'Forewarned is Forearmed.'" The taste of aromatic, nutty morsels slithery with butter is one of my earliest memories of taking my father's side in the name of science over emotion, courage over fear.

Gadgets were a problem, as they were part of the scientific establishment. Somewhere during married life my mother lost the nerve to make fudge (which did, after all, require a candy thermometer and a double-boiler). However, she fought to master the pressure-cooker, which greatly reduced the amount of cooking time required. Aesthetically inclined toward Slow Food, she could not stand prolonged contact with food of any kind, which with my father's help constantly reminded her of her failures (the eggs that stuck to the pan because she forgot to add butter, the raw pinto beans in the stew). In many ways the pressure-cooker symbolized their relationship, which was powerful, ready to blow, and produced meals rendered limp from the intensity of the heat exchange.

Her greatest technological success was with the percolator. Coffee was the one exception to the Cook as Seldom as Possible rule that governed her life, and she had the reputation for making the best coffee in the Sandia Mountains. She faced terror every time she made it (terror that the glass knob to the percolator would fly off and break, that boiling coffee would explode through the empty hole, that the pot would be left, forgotten, on the heat to dry up and turn red-hot and burn someone), but the rewards were sufficient to keep her going. It was my mother who poured me my first cup of coffee, half of which was milk. I was fourteen and felt that I had become an adult. To drink coffee was to join the conversation; to linger while morning light filtered through the piñon trees outside the kitchen window; to listen to my parents turn their psychological insights on other people and the world. I remember my mother's voice as hesitant, my father's as argumentative and assertive. My mother spoke of memories, my father of facts.

When my father entered the kitchen, he brought an aura of control and experimentation that reminded me of the gifts he brought back when he went on business trips (an industrial diamond with a smoky carbon core, postage-stamp-sized microfiche on which was printed the entire Bible that I could read only with my microscope, a bundle of rawhide strips with no discernible purpose). As he reached for the spices and combined foods in new and interesting ways (sardines with green beans, salsa on potatoes), he was not a cook but a Chef. On the one hand, he was showing off. But somewhere in that scientifically pontificating, show-off mind there lurked a child who wanted to play. When he added oregano to the peas, he was demonstrating not only knowledge but a willingness to experiment. So what if it tasted bitter? So what if it made you sick? Humans are not like rats, unable to throw up. It's okay to play with food.

Only rarely did my mother play with food. Over time she distanced herself from it. Her best recipes involved the least cooking: aesthetically arranged cheese, barely simmered apples, olives soaked in gin, a simple lemon chicken recipe[1]. As the marriage deteriorated, she cut down on eating. She ate like the proverbial bird, a bird that kept its leftovers in the freezer. When my four-year-old daughter and I stopped by for a visit when my parents were getting a divorce, all I could find for her to eat were frozen Fruit Loops.

When we moved from Albuquerque to the Sandia Mountains, I attended seventh grade at A. Montoya Junior High where I was required to take Home Economics. Like my mother, I did not know how to cook or sew. For my sewing project, I bought a pattern for a Western shirt

---

1 Coat chicken pieces with seasoned flour and fry briefly. Place in casserole dish, cover with lemon slices and brown sugar, pour in some chicken broth, and bake for 1.5 hours at 350 degrees.

that required knowledge of top stitches, one-way design fabrics, and nap yardages—things of which I had no knowledge whatsoever (and still don't). At the same time, I decided to bake a cake. It was not your usual two-layers-in-a-cake-pan out of the box kind of cake, with frosting made from butter and powdered sugar. It was a recipe I found (probably in a magazine with a name like "Cooking on the French Riviera") that required cooking the layers on the *bottom* of cake pans—at least eight thin, fragile layers—and after the layers had cooled, cementing them with sour cream and various jams and letting them coalesce under the heavy weight of a glass bowl in the refrigerator.

I sometimes wonder what would have happened if the cake had turned out as disastrously as the shirt. I was at a crossroads at that time, deciding what kind of life I would live. Watching my parents battle in the kitchen over oregano, mushrooms, courage, and self-esteem, I had given myself a reckless challenge: tackle life in full playfulness, whatever the cost, mess, or failure. I might very well have emerged from these experiments as fearful as my mother, as ready to retreat into the rigid structure of false but safe promises, an Eggs-a-la-Goldenrod kind of girl.

The cake, however, was delicious. It was different from anything I'd ever tasted. It tasted like courage.

Simplification and denial of food was, I now realize, my mother's own version of courage. When she decided to die, the first thing she did was to stop eating. No more meatloaf, mushrooms, or lemon chicken. My sister and I had been tempting her with the few foods she was still interested in eating, namely bacon and ice cream, but finally she said no to these too. When we insisted, she got angry, in the polite manner she always used. Not just "no" but "no thank you," in a way that told us she had come into her own mind and would no longer be bullied.

I wished that she had gotten the courage, on the threshold of death, to let loose and curse—at husband, children, friends, and body for their abandonment and condescension—but the closest she came to outrage was to say "no thank you." At that moment I understood that Eggs-a-la-Goldenrod were much more than a social hypocrisy. They were a refined person's article of faith that civilization was better than barbarism, that courteous discretion trumped rage.

She was, in other words, a classy broad.

An Eggs-a-la-Goldenrod kind of girl.

Mark Dery

À la Recherche du Taco Bell: One *Gabacho's* Run for the Border

I'm having a *Señor* Moment. Dinner, tonight, is the unthinkable: a Taco Bell Original Taco and Burrito Supreme®, abominations that haven't profaned this chowhound's palate since I was a kid in Southern California, birthplace of fast food. I'm committing this foodie felony partly because I'm *à la recherche du* whatever: the goldenrod-and-avocado-colored memories of my '60s-'70s youth, when dinner out, more often than not, meant Taco Bell.

Growing up white and middle-class in San Diego in those days meant that "cultural hybridity," as the postmodernists like to call it, was my birthright: Mexicans were "wetbacks" and "beaners," yet our shared historical (and often literal) genes, romanticized in elementary-school textbooks and on school trips to the region's Spanish missions, meant that Mexican food was "our" food, just as *piñatas* were a fixture at our kiddy birthday parties and Spanglish (*¿Qué pasa*, dude?) was an inseparable part of our teen idiom. A curious cultural alchemy transmuted the taco and the burrito, in my white, middle-class mind, into the soul food of SoCal culture the hybrid consciousness of the U.S.-Mexico borderlands, wrapped up in a tortilla.

Unsurprising, then, that Taco Bell outlets felt like home, in an Alta California, Father Junipero Serra, wrought-iron-lantern kind of way. Their cute little mission-style facades, scaled down to Disneyland proportions and topped by a hole-in-the-wall-style belfry, complete with fiberglass bell, were cozily familiar to Southern Californians like me. The Old California vibe was enhanced by trashcans shaped like saguaro cactuses and gas-jet fire pits (an inexhaustible source of entertainment for junior pyromaniacs, in that Lost World before iPod and Gameboy). Sure, the theme-parked architecture put a friendly face on the mission system, built on the backs of enslaved Indians. And the original Taco Bell sign the proverbial lazy Mexican dozing against a cactus, shaded by a cartoonishly huge sombrero just like the one my parents bought me in Tijuana—was to Mexicans what the golliwog lawn jockey was to American blacks. But we were clueless Anglos, and who knew?

The food, if not truly Mexican, was at least Mexican-ish. Not that my family scrupled at the difference: recently transplanted from Connecticut and resigned, in a Stockholm Syndrome sort of way, to my mom's unhappy homemaker cooking—the vaguely resentful, let-them-eat-Hamburger Helper cuisine of '70s mothers politicized by *Ms.* and *Maude*—we didn't know what distinguished a real taco from a Taco Bell taco, and didn't care to know.

But that was then, this is now. Which is the other reason I'm eating Taco Bell tonight: I want to sink my teeth into the culture clash between past and present—the whiter, more monocultural society we were, versus the hyphenated nation we've become. Taco Bell harks back to the Wonder Bread America of 1962, when the chain was founded on the assumption that real Mexican food was too slow, too spicy, too unpronounceably *foreign*, even in the Los Angeles suburb of Downey, where Glen Bell launched his chain. "Buh-*ree*-toh," I ordered, prompted by the painfully phonetic rendering on the early Taco Bell menu boards. "Toast-*ah*-duh." Ordering in *español* when you can't even *habla!* How bitchen is *that?!*

Paradoxically, even as its architecture and barefoot, serape-clad mascot, the "Taco Bell Boy," insisted on the Mexican-ness of the brand, Taco Bell was taking the "Mexican" out of Mexican food—destigmatizing it by deracinating it. Since the 19th century, the racial unconscious of white Southern California had projected its fear and loathing of brown-skinned people onto the food they ate. The racist commonplace that

Mexican food is *dirty*—a coded way of saying that our brown-skinned neighbors to the south are Third World *cucarachas*, peeing in the Great Race's gene pool—is a durable myth. In his essay "Tacos, Enchiladas and Refried Beans: The Invention of Mexican-American Cookery," the

Vintage Postcard
Postcard of Old Style Taco Bell

culinary historian Andrew F. Smith quotes John G. Bourke, a contemporary chronicler of frontier life. Writing in 1895, Bourke observes that the "abominations of Mexican cookery have been for years a favorite theme with travelers"—at which point Bourke promptly joins in the fun, deploring Mexicans' "indifference to the existence of dirt and grease" (not to mention their "appalling liberality in the matter of garlic" and their "recklessness in the use of chili colorado or chili verde").

In the turbulent wake of the Mexican revolution, Mexican immigrants poured into Southern California. Take Los Angeles, for example: in 1910, the city was overwhelmingly white; only 800 of its 100,000 residents were Mexican immigrants. By 1920, L.A.'s Mexican population had swollen to 21,000, making Mexicans the biggest immigrant group in the city. Then as now, the winds of demographic change fanned nativist fears and white supremacist sympathies, especially among the conservative Midwesterners clustered throughout greater L.A. and Orange

County. In the early 1920s, as Eric Schlosser notes in *Fast Food Nation*, the Ku Klux Klan ran Anaheim's daily paper, posted signs at the city limits reading "KIGY" (short for "Klansmen I Greet You"), and, for a year, won control of the local government.

Little wonder, then, that Mexican restaurants in the area chose to pass as "Spanish," as the *L.A. Weekly* food critic Jonathan Gold told me in a telephone interview. The owners of El Cholo, who helped engineer that genetic hybrid known as Cal-Mex cuisine, promoted their restaurant as a "Spanish café" when they opened it in 1923. Crucial to their success was El Cholo's open kitchen; visible from the dining room, it put to rest what *El Cholo: A Taste of History* delicately refers to as the *gabacho* "misconception that Mexican kitchens were not well maintained."

The equation of foreigners with filth and their cookery with "abominations" assumes its most gothic form in the old canard that Mexicans eat dog, an urban myth Craig Claiborne alludes to in his foreword to Diana Kennedy's *The Essential Cuisines of Mexico*: "I have always had a passion for the Mexican table since, as an infant, I ate hot tamales sold by a street vendor in the small town where I lived in Mississippi. (There were dreadful rumors about what the meat filling consisted of but, poof, I couldn't have cared less.)"

Truth to tell, there *was* a time when man's best friend was the *specialité de la maison*, south of the border. The Aztecs ate mostly vegetables — corn and beans were the twin pillars of their cuisine, which also made liberal use of tomatoes, squash, avocadoes, and chili peppers — but the upper classes fleshed out their diet with fish, turkey, duck, and, be it said, *canis familiaris*. Fattened in cages, small, hairless dogs known as *xoloitzcuintli* were the main ingredient in a dainty dish often set before the king: dog stew. That the *xolo* bears an unmistakable resemblance to the Taco Bell Chihuahua (a talking Chihuahua with a Speedy Gonzalez accent whose 1998 TV commercials charmed white audiences and infuriated Chicano activists) is what is known, dear reader, as a delicious irony.

Taco Bell made Mexican food safe for postwar white America by turning down the heat, translating alien ingredients into the *gabacho* idiom, and automating food prep: the *queso fresco* sprinkled onto Mexican tostadas were replaced by cheddar cheese; the fragrant, meltingly delicious *tortillas frescas* made by hand in Tijuana taco stands gave way to prefab taco shells mass-produced on assembly lines worthy of the region's aerospace industry, uniform as widgets.

Though the names of Taco Bell's allegedly "Mexican" foods might have been "new to many Americans, their contents were not," writes Andrew F. Smith, in his *Encyclopedia of Junk Food and Fast Food*. "Their components were similar to hamburgers—ground beef, cheese, tomatoes, lettuce, and sauce. The main difference was the tortilla, which most customers could easily understand as a substitute for the hamburger bun. As [the culinary historian] Harvey Levenstein wrote: 'It is questionable whether anyone but Mexicans should have considered it foreign food.'"

Most important, Glen Bell recontextualized the *experience* of eating Mexican food. In the gothic fantasies of white America, *taquerias* indifferent to the existence of dirt and grease served meat of uncertain origin and colon-scarring spiciness, calculated to exact Montezuma's Revenge from whimpering, backfiring *gringos*. Bell moved Mexican food to the right side of the tracks: brightly lit and spotless as operating rooms, early Taco Bells were staffed and patronized exclusively by Anglos, at least in my experience.

"At the time, Mexican restaurants were considered dirty," said Smith, in an e-mail interview. Raised in L.A. in the '60s, he recalled that "in racist Southern California, Mexicans and Mexican-Americans, then popularly known as greasers, were also considered dirty. Few suburban Anglo kids ate Mexican food until Taco Bell arrived. It sanitized 'Mexican' food (and in many ways, it also cleaned up the image of Mexican-Americans)."

But what's Taco Bell's reason for living in an America where public schools are adding mariachi to the music curriculum and *huitlacoche* is the new porcini? In the United States of 2007, Hispanics are now the nation's largest minority. As of 2006, the U.S. Census Bureau reckoned their numbers at 44.3 million—about 15 percent of the population. And 64% percent of them were of Mexican origin. Who needs partial-birth cuisine like the Meximelt® or the Crunchwrap Supreme® when The

Real Thing, in more and more American cities, is just a *barrio* away? Yet, defying all cultural logic, the chain "serves more than 2 billion [American] consumers each year in more than 5,800 restaurants," according to its website; in 2005, company-owned Taco Bells rang up $1.8 billion in sales, while franchisees tallied $4.4 billion.

Rather than replicate colonial logic by pontificating from on high, I decided to pass the mic to some Mexican-Americans who live in Southern California. Most of my e-mail interviewees agreed that Taco Bell's insanely cheap prices, made possible by economies of scale, were the primary reason for the chain's continued existence. Then, too, Taco Bell's late hours give it an edge with the young, male, beer-hose demographic. Gustavo Arellano, author of the syndicated column "¡Ask a Mexican!" calls the chain's food "hangover cuisine."

But opinions differed regarding the cultural politics of eating at Taco Bell. Luis Valderas, 40, a San Antonio-based Chicano artist, decries "the Americanization of Mexican culture based on corporate greed." He writes, "This fake Mexican food on steroids can never come close to the dishes my mother, *tías* [aunts], and *welita* [grandmother] used to cook for me and our family."

Francisco Bustos, 32, a "border-crossing writer" who lives in San Diego, remembers the words of a cousin who worked at Taco Bell: the beans "weren't real." Bustos wonders, "What did he mean by the beans not being real? I guess I simply thought, right, *claro que si*. If they're not cooked the way our parents and grandparents cook them...it changes everything in a plate. No real beans means no real plate."

Daniel Olivas, 48, on the other hand, seems to savor the cognitive dissonance of Taco Bell's "wonderfully wrong" gloss of Mexican cookery. "I admit to being awestruck by the warped brilliance it took to invent something like the Mexican Pizza," writes Olivas, a lawyer and fiction writer living in the San Fernando Valley. Obviously, he concedes, "it's nothing like the food my mom makes, but I'm not expecting that...I'm not one of those Chicanos who believes that Mexican food is sacred. I'll leave such snootiness to the French."

In many ways, Perry Vasquez's wry, ambivalent take on Taco Bell captures the brand's polyvalent slipperiness, as well as the deeply personal, sometimes paradoxical ways in which we negotiate the Deeper Meanings of Things in consumer culture. To Vasquez, 48, a San Diego-based artist whose work explores border culture, Taco Bell's "corporate caretakers swallow up every exploitable image of the Spanish history and *Mexicanismo* and turn it into something like Hello Kitty."

Ironically, Vasquez "had very good feelings" associated with the brand when he was growing up in conservative, fundamentalist High Point, North Carolina. He and his mother and brother had moved there from Escondido, California after his parents divorced, and when a Taco Bell opened "in the late '60s or early '70s, I actually took some pride in it," writes Vasquez. "For me, it was like having a small part of California in North Carolina. Much of my identity was built around being from California. It was fun for me to go there with friends and say, 'Yes, this is what a taco is like. We eat them all the time in California. Aren't they good?'"

They *were* good. Or, at least, I remember them that way, in defiance of my gastronomic superego's insistence that since Taco Bell food is a dismal simulacrum of The Real Thing, there could never have been a time when its tacos were not, as postmodern philosophers like to say, "always already" sucky. That's the perversity of memory: no matter how sophisticated my palate has grown or how politicized it has become, I still feel a nostalgic fondness for Taco Bell tacos, triggered by sense memories of that first bite, when the shell would disintegrate into a heap of tortilla shards and meat on the orange wrapping paper that doubled as a tray. The sublimity of that crunch, the sensuous contrast between brittle, ultra-thin shell (worlds away from the chewy, chamois softness of the griddle-warmed tortillas served by Tijuana *taquerias*) and moist, spicy-sweet meat: Taco Bell tacos combined the delights of Pringles chips and Sloppy Joes. For a kid in the late '60s and '70s, what could be better?

But why am I, a *gabacho* who barely speaks Jell-O-shooter Spanish, so devoted to the pursuit of the One True Taco? Lately, my jones for *echt* Mexican has gotten more extreme than ever. I find myself cruising the

Web for foodie-porn photos of pre-Columbian holdovers such as *tacos de chapulines* (grasshoppers) and *escamoles* (ant larvae). What's *that* about? Is this one *gabacho*'s ironic dream of Making a Run for the Border, as the Taco Bell tagline has it—leaving behind the Wonder Bread soullessness of white, middle-class culture for the mythic richness of *Mexicanismo*? Isn't that just the old Orientalist fantasy of going native, equal parts Mistah Kurtz and Cabo Wabo?

But if my never-ending search for the One True Taco is just another manifestation of the Anglo obsession with Mexico the exotic, the earthy, the primitive, the unimpeachably Authentic (think of the *gabacha* feminist sanctification of Frida Kahlo as Our Lady of the Unibrow), it may mask a gnawing anxiety: the pervasive fear that reality is morphing into virtual reality—that Authenticity is just a philosophical mirage in the Desert of the Real, to use the philosopher Jean Baudrillard's term for the media-warped, culturally remixed world we live in. It's a world where tortilla consumption is up in the States but down in Mexico, and where, as the *gabacho* popularizer of Mexican cuisine Rick Bayless told a reporter for the Associated Press, "they've started opening Taco Bells in Mexico now and people consider it American food." He added, "A friend of mine in a Mexican city said to me, 'You've got to taste this dish, this American dish. We've got it all over the place in Mexico now. It's nachos.'"

Who knows what Mexicans will make of the nacho? Consider the *paste*, a meat-filled pastry native to the Mexican state of Hidalgo—native because the Cornish miners who worked in the region's silver mines brought the meat pie known as the pasty with them. Of course, the Mexicans hot-rodded it with *tinga* (stewed pork) or *mole* sauce, chipotle or habanero chili peppers. Another example: according to the Mexican cultural critic Francisco Carballo, there's a sushi restaurant in Mexico City called Sushi-Itto where the chefs accessorize the raw fish with plantains and chilis.

In a globalized world, the Dream of the Pure is an embalmer's fantasy. I think of the philosopher Kwame Anthony Appiah's essay "The Case for Contamination," in which he quotes Salman Rushdie, "who has insisted that the novel that occasioned his fatwa 'celebrates hybridity, impurity, intermingling, the transformation that comes of new and unexpected combinations of human beings, cultures, ideas, politics, movies, songs. It rejoices in mongrelization and fears the absolutism of the Pure. Mélange, hotch-potch, a bit of this and a bit of that is how newness enters the world.'"

Then again, maybe my hopelessly overdetermined reading of Mexican food is simply the product of a Proustian preoccupation with lost time, an attempt to beam back to the Endless Summers of my San Diego youth.

Before I bite into my Original Taco, I perform a *CSI*-like necropsy on it, anxiously examining what the Taco Bell menu insists is "crisp, shredded lettuce" and what I insist is limp, dispirited lettuce. Dissecting it with my fork, I probe the "real cheddar cheese" (accept no substitutes!) and tiny mound — a tablespoonful or two, at most — of what my unreliable informant claims is "seasoned ground beef" but which looks suspiciously like earthworm castings.

I think of the Carolina highway patrolman who found a freshly hawked lunger, courtesy one disgruntled employee, dangling from one of his Taco Bell nachos. I think of the scores of people poisoned, in 2006, by the E. coli outbreak in Taco Bells throughout the nation. I think of the rats gamboling contentedly around a Greenwich Village Taco Bell. (NBC reporter Adam Shapiro described one showboating rodent climbing onto an upside-down stool, then dangling from it "like a gymnast." Cute, in a *Willard* meets *Ratatouille* sort of way.)

With these thoughts as an *amuse-bouche*, I take my first bite. I chomp through the millimeter-thin shell, flavorful as corn-fed cardboard and eerily crunchless in the soggy-armpit humidity of a New York summer. Chewing, I ruminate on the food writer Jonathan Gold's comment in an e-mail to me: "I don't think there's any such thing as authentic Mexican food." This from a Pulitzer prize-winning critic who also told me, with palpable excitement, about his lard connection, a guy who sells "*manteca de carnitas*...the liquid lard rendered in the process of making *carnitas* [fried pork], liquid gold. I fried a few batches of chicken in it last night, accompanied by fiery red salsa and homemade tortillas, and I'm pretty sure I saw god herself." So what is Gold, a guy who admits he "did plow through most of the Semiotext(e), Frankfurt school, poststructural stuff" when he was in his '20s, saying? That Derrida had it right when he Dropped the Chalupa on Western philosophy, arguing that meaning is not, in fact, anchored in some Transcendental Signified but is forever deferred? Ask a Gordita Supreme® what it *means* and it will simply point to a signified that points to other signifiers—or, in a pinch, try to distract you by asking if you want to upgrade to marinated and grilled all-white-meat chicken. Maybe I need to lose my bobo-intellectual illusions of an authentic Mexican-ness, somewhere over the border.

But not before I've mainlined some of Gold's liquid gold.

I reflect on all the psychobiographical and cross-cultural meanings I've tried to stuff into a folded, fried tortilla, symbolically speaking. Then I recall Perry Vasquez's mini-dissertation on the subject: "What is a taco? It's a fast food entrepreneur's task to ask that question, much the same way a modernist painter might ask: What is a painting? A 'taco' is an empty form, a genre, a shell that can be stretched, expanded, recombined, redefined, and recontextualized...up to a point maybe, until it is no longer a taco and then apparently it becomes a wrap. And that's the ingenuity of it. But is it worth eating? In my opinion, no...Unless you're faced with starvation...and even then maybe not...*Orale!*"

As I munch, one thing, at least, is instantly clear: You can't go home again.

Jennifer Cost
Taco Bell El Cajon Blvd
Taco Bell, El Cajon, CA

Alys Masek
I'm Taking It with Me

I'm taking Kendra's raucous laugh, and her beautiful
CatherineJane coats, our walks to 9th Avenue, and the stop
at Arizimendi Bakery for a slice of blistering pizza.
I'm taking the Christmas parties at Kevin and Joe's,
the long black dress with the spiderweb back,
pretty boy bookends on either side of me,
necking all night, then zipping my dress,
and slipping out as sun starts to rise.
I'm taking the walk home from the N Judah,
the Grateful Dead house at 710 Ashbury, and the way
the windows light up when the sun hits in this city of gold.
I'm taking Polk Street and the aging queens and runaways
huddled against storefronts, and the Vietnamese sandwich place
on Larkin that closes at 5 but makes the best
meatball sandwich in the world. I'm taking Camels unfiltered
and Miller light and the scratchy
wool sailor's sweater that is all I have left of my Dad.
I'm taking the waterfall at Big Sur that day
we were high and I almost jumped. I'm taking my disastrous
first marriage and the time I cut all my hair off
and how Alan lied and said it looked good. I'm taking the pine tree
in the canyon and the cactus and the dry farmed early girl tomatoes
from Ferry Plaza farmer's market. I'm taking the Chilaquiles
from Primavera and their thick homemade tortillas
and chilies roasting in October at the Santa Fe farmers market
and Kit Carson's grave in Taos. I'm taking my Mom dancing
to *Begin the Bguine* just days after we lowered my brother George
into his grave. I'm taking all of his old Sam Cooke tapes
and how he beat the professionals at poker.
I'm taking the way he never gave up on anything,

even his anger. I'm taking that night with him
at the Dana Point harbor, the last time I saw him
alive, the two of us talking about work and how he still missed the city.

Alys Masek

❧ Summer Salad

If you find yourself at the Ferry Plaza Farmers' Market in San Francisco in the summer, make your way to the stand where they sell dry farmed early girl tomatoes. They are, bar none, the best tomatoes I have ever tasted; a perfect balance of acid and sugar and so flavorful, I happily eat them out of hand. After you have your fill of eating tomatoes straight, consider putting a few under the broiler until the skins are blackened and then tossing them into a blender along with chopped cilantro, garlic, onions, Serrano chilies and lime juice. Whirl until you have a finely mixed salsa which tastes of the sun, heat and summer—a welcome respite from the cold and fog of San Francisco summers. Or you can make this salad, which is a combination of a Greek Salad and Fattoush—a Middle Eastern salad of tomatoes, cumbers and toasted pita. This salad is all about crunch and contrast, the heart of romaine, and the cucumbers, red onion, and toasted pita provide the crunch while the saltiness of the feta cheese and the olives contrast nicely with the sweet tomatoes. The sumac, which you sprinkle on at the end, lends a pleasantly tart, citrusy note.

1 head Romaine hearts, cut into fine ribbons
1 whole wheat pita
3 to 4 tomatoes, finely chopped
3 Persian cucumbers or half of a regular cucumber, thinly sliced
¼ of a medium red onion, thinly sliced
½ cup kalamata olives, pitted and sliced in half
3 T mint, dill or cilantro, roughly chopped

4 oz. feta cheese, crumbled
sumac to taste (available at Persian markets)
Olive oil
Seasoned rice vinegar

Start by opening up the pita bread and cutting it so that you have two thin slices of bread. Lightly brush with olive oil and broil until both sides are nicely browned. Reserve. Combine the romaine lettuce, the tomatoes, cucumbers, red onions, kalamata olives and herb of your choice in a salad bowl. Add ¾ of the feta cheese. Then add the reserved toasted pita. Dress with the olive oil and rice vinegar. I like to first add the olive oil, toss thoroughly, and then add the rice vinegar. Sprinkle the salad with sumac and toss again. Place on two plates, sprinkle with some of the reserved feta and serve.

Serves two as a light lunch or dinner.

Lauren Guza

A Brief History of Birthday Dinners

Two
Picnic tables, San Gabriel, CA

I wear my new swimsuit, lavender and turquoise stretched tight over a bongo drum of a stomach, dumpling legs. Hair like Billy Ray Cyrus meets E.T., wriggling on the kitchen table while my mom and her sewing scissors have their way with his bangs. My favorite uncle is there, bearded bear of a man who cares about books and the Dodgers and everything else I don't yet know I will love. At the moment, I know I love cake.

And here it comes, like a pink-iced Disneyland. I've figured out that candles mean you're somebody to celebrate. On Christmas, we lit a candle for Jesus, and they've lit *two* for me! For a moment, there's just me thinking how soft and squirmy that cake will feel in my fists as I jam it in my mouth and probably under my nose to make a mustache like Daddy's and maybe in my hair if Mom's not looking. But the frosted fantasy crumbles to bits, because the guests, all of them crowded around the picnic table in the orange sky, mesquite air, all of them suddenly look at me and begin to sing. I stare. Open a quivering mouth. Begin sobbing and try to hide in my mother's shirt.

Nine
Rocky Cola Café, Montrose, CA

I come here for the chicken fingers. Salty, battered, dunked in yellow cream honey mustard that drips to the floor like brush paint on a canvas of black and white tile.

And a strawberry shake, obviously. If you're lucky, they make too much shake and give you the extra in a metal canister with a wide open top. Once I tried to drink straight from the canister, lifting it high above my mouth to show off. Lifted it just long enough to watch it avalanche onto my face and down my shirt.

In time, Bill Clinton will eat in this restaurant, maybe at this table. The Backstreet Boys will film a music video in here, windows draped with sheets so the gathering crowds don't see the magic until it's on television. But politics, entertainment, sleight of hand: they're all to come. Right now, Bill Clinton is a governor I've never heard of, in a state I won't know until next year when I memorize its name for a map test. "Boy band" is a term uncoined. I'm nine, and I order an extra helping of honey mustard.

In the corner, a creaking metal jukebox plays songs that make my father look backwards into his own eyes. I see him in those backward eyes, a long-haired kid lying on his back on a bed in Virginia, guitar on his stomach, playing along to Beach Boys albums. Forty years later I will take him to a Beach Boys reunion concert. We will watch Brian Wilson, a swaying, age-ridged oak, try to swagger across a stage, and he, like my father, will be young again. Dad will get lost in chords for a moment, and, for the first time, I won't want him to come back. I will want him to stay a little while in a place with guitars made of old trees.

Fifteen
The Flintridge Inn, La Cañada, CA

It's the building that's always changing hands. Always a restaurant, always different, always cleared out and scraped bare within a few months. Pockmarked with forgotten chairs, wire ribs in the walls, a small fork in the corner of the kitchen, rusting in the dark. Giving birth to a new name, new menu, but never quite solving the riddle of what makes people come inside and stay.

But the roast beef is rosy and warm, sunset on the desert sliced thick, and here butter and sourdough settle in together naturally, like they know and don't need a knife to force them around. They're why I chose this place this year. Because of the prime rib and the soft rolls and the families sitting around tables and how those things make my mom happy.

Dad is late. But he'd called to tell us he would be, so it's not rude; it's work. Mom smiles at him when he walks in, and I want to ask him to tell her she is beautiful. I used to do that when I was younger. *Daddy, don't you think Mom's new necklace looks nice? You know, you should tell her you think so.* But he says Sorry I'm late, and is looking at me. Happy Birthday, kiddo, and kisses my forehead. Walks around the table and kisses my sister, who's blowing milk bubbles.

Where's my kiss? Mom asks, smiling shyly, teasing him.

It's not your birthday, he says, and sits down.

Twenty
The Ivy, Los Angeles, CA

Beverly Hills: Land of the Lettuce Eaters. I eat a salad twenty yards from where Lindsay Lohan once crashed her car. Disappointed that I am eating salad when I wanted pizza. Ashamed that my dad's wife, size zero and not one to splurge, makes me more likely to do this. And ashamed that I write things like she's a size zero, when really I should note that she knows about books and that she's brave enough to stand on a stage in auditions and cancer hospitals and that she makes my dad laugh. Ashamed that I've chosen a restaurant twenty yards from anywhere Lindsay Lohan has been. And then that I have thought a thing like that without ever having met her. She might like books. She is probably brave.

Twenty-four
Kahurangi National Park, New Zealand

First birthday in the southern hemisphere. First in a forest of wet, black leaves. First in love, I admit to myself in the quiet.

Finding nothing, we eat what we crammed into the corners of our packs. Granola bars bought in Los Angeles and crunched under camera batteries and wallets and shampoo bottles until they come out in battered, pasty pieces sifted from the cellophane. Granola bars served with a side of breath mints, a wrinkled foil package courtesy of Qantas Airways, eight days ago above the Pacific. We toast with water bottles filled at the pump seven miles up the trail. To adventures, we say. And to hell with fancy restaurants. We twirl the plastic bottles like wine glasses, take a moment to savor the aroma (ah, what a particularly buttery, fruity, woodsy, full-bodied water!), then sip it and nod as we let it trickle down our throat, drunk on pretending.

We eat quickly, he and I, shoulders pressed together at the rough table, ten miles uphill and through rain from the clearing where we parked our car. The only place besides our bodies and backpacks that has everything we own in New Zealand. We eat quickly because this hut we've found in a crevice in the hills, this hut whose website spoke of reservation requirements and local convenience stores, has no light beyond the waning breath of a purple sun in the edges of the windows. No people, no one to take our ticket, no food to sell for the shiny dollar coins that have become less and less foreign to us. There are only our voices, also less foreign to us than they once were, and the soft weight of our socks on wood as we pad around in tomorrow's clothes, today's hanging like wet salamander skins on scattered railings and strings.

We slide our fingers down the pages of the guest book. Who has come before, and were they as alone as we are? Addresses and dates and a thin, white rectangle for comments. Find an adjective, maybe bind it with a noun or two if your handwriting is small, an adjective that tells them every fragmented, trumpeted thought you invented on this mountain. We leave it blank, knowing the limits of adjectives.

For dessert, a chocolate bar, which we eat on the crest of a hill, listening to a waterfall and certain we can see the wind. We watch a bird, layered brown like wet thatch, poke its bill among the scrub bushes, miniature rainforest. Prehistoric almost, in its ability to not imagine our existence. We try, but can't name it.

Ilya Kaminsky
A Toast

> If you will it, it is no dream.
> — *Theodore Herzl*

October: grapes hung like the fists of a girl
gassed in her prayer. Memory,
I whisper, stay awake.

In my veins
long syllables tighten their ropes, rains come
right out of the eighteenth century
Yiddish or a darker language in which imagination
is the only word.

Imagination! a young girl dancing polka,
unafraid, betrayed by the Lord's death
(or his hiding under the bed when the Messiah
was postponed).

In my country, evenings bring the rain water, turning
poplars bronze in a light that sparkles on these pages
where I, my fathers,
unable to describe your dreams, drink
my silence from a cup.

Vi Dutcher

Grandma's Sugar Cookies

For particular Amish and Mennonite women, the kitchen, which endures as a created space in the home, is the center of activity for the family in general and for the women in particular. Historically, within this social hub, we took our baths in the galvanized metal wash tub on Saturday nights, boiled our water in copper tubs on the stove for Monday wash days, heated our irons on the stove for Tuesday's ironing, frosted Saturday's cakes and fluted our pie crusts, and butchered our chickens outside and brought them inside to pluck and dress them. Although, in recent years, we have relegated some of these activities to other rooms such as the bathroom and laundry room, and have transformed some rooms in the family dwelling from a parlor to family room, we keep our kitchens, with its stove, table, chairs, and cupboards, situated as the located centripetal force of much of our activity. Women occupy kitchen spaces and, in so doing, represent to themselves as a lived stability that endures via socio-religious cultural roots in the Amish and Mennonite tradition. This representation shows up as everyday actions materialized in providing meals for the family and community and in maintaining robust social relationships through recipes and letters, which merit investigation in their own right.

Recipes are usually thought of in conjunction with food, and that *is* primarily how they are used. However, more broadly, a recipe is a set of directions for preparing something—anything—a prescription—denoting the way something ought to be done—for best results (*ought* and *best* are operative words here). And in this community of Anabaptist women, as in many communities, their recipes are an example of and serve a social purpose—prescribing most activities of daily living.

As such, these recipes, then, are not just objects—pieces of paper—standing alone but are connected in complex ways to tools, machines, women, men, children, social customs, values, and core beliefs about life. Indeed, they may be seen as cultural units arising, growing, and changing over time. In our twenty-first century kitchens replete with several cookbooks, we often take for granted that a recipe is found stuck between the pages of cookbooks or on cards, even hastily scribbled on scrap paper.

In the Amish and Mennonite culture represented in this article, a recipe is also oral. And a recipe, whether oral or written, is not the basic unit of food preparation in these familial settings. Rather, the recipe is a basic unit of instruction—a system of teaching fundamental elements to the larger community in which these women are an integral part. First, of course, the recipe instructs these women on how to prepare food. However and more deeply, as we shall see, the recipe, through oral narrative, equips a woman with and entrusts to her important Anabaptist values.

My great-grandmother, Lizzie Yoder, known in her community by her first name preceded by her husband's name, Sam Lizzie, set up housekeeping in 1906 at the age of eighteen. Her twenty-one-year-old daughter, Katie Coblentz or Andy Katie, began her own kitchen in 1930. Ten years later, both women were widowed, and they combined their households for economic strength during these Depression years. Since my mother was eight years old at the time, and able to do her share of the work, three generations of women with intergenerational divisions of labor and apprenticeship pursued interdependent living on the farm. By 1950, my eighteen-year-old mother, Crist Betty, set up housekeeping and relied heavily on her mother and grandmother who by now lived in separate homes just down the street. Although these women carved a space for their kitchens in different decades, prevailing cultural attitudes regarding their roles in the home endured. However, by the time I was married and left home, much had changed and continued to change. I was never called Jon Vi, and I lived in a southern state seven hundred miles away.

My Amish great-grandmother's kitchen encompassed the traditional one room as part of the larger house, a summer kitchen set up in the breezeway between the house and the woodshed, a combination vegetable, flower garden bordered by a grape arbor, and the basement cellar where her fruitfulness was packed into glass, quart jars. Her recipes are handwritten in English on the pages of a bound black and white composition notebook. Of her fifty-four recipes, twenty are for desserts and fifteen are for pickling either fruits or vegetables. Other recipes include how to sugar cure a ham, how to make red beet wine, and two fruit salad recipes. Directions are given to herself to include a pinch of salt and a scant 1½ cup of flour. However, most recipes do not give instructions but only list ingredients.

Some of her recipes include other inscriptions that have nothing to do with how to make the food item but have everything to do with the social milieu and the exchange system of recipes. The vegetable soup recipe is from Sol Sevilla Schrock, and the red beet wine recipe is from Emmanual Katie. The spice cake recipe is from "Eli Stutzmans [sic] youngest daughter from his first wife." Other comments have to do with the success of a particular recipe. For example, the peanut cookie has this statement at the end of the ingredient list: "They are good."

Other recipes reflect the diseases and do-it-yourself conditions of the culture. Recipes follow for "A filler for the Floor," "Master Mix Laying Mash" for her chickens, and "Death to Quack Grass."

Only one recipe from my great-grandmother is found in the green card file recipe box of her daughter, my Conservative Mennonite grandmother. And it is for grape nuts, a cake made with wheat flour that is cooled, cut in squares, grated on a wooden-framed screen, laid out on a baking sheet, and dried in the oven for one day. It makes a delicious cold cereal for breakfast that is still enjoyed in the extended family. My grandmother's box contains one hundred and sixty-one recipes with 75 percent constituting dessert recipes. Few, if any, written instructions, including baking times and oven temperatures, accompany these recipes. A few casserole recipes are included and some pickling recipes. Meat,

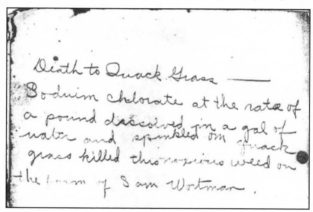

vegetable, and fruit preparation are absent. Unlike her mother's collection, recipes for treating diseases, aching feet, animal husbandry, and floor repair are nonexistent. Several recipes include information on who gave her the recipes, and it is always in the form of the woman's first name preceded by husband's name. One recipe for a drop sugar cookie is named Orus Katie Cookies.

My grandmother's sugar cookie recipe includes a list of six ingredients with little or no detailed instructions for mixing, no instructions

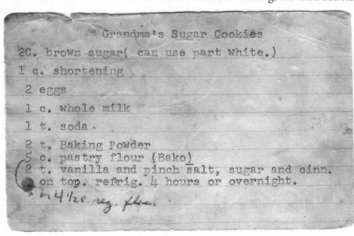

for what utensils to use, and no baking instructions. My grandmother's family role or *Grandma's* is included in the title. She makes the assumption that the users know standard measurement equivalents.

Although its origin is my grandmother, who says this recipe is "in my head," the written sugar cookie recipe comes from my collection, and I typed it with revised instructions handwritten at the bottom. My grandmother's recipe does not exist for her in written form, and when I met with her to make these cookies, she took time to remember the recipe she is accustomed to using. However, because of her recent decrease in memory retention, she was not successful in recalling it. I, therefore, produced mine, which I had written down during a telephone conversation with her many years ago. I find no complete sentences in either recipe: No mixing instructions, and no oven temperatures or baking times. The ingredients are listed in the order in which they are used except that the instructions call for the cook to add the milk alternately with the dry ingredients. These specific instructions are not written, but they are usually learned by young females in kitchen conversation in the form of oral recipe.

Because the written form of the recipe is sparse in nature and demands contextualization and shared knowledge, face-to-face conversation is a pre-requisite to recipe usage. These interpersonal relationships—the notion of community—are so valued that the giver's name is often assigned to the recipe's name. Thus, a plain sugar cookie becomes Grandma's Sugar Cookie. Katie Hershberger, my grandmother, by being the sole maker of these cookies over the years, has transferred this variety of sugar cookie to her ownership. One of her major roles in the family is being grandmother to her grandchildren, and this status is overlaid on this recipe. With the giver's name a part of the title, there is a reciprocal relationship between name and product that endures over time. Indeed, the identities of food and my grandmother become exchanged and wedded so that the she becomes the product and the food takes on her personality.

The recipes of my grandmother allow for improvisation, substitution, and experimentation. Because my grandmother knew three languages

(Pennsylvania Dutch; English; High German, used only in some church services) and because Pennsylvania Dutch is an oral dialect of German used in many Amish person's everyday conversation, recipe literacy events are often marked by the usage of two languages—English usage for the written recipe and Pennsylvania Dutch for the talk mediated by the written recipe. In other words, often the participants in the literacy event are reading English and explaining it in Pennsylvania Dutch. In the recipe event that included my grandmother and me, a Pennsylvania Dutch word was used to give me further instructions for creaming the first few ingredients:

Vi: Creamier than this? Is that about right or should I do it more yet?

Katie: *Knotch* it a little bit yet. [Both women laugh.]

Vi: *Knotch.* I know what that means, but how would you say it in English?

Katie: Oh [her voice trails off]

Vi: Like, you *knotch* a baby, fuss with them, and spoil them.

Katie: [sifting flour] *Knotch* or smooch (loving caresses given to babies and to young children).

This culture, based on German influences and marked by its regular usage of Pennsylvania Dutch in certain everyday speech situations, uses English as the language of writing in recipe genre. Yet, it relies on this dialect of German to carry over certain means to insure the product's outcome. Babies and food alike receive tender, loving care from these women.

The genre of recipe is not only a cultural representation of food preparation, but we can include how-to accounts of survival and of ways to make decisions in life. Embedded in these interviews and in the kitchen conversation between my grandmother and me are stories collecting recipes that list ingredients for survival, for the reification of the existing societal milieu, and for a resistance discourse regarding gender issues, material inequities, and religious dogma. In 1952, my Amish great-grandmother encapsulates these ingredients and writes from her winter home in Sarasota, Florida to her Conservative Mennonite daughter (my grandmother) in Uniontown, Ohio:

Great-grandmother hosted two meals that particular Sunday. She lists what and who she served at both dinner (noon) and supper (evening). Prior to these meals, she attended church where Eli Bontrager preached. She pronounces both her food and the sermon "good." For my great-grandmother, and many Amish women like her, the evaluation of food and religion is tightly linked.

The woman's role may be to provide for the physical and spiritual health of her family, but it was the man's role to provide the funds so this health could occur. He was the provider for her materiality, and it is his name that is inscribed upon her recipe. It was the man who was poor, not the woman; however, her lived experience—her materiality is poor. His impoverished condition did not necessarily bring him shame since these were the years directly following the Great Depression. Prior to the year when the above letter was written, both women, my great-grandmother and my grandmother, experienced widowhood one year apart, and hard times hit. Since the man in the family provided for the family's monetary income, his absence meant lean times for everyone. One recipe found in my grandmother's recipe box for Poor Man's Steak is testimony to this moment in family history. Not only were there no steak recipes found in this box, but this was not steak. Instead hamburger mixed with crushed soda crackers and water simulated steak.

My grandmother worked as a maid cleaning one home per week until she was in her mid-seventies. By then, she had long passed the time when she needed the money, but she states that it was very important for her to have her own spending money so that she wouldn't have to ask her second husband for it. This she states in spite of the fact that my grandfather was generous to a fault with his money and would have given her any amount she asked.

Many years ago, my grandmother's first husband died, and she became employed outside the home killing and dressing poultry in a butchering business. This employment was acceptable in the Amish church/community for pragmatic reasons in order to provide for the family's daily needs and to make ends meet. She recounts a time when a neighbor man gave her a brace of live rabbits, and she was grateful for the meat since she had three hungry children. The neighbor presumed that she knew how to butcher them since she worked in a poultry butchering business. But she had never butchered rabbits, and she had heard that when their throats were slit, they cried like newborn babies. She is a strong woman, but she shrunk from this task. When I asked my grandmother why she did not ask the neighbor man to kill the rabbits himself, she replied, "I wouldn't let him think I couldn't do it." A good woman makes it somehow; no matter how much she suffers, she provides. This woman says she prayed, and the rabbits made no sound as she strung them by their feet on the clothesline and executed the deed. The relief is still mapped on her face as she tells the story. Her prayer provides a refuge and a safety net for this deprivation of materiality. God could know her weakness, but not men who are directly under him.

Moreover, religion and food are inextricably linked in other ways. One way this linkage is represented is that religious instruction and food instructions are given to the very young, and they construct reality for the young girl in the family. When I was eleven years old, I stood in a line of other young people full of nerves, fear, and wonderment as we

#736   07-31-2010 1:31PM
Item(s) checked out to 28055000013377.

TITLE: The outermost house : a year of l
BARCODE: 37535000633208
DUE DATE: 08-21-10

TITLE: Four fish : the future of the las
BARCODE: 37535000961526
DUE DATE: 08-21-10

TITLE: Les plages d'Agnès [videorecordin
BARCODE: 36014000596741
DUE DATE: 08-07-10

Tivoli Free Library
http://www.tivolilibrary.org/

were baptized and made members of our local Conservative Mennonite church. It was in this year that I had grown into the "age of accountability," knowing right from wrong and being accountable for my behavior alone before God and his church. I was eleven years old and the church leaders placed upon me full membership into a community of faith. This baptismal rite of passage was accompanied by another rite granting me full membership into the community of Conservative Mennonite women: The time had come for me to learn how to cook and bake. My grandmother said so. And thus it happened. As an eleven-year-old, I stood by my grandmother and learned to roll out pie dough.

To this day, my recipe for a flaky crust has no instructions, but I hear her voice over my shoulder every time I wield the rolling pin. As in religion, food preparation has an order, a pattern, a certain way of doing. My grandmother embodied right and wrong ways to practice behaviors relating to moral character so that what she practiced became ethical practice. Before I could learn how to make Grandma's Sugar Cookies, I had to drive to three different stores to get the specific ingredients needed. For my grandmother, there was no compromise for the special flour, lard, and buttermilk required. While mixing the dough, she pressed the creamed mixture over to one side of the large, stainless steel bowl so that she could break four eggs into the other side and beat them. This, my grandmother stated, is to save using another bowl for beating the eggs. I attempted to scrape every trace of lard from the measuring cup, but she still found lard I missed. She must use every drop. She must waste nothing. Through food and its production, young girls and women learned the right way to prepare food and the right way to behave to achieve just the right effect. These *right ways* make up the work expected by these participants as they labor today to achieve salvation among their peers and tomorrow in heaven.

Luciana Lopez

Love Me Tender

The year I lived in Japan I always parked my bike at the low wall outside Shiki station whenever I caught the train to Tokyo. I took the 30-minute trip three or four times a week, going into the city to meet friends or shop after work. Each time, the old man at the food cart, his white clothes immaculate, cheerfully pointed to the signs nearby. Though I read almost no Japanese, I understood: No parking. I'd smile and shrug and laugh, and the man would laugh back. I trusted my bike lock to deter thieves, and the dozens of other bikes parked at the pedestrian alley's end to keep the police from singling me out for a ticket or worse. At the old man's food cart, the salarymen grabbing a bite and a beer after work paid us no mind. Our exchanges were regular but brief, limited by our lack of language. A quick greeting, the man pointing at the sign, my sheepish laugh; then I'd go into the station and catch my train

I knew why I'd caught the man's eye: Though near Tokyo, Shiki, where I taught English on a government-sponsored program, was a small town. Americans were rare—to say nothing of brown-skinned Latina-Americans. By October, when the man motioned me over to his cart on my way home, I'd lived in Japan for more than two months. He was a small man with close-cropped gray hair and a sun-leathered face, perpetually good humored, his age hard to tell. The man waved his hands and burst into Japanese, and I saw that one of the beer-drinking men at the cart this time was a Westerner, who then began to translate.

"He says he's been wanting to talk to you," said the other gaijin, who introduced himself as an American university professor named Paul. "You always flirt with him when he tells you you're parking your bike illegally."

This surprised me: I'd never thought of our pantomimes as flirting. My actions had been, really, more of a brush-off than anything: Sure, I'd been nice, but in the end I was still parking illegally. I tried not to react, fearing I would say or do something that would be taken, as my smile and laugh, as more than I meant.

Another rapid exchange of Japanese. "He thinks you're cute, too." I was flattered. In Japan, cute is a big compliment—Hello Kitty is a national icon, and even such sober institutions as banks employ cuddly cartoon mascots. More than that: I'd grown starved for male attention in Japan, where not only did I not fit the local standard of beauty, but, as a non-blonde, I didn't even meet the foreign standard.

Yet pleased though I was, I didn't know how to take it, what might constitute an over- or under-reaction. I stalled for time by laughing and trotted out a stock thank-you: "arigatou gozaimasu." The stall owner's name was Sato, said Paul. Sato urged a cup of beer on me. "Alcohol nomanai," I declined, for once grateful for the slight liver condition that kept me from drinking. Persistent, he took out a 2-liter plastic bottle of unsweetened brown tea. "Take the tea," Paul suggested. "It's only 100 yen a bottle, anyway." I was grateful for Paul's guidance, even though I didn't understand why he offered it. I accepted a plastic cup with both hands, the politest motion I knew how to make, and took a small sip after saying a ritual "itadakimasu," the Japanese courtesy spoken before receiving food. I didn't drink it all: If I finished it, I might be perceived as greedy, I thought. And holding onto the half-full kept gave me something to do with my hands, so that I didn't feel quite so awkward.

Sato wasted little time; "I love you," came his heavily-accented English. The salarymen drinking at his counter chuckled appreciatively. He pressed his suit. "His wife died last year, and now he wants to marry you," Paul translated. Sato must have been 60; I was 25. In the States a man like Sato would have come across as creepy, and I would have cut him off quickly. But in Japan, where I'd grown used to the safer atmosphere, Sato's amorousness charmed me. More than that, it stroked my undernourished female ego. As an average-sized American woman (around a size 8), I often felt ungainly and unfeminine—almost Amazonian—in Japan, where much of the population was shorter than me. It mortified me to admit it, but I missed the admiration of men.

But if Sato's overtures caused me little fear as to my physical safety, socially, I had no idea how to respond. My consternation must have showed, as Paul again advised me. "You're supposed to say thank you," Paul informed me.

"Domo arigatou gozaimasu," I said, bowing, the most formal thank-you I knew how to say, preferring to be thought over-polite than rude. I added a small laugh, a nervous reflex easily accepted in a country where laughter conveys embarrassment as often as amusement. The men around me nodded their approval and turned back to their cups of beer. I relaxed a little, grateful for their approbation, though still unsure of what would come next.

Showing his prowess as a provider, Sato asked me if I liked oden, if I wanted dinner, gesturing towards the stew-like dish of boiled vegetables, eggs, and fish cakes which made up his Tuesday night menu. I told him I liked oden but had already eaten. In truth, I was wary of accepting dinner, of triggering the calculus of gift-giving and—receiving in Japan. I didn't want to incur obligations and responsibilities beyond my understanding.

Then Sato asked me if I liked takoyaki, fried dough balls with octopus at the center. I thought it was safe to answer yes, as there were none at his cart. But I had underestimated him. Sato walked a few meters to a small white takoyaki stand I hadn't noticed and bought an order of half a dozen, each smaller than a hen's egg. Over my protestations, he presented the clear plastic case to me with a small flourish. "Spending money on you is his way of making a point," Paul emphasized. What point, I wanted to ask, and can he unmake it? Please? I gave another bow, another "itadakimasu," and opened the case. I offered the dough balls to the men around me, trying to dilute the debt of Sato's present.

As they speared the seaweed covered balls with toothpicks, I felt glad not to be alone in partaking of Sato's generosity.

"Do you like karaoke?" Sato asked me, his English halting. I said yes—my biggest and most constant lie in Japan. I hated singing before others, my voice always off-key no matter how hard I tried. But karaoke wasn't about what I wanted so much as about taking one for the team, so I'd learned to take a deep breath and accept the microphone.

Sato furrowed his brow as he formed his next question. "What is your karaoke song?" he asked.

"Hey Jude," I answered promptly. I'd come to appreciate the virtues of this song: a simple tune, well-known lyrics and a moderate tempo that virtually guaranteed enough audience participation to mask my weak voice.

The salarymen joined Sato in encouraging me to sing, and I warbled a few bars, trying not to cringe. The men applauded, obviously for the effort and not the skill.

Sato returned the favor with a rendition of "I Left my Heart in San Francisco," the lyrics occasionally metamorphosing into an indistinct but enthusiastic "la, la, la." He moved on to "New York, New York" with the same verbal haphazardness. When he meandered into Presley's "Hound Dog," I joined him. Despite my usual embarrassment, Sato's good humor drew me out, and, to my surprise, I found myself enjoying the song. He ran through an impromptu Elvis medley, extending one hand to me, the other placed over his heart.

When I finally begged off for the night half an hour later, I'd run out of Elvis songs and had drunk my fill of tea. As I said goodnight, Sato gestured as if to shake my hand, and I reached across the broth-filled tubs of oden. The singing and camaraderie had made me happy, and I was proud, too, of how I'd handled Sato's declaration of love, his good-natured flirting. I felt pleased with myself, like I had passed a social pop quiz. I had turned Sato's advances into a friendly, low-key exchange, an interlude and nothing more, I thought. But at the last moment before our handshake, Sato turned my palm down and kissed the back of my hand. He grinned at me, his face a mix of mischief and glee, as if he knew—had known all along—how I'd tried to divert his attentions. *See?* he seemed to say. *I have lessons for you yet.* I smiled back, and the laughter of the salarymen followed me as I withdrew my hand.

Joseph Zaccardi

Recipe

Parts of the Skillet:

The hanging ring, the handle and tang, the iron side and bottom,
the seasoned surface, the weight.

She's showing me how to make golabki, she says the word
slowly, ha-loop-kee, so I'll understand; how to scald the cabbage,
how much rice to cook up, the pinches of salt and the measure
of thyme, what cut of pork and beef is best, what attachment
to use on the meat grinder that has the raised foundry's name
under the lip of the hopper.

What's golabki mean, I ask, I mean literally.

Parts of the Knife:

The neb and rivets on the handle, the bolster, guard and heel,
the back of the blade, the blade, the free edge, the point.

Golabki means golabki, she says. She sniffs. Some people call it
pig-in-a-blanket. But that was after the Nazis and Stalin. Now
here's how to make the sauce, my secret: sour cream,
Hungarian paprika, and the fat from the pan juices,
and flour.

Without this, they lie like unclothed bodies side by side.

Teresa Barnett

Food for Thought

"Next to eating good dinners, a healthy man with a
benevolent turn of mind must like, I think, to read
about them.

— *Thackeray*

It was my second-grade teacher who introduced me to *Charlotte's Web*.
"A reader like you," she said, "you can't pass this one up," and she thrust
the book into my hands. I know now what she hoped I would find: the
naive but true-hearted Wilbur, the book's loving homage to friendship,
the wit and grace that even a spider can reveal under pressure.

And indeed I did like *Charlotte's Web* — devoured it in one single cross-
legged-on-the-bed, arms-drawn-tight-around-my-knees, don't-come-up-
for-air-until-you're-finished sitting. But what I remember about it is neither plot nor theme nor character. Not the humor of quasi-human per-
sonalities in vividly egg-laying, blood-sucking bodies. Most certainly not
the artful demonstration of how the right words in the right place can
triumph over even the meat cleaver. No, what I remember is both more
abstruse and infinitely more direct: I liked the descriptions of Wilbur's
slop.

> Breakfast at six-thirty. Skim milk, crusts, middlings, bits of
> doughnuts, wheat cakes with drops of maple syrup sticking
> to them, potato skins, leftover custard pudding with raisins,
> and bits of Shredded Wheat.

Or later in the day:

Skim milk, provender, leftover sandwich from Lurvy's lunchbox, prune skins, a morsel of this, a bit of that, fried potatoes, marmalade drippings, a little more of this, a little more of that, a piece of baked apple, a scrap of upside-down cake.

Who could resist it, this roll call of the edible? Each item present for a moment in all its specificity, each dense with objecthood, with texture, smell, and taste. Food, food, food, food, as literal as life and twice as much.

For if I should suspend my reading long enough to visit my mother's refrigerator, I knew what I would find: containers of leftover Campbell soup casseroles, neatly stacked bins of carrots and celery, shelves unstickied by sweet, sugary desire. The cookies would always be locked in cupboards beyond my reach, the food portioned out in three restrained and well-balanced meals. While here in Wilbur's trough, the foodstuffs dripped like honey, like heaped chocolate sundaes, shelves of bright candy, acres and acres of frosting-glopped cakes. It was inexhaustibility, satiation. It was every pleasure my mind could muster, world without end.

So there it was, short and to the point: what you could not have in life, you could in books. Literature as compensation, pure and simple. But then there was that other thing — the fact that I need not have tasted a food to be tantalized by its name. What, for instance, was marmalade? Or that storybook staple custard pudding? And what about that prodigy known as upside-down cake? Swap the two sides of a cake and taste itself goes topsy-turvy? Alice's Wonderland sudden, perhaps, and startling on your tongue?

Reading these lists reminded me of that other list: the catalog of luscious foods I had encountered only in books. There were chocolate phosphates, crumpets, dumplings, peach cobbler, popovers, and shoofly pie. The puddings — Indian, Yorkshire, tapioca, and plum. Drinks that promised infinite contentment — wassail, mint juleps, hot toddy, and spiced rum punch — like soda pop, I imagined, and hot chocolate combined. Those substances as smooth as ice cream and as tasty as all of its flavors in one. In their silky names you could hear it: blancmange, syllabub, ambrosia, and manna. And of course there were the candies I scouted the penny-candy shelf for in vain: toffee, horehounds, Turkish delight, salt water taffy, and—name that said it all—sugarplums. Then besides all these, in sonorous roll: pemmican, clotted cream, hors d'oeuvres, fritters, egg creams, cream puffs (anything with cream), Welsh rarebit, sarsaparilla, turnovers, tarts, truffles, trifles, souffles, and hot-cross buns. Not to mention the never before heard of candies that Pippi Longstocking bought by the pound; Mary Poppins' medicine, able to take on any flavor you chose; and the food pills of the future that made you taste an entire spaghetti dinner.

Such words—devoid of referents, complete within themselves—reminded me of a pleasure I had recently discovered in a Sunday school song. "Apples red and apples yellow," the line ran, "round and juicy, sweet and mellow." "Round" and "juicy" I knew—they were good words, right words for an apple. But this word "mellow" was new to me. And yet, though I had never heard it before, instinctively I grasped its cool, vintage mouth-fillingness, the way it wrapped up in two bursting syllables what "round," "juicy," and "sweet" had to limp through in more halting and imprecise fashion. Apples were good, but far better to say this word. If I longed to devour apples, now I knew I longed even more to describe them.

W. H. Auden writes of a similar childhood preoccupation. As a young boy, he says, he showed an inordinate interest in machinery, and his parents naturally assumed that he would become an engineer. But a more profound observer, he argues, would have noted that he had no mechanical aptitude whatsoever and would have realized that his interest was thus a symbolic one. It was not the literal cogs and belts and turbines that Auden loved, but the way they could be used as symbols. Not the world but its metaphors. And it is precisely that preference for the non-literal, he says, that ensured that he would become a poet.

But I, alas, was no Auden. I was nine years old, caught between the world and its representations, dreamy and grasping and all too ready for a fall. My grandmother had a gingerbread castle, kept like fine china in a tissue paper nest, brought forth with ceremony every Christmas time. It was the stuff of imagination: turrets and spires and stained-glass windows. It was the stuff of here-and-now reality: thick, swirled frosting and Necco wafers and M and M's. There I was, nine years old, and what I could not do was merely look. Now that the castle had sat on the mantle through every Christmas I could remember, one day I persuaded my grandmother to let me eat it. All expectation, my mouth opened around the realm of fairy-tale magic, and, inevitably, closed upon the ashy texture, the non-taste, of decade-old candy. There I stood, dust in my mouth, my poetry irrevocably deformed by a huge, tooth-pocked bite. And intuiting, this too irrevocably, that perhaps metaphor is metaphor and should be left as such.

So undoubtedly I would have done better to have been Auden, to have known my literal from my metaphorical and, if I could not have been a poet, at least been happy in my literal munchings. To have either inhabited that castle in imagination alone or stuffed myself on fresh and unpoetical gingerbread. But, in truth, the dilemma still seems to me unsolvable. Thrust back into my grandmother's kitchen, that castle regenerated before my eyes, what would I do?

For maybe Auden can say "food" and mean all things else, but when I say "food," I mean food. I mean the French bread I tear off in hunks and stuff in my mouth as I run out the door. I mean the brownies a friend bakes for me and which I parcel out in slivers for weeks. I mean the soup, freighted with its nuggets of onion and squash and potatoes, which I spend all afternoon making and whose aroma rises, steaming, toward my face at dinnertime. And when I say "food," I mean too that stuff that foams like endless verbal meringue across the pages of cookbooks and novels and menus. I mean the liberally sprinkled adjectives: "freshly ground," "extra spicy," "braised to perfection." The lingering step-by-steps: "sauté until golden," "whisk until light and fluffy," "season to taste." I mean the groaning, page-long tables of Thomas Wolfe, the banquets spread before Odysseus and that wine-blue sea, Levin and Oblonsky's dining, William Carlos Williams's plums, the catalogs of the young Gargantua's meals, Proust's madeleine, the Ghost of Christmas

Present's puddings and chestnuts and stuffing and cakes, and the fact that Babette spends all her fortune on one supernal meal.

And even now, now as I write these words, I cannot choose. I write. The words refuse to flow. I reach for a bag of tortilla chips. I munch. I write. I cross out. I tear open another bag of tortilla chips. For words that will not fill my senses, I stuff in chips that will. Or perhaps the words do flow, and then, reveling in twofold pleasure, I stuff in food even while I write. Words/tortilla chips. Words/Snicker bars. Words/double-decker lasagna with three kinds of cheese. And finally, when even that is no longer enough, as I eat I take to writing about food. This essay whose crunchy, whose adjective-rich sentences sustain me, this essay in which perhaps, finally, my literal and my metaphoric worlds will merge. If I had enough food, would I cease to write? Give myself over to days of gorging and never once think of touching pen to paper? Or if I could write well enough, would I cease to eat? Would I then have mastered desire? Have learned to live in the castle without fear of devouring it? "Cilantro" and "ginger." "Succulent" and "caramelized" and "tart." The way "marmalade" smacks its lips twice and then smugly closes its mouth around its fullness, while "dollop" simply plops itself down, lolling in its pleasure for all to see. "Creamy" and "toothsome," "cinnamon" and "dill." All the rich, ripe broth of edibility comes pouring down.

Wilbur stood in the trough, drooling with hunger. Lurvey poured. The slops ran creamily down around the pig's eyes and ears. Wilbur grunted. He gulped and sucked, and sucked and gulped, making swishing and swooshing noises, anxious to get everything at once. It was a delicious meal—skim milk, wheat middlings, leftover pancakes, half a doughnut, the rind of a summer squash, two pieces of stale toast, a third of a gingersnap, a fish tail, one orange peel, several noodles from a noodle soup, the scum off a cup of cocoa, an ancient jelly roll, a strip of paper from the lining of the garbage pail, and a spoonful of raspberry jello.

At the Kitchen Table

Edward Espe Brown

Nurturing the Heart

One of the primary ways we connect ourselves, one to another, is by eating together. Some of the connecting happens simply by being in the same place at the same time, sharing the same food, but we also connect through specific actions such as serving food to one another or making toasts: "May I offer you some potatoes?" "Here's to your health and happiness." Much of our fundamental well-being comes from the basic reassurance that there is a place for us at the table. We belong here. Here we are served and we serve others. Here we give and receive sustenance. No small matter.

I found that serving food in the meditation hall at Tassajara was an extremely powerful practice; powerful because it was a deeply intimate activity. Taking place in silence, the basic transaction of serving food is vivified, so that the subtle inner workings become apparent. The mind of the server and the mind of the recipient are transparently revealed — you don't have to be a genius.

Suzuki Roshi often said that when we all sat in the same posture, as we did in meditation that it was easy to tell the differences between people. Sure enough, serving one person after another, the flavor of each was apparent: anxiety, greed, calm, respect, anger, fatigue. We were all so nakedly revealed for what we were. And people receiving their food could tell the mind of the server: ease or awkwardness, nervous or composed.

Suzuki Roshi's mind was unique, vast and spacious rather than small and petty. He seemed to be neither conniving to produce particular results nor struggling to avoid other outcomes. His movements were ordinary and unremarkable, yet he was vitally present and precisely responsive. Without rushing or being hasty, his bowl would be in exactly the right spot to receive the food, to receive me. Over and over again, when I served him he was like this. A wave of tenderness would come over me: he was just there, ready to be with what came.

Once in the question and answer ceremony after sesshin someone asked Suzuki Roshi what he felt when she was serving him food. Yes, I thought, what is his mind at that time? "I feel like you are offering me your most complete love, your entire being," he answered, and I knew it was true, because that's what I was doing when I served him, and I knew he was receiving me thoroughly and wholeheartedly, without reservation. I felt healed each time I served him.

It wouldn't last long though. As I proceeded down the row after serving the Roshi, my more ordinary mind would return, and I'd become progressively more speedy, running a silent critical commentary: "Can't you get your bowl out here more quickly? Where's your mind anyway?" "Do you have to be so greedy?" "Stop being so picky." I had something to criticize about everyone except Suzuki Roshi.

A part of our training was learning to move energetically, the Japanese Zen ideal of movement with vigor and enthusiasm. So I would try to serve as many people as I could as quickly as possible, which is not the same you might note (as I was studiously not noting) as being polite or gracious. Basically I would be racing the server on the other side of the meditation hall to see who could finish first.

The people being served tended to get in my way and not cooperate as effectively as they might to see that I got down the row as quickly as possible. Once in a while I would remind myself to try to see virtue. Calm down, I'd tell myself, don't be in such a hurry to get to the end of the row. Yet this was difficult because I prided myself on being the fastest server.

I wasn't happy being caught up in this obsession, but I didn't know what to do. Then one day I had a sudden inspiration, "Why don't I treat each person as though he is Suzuki Roshi?" Is there fundamentally a real difference between people or are there just these differences that I make up and believe are important? Isn't everyone basically worthy of respect and careful attention? Why don't I treat everyone as if she is Suzuki Roshi, because each person is at some level Suzuki Roshi. I saw that I could bring the same mind which I brought to serving the Roshi to serving each person: the same respect, courtesy, tenderness, and patience.

Doing this was difficult at first. By the second or third person after the Roshi my habitual mind was back in play, but gradually I slowed down. I don't know if anyone noticed a difference — no one commented to me about the change — but I felt lighter and more connected, not only to others but also to my own being. The fact that I was no longer belittling and demeaning others meant that some part of me could relax and be at ease as well, no longer in fear of being attacked. To honor the person being served is to grow larger-hearted and honor oneself as well.

I have kept up this practice for many years now, so that even when I became a waiter at Greens I continued to make this effort to serve each person as I would serve Suzuki Roshi. I did my best not to get involved with who was who, how they behaved, or how they 'deserved' to be treated based on how they treated me. "Here is your food, my heartfelt offering for your well-being." "May your heart be at peace, and may you grow in wisdom and compassion."

Kathryn Law
Twig and Dried Leaves

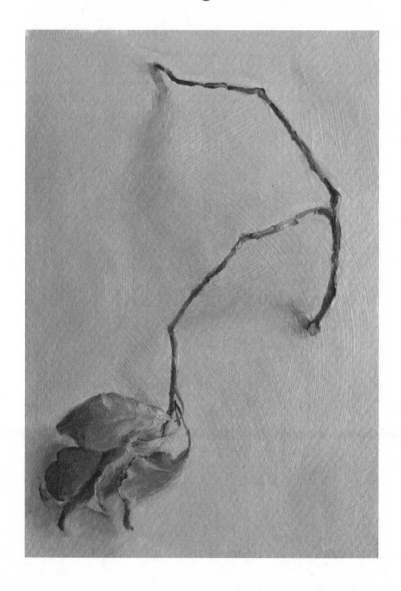

June Cressy

Tonglen

I went to Denver for Christmas, something I love and hate to do. I love seeing my brother and mother. Most of the time. And I hate to be caged indoors in frigid weather. The house shrinks. So after seven or eight days of visiting with each other, and the temperature now a blistering twenty above, we all decided to "go somewhere." As the visitor, I got to choose. Somewhere was Boulder. In the back of my mind I wanted to visit Naropa Institute, a college founded by Tibetan Buddhist, Chogyam Trungpa Rinpoche, several of whose books I had been reading lately. His message of compassion spoke to me. Several times I had practiced his breathing meditation called tonglen, in which you visualize taking in the pain of another on the inhalation, and release your own peace back to the other on your exhalation. Naropa was in Boulder. But it was Sunday, so I really didn't expect the place to be open; and even if it was, there weren't any specific questions I wanted answered. I wasn't going to move to Boulder and enroll. It is a cold place, and I am in a poor state. Part of me loved the fantasy of going to an "away" college. Especially one that spoke to my heart and soul, as well as my mind. But I am middle-aged, with a steady job, a pension and a mortgage.

The college was so small we passed it by the first time. On the way back, we slowly rolled up to a very old, burnt-umber stone building with small turrets all around. It reminded me of half-scale castles at theme parks. It had probably been an elementary school at the turn of the century. I couldn't see how great minds and spirits like Trungpa and Allen

Ginsberg and his fellow beat poets and artists and writers and those others bringing Tibetan Buddhism to America could possibly fit into so small a space. How could such big sky minds crowd into tiny rooms with tiny desks and tiny chairs? I never went up to the door to find out. It might have been open, but I didn't get out of the warm car. My brother looked at me. "Well?" I passed the baton. "Your call."

We ate in a trendy brewery restaurant with shiny chrome beer bats behind the thirty-foot long bar. Five twenty-five inch televisions blasted hungry patrons with the day's football drama. Sated, we three bundled up again, and headed out to the pseudo-posh shops of this neck of Boulder. One shop sprouted two-thousand-dollar lumberjack-split, varnished pine couches, with attached deer antler lamps, perfect for snuggling up on with sweety before a lush fire and warm brandy. Another bragged two-hundred-dollar Angora wool sweaters to cut the seasonal chill. This was not my neighborhood. And there was also enough piercing air outside to nip my nose and make my eyes tear each time we left one store and headed thirty feet to the next one. I kept my head down and my arm wound through my mother's to brace her from slipping on the ice beneath the snow-covered cobblestones.

I was thus focused on the upcoming warmth when she jerked my arm and stopped me in mid-step. Annoyed with that and the cold, I looked up at her pointing to a man I had ignored as we walked past. He sat on the edge of a large, red brick planter box that held a young Spruce tree and three wire reindeer strung with red and white lights. Somewhere in his past, this man's bland face had been badly burned. His lips were several shades of scar tissue. His eyelids had not been successfully reconstructed. His colorless hair, matted by a once-blue watch cap, was missing in places. A gray, worn aura surrounded him. There was an emptiness in his eyes that both grabbed me and made me want to run.

"Go get him a cup of coffee." My mother's voice snapped me back. Part of me thought coffee a too-little-too-late solution to this man's future. Another part of me remembered recently re-reading one of Trungpa's Buddhist stories of the little girl walking along the beach, throwing back into the sea one of thousands of starfish that had washed ashore the night before. The adult with her said her efforts would make no difference. The girl, tossing another starfish back home, looked to the adult and said, "Made a difference to that one." So I walked into the deli a couple doors up and ordered a large container of coffee.

As I looked around and waited, the surroundings and my thoughts pulled me back to the donut shop my parents owned when I was young. Depression-raised, they worked seven days a week for many years, and were always paying off one debt or another. Yet my father was forever cashing checks a little earlier than their due date, and running tabs on those who were a week short of their next Social Security payment. The little old homeless lady, a regular, never paid for her coffee and donut with cash. There was an unspoken sweat equity arrangement between her and my mother. She wiped down all the stools with her napkin, and then, with a big toothless grin, accepted the bag of donuts waiting for her mysteriously at the end of the counter. The church got the leftover donuts to distribute.

Again and again, my mother's hand tugging on my arm speaks to me. On this particular visit my brother and I had already contributed several dollars to people shivering at nearly every stoplight in Denver, all clutching small cardboard signs describing their plight.

Hot coffee in hand, I went outside and walked up to the man on the planter box and gave it to him. His hands had been cold and dirty for years. I wish I could say it was a spiritual moment. I wish I could say he looked into my eyes and we both beamed. We didn't. We didn't speak. We each nodded, almost imperceptibly. I can't rightly say I would love to have invited him home to dinner, or even to a restaurant meal. I can't say I wished I had done something to improve his greater life situation. I wish I could have wished that in the moment. I only gave him a cup of coffee.

I turned and rejoined my brother and mother. She told me that while I had been in the deli, she went into the bakery next door and got a bag of day-old pastry, which she gave to the man before I returned with the coffee. I put my arm through hers as we walked toward the next shop. And again, it mattered to this one.

Janice Levy

The Bottom of Her Feet Were Pink

My mother was not from the cooks. Her measuring cups were chipped, her pots dented, her pans blackened and bruised. She used the bottom of her shirt as a potholder. When she burned or cut herself, she'd give a yelp, but never put on a band-aid. She was always in a hurry.

While my mother cooked, I spun on a rusty stool, my legs kicking a counter, and watched music videos. My mother fried the meat patties until they looked like charred shipwreck, then plopped them on a paper plate where canned peas and carrots swam. I had to eat fast, before my dinner sprung a leak.

My mother unhooked the safety pin cinching her waistband and ate standing up, digging her hand into a box of Ritz crackers. When my father's car pulled into the driveway, she swept the crumbs into a corner and pushed bobby pins through her kinky hair. "Next shift," she announced, taking my plate away.

My father sat alone at the table on a cushioned chair and ate off a real plate; his peas and carrots were even hot. But still he griped, scratching his stomach like a bear. "Again no napkins? No ketchup? No fork?" My mother scurried back and forth like a kitten on glass.

My father gave me the change in his pockets, then waved me away; he said he liked to hear himself chew. While he grunted into his newspaper, my mother leaned against the stove, dipping Oreos into black coffee. She didn't split them open to lick off the cream. Until she shooed me out of

the kitchen, I watched her watching my father and swallowing her cookies whole, like a snake.

My family didn't "do" Thanksgiving. As far as I knew, you did Thanksgiving only if you were a Pilgrim or could cook like Martha Stewart. But
when I was six, my father invited his boss to Thanksgiving dinner at our
home.

"We never — " my mother protested. "Really, Richard, you don't even
like turkey." She picked at her cuticles. "I don't have what to wear."

My father suggested a flour sack. He was more concerned with his
boss choking on a bone or the roaches carrying away the food. He said
my mother cleaned with her eyes shut.

I said I'd dress up as a Pilgrim and mash cranberries in the bathtub
with my feet. I danced with a broom and flapped my arms like a turkey.
My mother reached for a bag of chips. My father massaged his forehead.
Then he opened the Yellow Pages and called "the agency."

Though I'd never met Dora-from-the-agency, I knew she had to be
someone important, because my mother taped tissues around the toilet
seat and copied down the license plate numbers of Dora's car. I was
puzzled, though, when my mother hid her gold watch in a Cheerios box
and followed Dora from room to room as she cleaned.

Dora sang to the turkey as she rubbed it with spices. She taught me
how to roll out dough for the apple pie. I traced my hand on construction paper and colored the fingers like turkey feathers. Dora didn't yell
when I spun across the floor in a big wooden salad bowl. I asked her why
the bottoms of her feet were pink, and she said the skin had rubbed off
from so much standing. I laughed when she took out her front teeth.
Dora braided my hair and stopped a run in my stocking with clear nail
polish. She said I was the prettiest Jewish girl she'd ever seen, and that
my nose wasn't even that big.

"Dora," my mother said, "you'll do the dishes after the company's
gone." Then she squeezed my arm. "Don't you come downstairs until
you're called."

Dora and I sat on the floor in the corner of my bedroom, picking up
the conversation through the heating vent. "Your wife's quite the little

lady, isn't she?" the boss said. "You must have slaved all day," his wife said to my mother. "Everything is just perfect."

I asked Dora why she didn't go downstairs and tell them the truth. She said there wasn't any point in trying to take credit, because you could wait a lifetime for them to give it to you, and she'd rather have the time of her life than wait a lifetime, any day. Then she told me to name all the things I was thankful for, and when I got stuck after cell phones, my fish Goldie, and Big Macs, she said I should be thankful it was the turkey in the oven and not me.

Dora and I had our own Thanksgiving. We ate an entire box of Malomars, picking off the chocolate shell and scraping our teeth against the graham-cracker bottoms, then stuffing the marshmallows into each other's cheeks.

"Happy Thanksgiving," Dora said, and she gave me a sip from a bottle she'd taken from my parents' "keep-out" closet. I asked her to wake me when they called for me to say my 'How-do-you-do's.' Dora smiled, then took off my glasses and kissed the part of my face that nobody ever touched.

Mimi Moriarty

Sipping Lemonade

Imagine sitting under an apple tree
sipping lemonade from glasses, red rimmed,
supermarket tag faded on the bottom,
undissolved sugar resting under a slice.

She is about to tell her story around a truth
she has imagined, a truth she cannot bear
without a story surrounding its edges,
pulling it in, folding cheesecloth around it.

She clears her voice, holds the glass in two hands,
sighs with the weight of the story.
Then a tear, one solitary warning, breaks
the surface of her downcast eye.

You notice hesitation, then a glance toward
the kitchen. She leans against the weight,
"This," she whispers, "can go nowhere but here."
She points to your heart, then back to her own.

You lean forward, elbowed, your own glass
makes the sound of ice cracking, and your eyes
meet hers, a pact. The story of your father
streams out, a tart taste to the tongue,

runs a rivulet in the grass until it reaches the porch,
slips under the house he built with hands
calloused from chopping wood, planing wood,
framing wood around a kitchen window

so the light will shine through.

Stephen D. Gutierrez

Who's TJ, Who's What?
Tamales on Christmas Eve

It's a tradition, more than a tradition, a way of affirming who we are. Despite the protestations of who we aren't—TJ's, a bunch of fresh, over-the-border Mexicans with no couth, unsophisticated and unprepared for the big city, L.A., and all its glamorous trappings, such as are represented in the little holes we occupy there, lower- middle-class enclaves with little to recommend them except warmth and shelter (maybe that's enough! One year you're in Mexico suffering under a palm roof on the outskirts of the *rancho* you don't even own, complaining about the brutal *jefe*, and the next year the clouds clear and you're in California with enough to eat until you look up and see your family around you, and, *hijo de la chingada*, nobody has starved in so long you mustn't be *un pobre* anymore, let alone your grandchildren seeming so American it's almost painful to watch but for the blessings of food, shelter, work, clothes, and a little left over for a good party on Christmas Eve)—we eat the ancient foods and claim some connection to *raza*, to the people, no matter how disdainful. Seated in a living room festooned for the occasion ("Merry Christmas!" "*Feliz Navidad*," provided the soundtrack early on, aunts and uncles and cousins and relatives so distant you barely knew they existed bursting in with food and drink and taking their places comfortably), on couches and in chairs set up in a loose oval, we struggle with *tamales* on paper plates in our laps, poking at the *chili*-colored husks until they unravel to reveal the beauty of a burnt-orange mound of *carne* wrapped in *masa*, done the old way, not with prepared cornmeal ("*masa preparada*," the concession to the modern age still sounding a bit ignominious to the purist, the connoisseur of real Mexican food), the *masa* ground by hand this year by fiat of an obsessed *viejo* drooling in the corner. He's doomed to die of a rare cancer within months, so he has demanded of the women an authenticity within arm's reach.

He has seen it all, the leap from the most perilous poverty to this nighttime scene of joy and a table so plentiful we must have never been that poor after all, really, come to think of it. It wasn't so bad back then in the old days, the days of the crossing and afterwards of working and living in L.A., the slick stone-castled place above the smog-line that everybody fit into easily. Paradise was our natural destination.

We were angels with our style and debonair grace. Our classy wings flapped so hard nobody could notice the *huaraches* on our feet when we left the ground and hung out in the blue-tinted porticos, getting along with anybody with a pipe and an ascot.

"I remember when…" And Grandfather and uncles were more sophisticated and elegant than in the pictures you've seen of them, average Mexican men, workers in denim jackets and dungarees, leaning against posts in the greater L.A. area between jobs or looking awkward, not quite right, in Sunday suits. Big smiles, thin mustaches, ropy muscles, not at all the Clark Gables they're made out to be.

"We weren't TJ's like these new ones around here."

"That's for sure, pass me the *sal*, honey, these beans are a little bland… *Sin sabor.*"

"Rita! Tutti's complaining about your beans again!"

"*¡Ay, tú!* Shut up! On Christmas Eve! They're delicious, Rita, just… yummy. *Sabrosos.*"

"Here come the TJ's, ssshhh." Down the street, a group enacting *Las Posadas* stops at a house and knocks; a patch of dirt separates us, and then there is the hall for community events. We see them out the front window standing under a porch light.

"I wonder if they'll come here."

"Naw, they won't. They know who's Mexican on this street."

"*¿Cómo qué* who's Mexican?" Grandmother pipes up bringing in another plate of *tamales* to offer around. "We're all Mexicans here but you, Tutti. You think you're what? *¿Princesa de esta calle de tierra? ¿Carlotta aquí en mi barrio?* Sheesh, don't tell me Mexican. *Soy mexicana.* I'm proud."

Munch munch. Silence.

"Still, we're different…"

"What do you mean, different?" A cousin wants elaboration. She scrunches up against the couch and asks honestly. She holds her hair up in a twist and listens.

"Well…"

"I heard on Independence Day they threw parties, our grandparents back then, great grandparents." I wink at another cousin across the room. "Roasted goats and flew *la bandera mexicana* proudly. Wasn't that true, Mom? They threw big barbecues in your backyard celebrating *el dieciséis de setiembre*?"

"Yeah, and they got drunk and got all sentimental over *el grito*, they sure did."

"Sound like a bunch of…*un poquito*," I nudge my grandmother because we understand each other, "TJ to me."

"*Ay*, enough. Don't talk about my *abuelo* that way. He was a good man."

"He was." Grandmother assents to the goodness of her father-in-law.

A knock at the door, and we all spring up. On the porch, Mexicans dressed in traditional costumes crowd around us, Joseph and Mary asking for entrance. And we, the non-traditional, not-Mexicans that we are, bow our heads and listen.

We smile gravely at the pitch.

"*No tenemos espacio en la casa.*" Grandmother handles them, and when she's done, turning to us with a smile of satisfaction on her face, asking us, "Who's TJ, who's what?" we bury our faces in the food, scooping up the beans, the rice, the *tamales* on the plates under our noses.

"*¿Estos tamales están buenos, no?*" The ancient in the corner pipes up in exaggerated Spanish. "*Tan sabrosos como en méxico.*"

And we all laugh.

Kathryn Law
Chili Pepper with Knife

Christine Huynh
Notice the *Ha Gow*

My mother knows the difference
Between eating shark fin soup
And love,
But she doesn't distinguish.
It's easier to feed me soup,
Give me money,
And stay up late waiting.
She does this as if
She's done it all her life,
As if when she was born
She was waiting for *me*
To be born,
To give me lectures,
Play games with me,
Cry when I stopped paying attention,
Stopped noticing the *ha gow*
And the rice
She'd leave on the kitchen table,
Still warm to the touch.
She knows the difference,
But can't distinguish.
She makes fried broccoli
With oyster sauce
Sautéed in tears and silence.
We hardly speak.
Rice has been steamed twenty-two years
In regret,
In a large pot
All spooned into a bowl
Ready to eat

Whenever I want.
She will still look at me,
Dying to ask,
Have you eaten yet?

Sharon DeBusk

The Chicken Wars

Two years ago, my 16-year-old daughter McKenzie and I were having breakfast in the kitchen when she read this headline from the morning paper: **Ocean fish slide toward doom. Over fishing and pollution threaten global disaster by 2048.**

With that, she looked me squarely in the eye and said: "I'm not eating fish any more. Or chicken either."

This wasn't the first time she had denounced eating fish, pig, cow or chicken. The girl who once loved cheeseburgers had become a devoted vegetarian at 13, citing the cruelties of eating animal flesh. Recently, she had allowed chicken and fish back into her diet, only because our doctor warned that she needed to bring up her iron counts to avoid anemia.

From the beginning, I feared her growing body wouldn't get the proper nutrition if she went vegetarian. I couldn't resist asking her, "How can you be a vegetarian when you don't even *like* vegetables? To which she would reply: "You're not the boss of me, I'm going to do what I want ... and you shouldn't eat meat either."

And just to set the record straight: I love vegetarian food. I just like a little meat on the side.

❧

Our kitchen became the stage for many a power struggle between us, mostly centered on her vegetarianism. I consider chicken to be one of nature's healers, and all I really wanted was for her to eat some—for the sake of her health. She just wished I'd stop trying to get her to eat chicken. Over and over, we played tug-of-war with the brittle wishbone, each hoping it would snap in our favor and we'd get our wish.

Then she started getting colds and coughs, followed by strep throat, pneumonia, mononucleosis and finally an infection following removal of her wisdom teeth. I was at my wit's end. This kid needs some protein, damn it! If she would just eat some chicken...

I was worried for her health, but the truth is, when she was sick, her surly moods subsided. She would let me comfort her, stroke her feverish brow—and yes, she would even eat my homemade chicken soup, swimming with pillowy matzo balls. She let me love her in a way that was natural to me—by nourishing her.

I remember the baby books that I read when my daughters were infants. The authors counseled new parents not to take it personally when their child refused a certain food they had offered. The books said, "Food is not to be confused with love."

But food and love are surely intertwined. Doesn't the most inspired cooking have love at the source?

Anyway, the food-love connection is set up from the beginning. How do you breast-feed your baby and not equate that with love? I can roll the years back to 1990, when my daughter breast-fed for the last time. We are sitting at the side of our quaint outdoor neighborhood swimming pool. McKenzie is 15 months old and nursing, her shock of dark hair billowing in the summer breeze. She suckles away. The love is flowing. Then she pulls off, head craned toward the excitement in the pool. She scoots from my lap and toddles away—the first of many steps toward independence.

⁊

McKenzie turned 18 recently and moved into a nearby apartment with friends. During her last year at home, we found plenty of topics to argue about (boyfriends, curfews, college). But I also began to embrace the difficult process of letting go. I stopped fighting her vegetarianism, for one thing. We found we had a shared love of cooked spinach, especially if it was sautéed with olive oil, garlic, feta and toasted pine nuts.

Shortly after she moved into her new place, she called me to say she had developed a bad sore throat. I found myself at the store buying a roasted chicken.

When I appeared on her doorstep with it, she rolled her eyes. But she politely took the chicken and put it in her refrigerator. I'll never know if she ate it.

These days, we get along better and even share dinner together once in awhile. She always eats the same thing, though, which is never chicken. It's salmon.

Perhaps I should just take a little comfort in that, and offer you a recipe for salmon chowder. But no, I'm going to wave the long end of the wishbone, and give you my recipe for chicken matzo ball soup instead. Enjoy—and be well!

Sharon DeBusk

⅊ Chicken Matzo Ball Soup

For the soup:

1 whole chicken
2-3 boneless, skinless chicken breasts
Onion
6 to 8 garlic cloves
Carrots (you'll need a few for making the broth and a few for the
soup itself)
Celery (same as carrots)
A few pinches of herbs de Provence, or Italian herbs to taste
Red pepper flakes

For the matzo balls:

1 cup matzo meal mix
6 eggs
2 T vegetable oil
2 tsp salt
6 T of the chicken soup

First make a chicken broth by boiling the chicken, along with coarsely chopped garlic, onion, carrots, celery, herbs, and salt and pepper. When fully cooked, strain chicken broth into a 6-quart pan with lid. Remove and discard carcass (or clean it and use meat for something else. The boiled chicken tends to be too stringy for the soup). Also, strain out chunks of fat, skin, bones or other undesirables from the broth.

To the broth, add 1 freshly chopped onion, 3-4 sliced carrots and 3-4 sliced celery ribs, a few whole garlic cloves (if desired), and more season-ing, to taste. Let the soup simmer awhile to cook vegetables and allow flavors to mix.

While the soup is cooking, make the matzo balls. Using two bowls, sepa-rate the eggs into yokes and whites. To the yolks, add 6 T of chicken soup, 2 T of vegetable oil and 2 tsp salt, and mix well. Beat the egg whites until they are stiff.

Very gradually stir the matzo meal into the egg yolk mixture, and then fold in the egg whites. Refrigerate for at least an hour so that the liquid can absorb into the matzo meal.

Sauté the chicken breasts and slice into bite-sized chunks. Set aside to add at the end.

Now it's time to cook the matzo balls. Bring the chicken soup to a boil and then reduce to simmer. As quickly as possible, form matzo mixture into roughly 1½ inch balls, and drop into the simmering soup. Don't worry if they look a little unformed in the pot. Just quickly put the lid on and trust that they will look more like balls when they are done! Simmer 60 to 70 minutes, and refrain from lifting the pot during the simmering period.

Then, add chicken pieces and season with salt, pepper and red pepper flakes, to taste. Enjoy!

Kathryn Law
Feather

K. Nadine Kavanaugh

Bread Machine Blues

Downstairs, in the kitchen, my new bread machine is baking a loaf of whole wheat bread. Its crust will be golden brown and it will smell wonderful. My husband and I will eat it all week, as toast for breakfast, surrounding turkey and cheese for lunch, and to sop up any plate leavings toward the end of dinner. Unlike plastic-wrapped, pre-sliced, store-bought sandwich bread, it won't last too long, because it has no preservatives in it—I know, because I added all the ingredients myself. But we'll finish it in good time, and then I'll make another.

All this is clearly great—so why do I feel so equivocal toward that lumbering chrome box?

The Bread Machine Comes Home

We received the bread machine as a wedding present this past summer, and we had it for a good three weeks before I shook it out of the box. We had registered for it, certainly, but then we registered for a lot of things. Registering is fun. Now here it was, enormous, shiny, and expensive, and I wondered if we'd really use it. Weren't bread machines the epitome of the useless wedding gift? I'd read magazine articles about the dread single-purpose gadget which, once put on its high shelf, would justifiably molder for years, only to be guiltily noticed once a year when, stepladder out, the great hunt for the Christmas decorations was in full swing.

I resolved that this would not happen to me and my bread machine, and so I dutifully read both booklets that came with it, washed the moveable parts with warm water and a gentle cloth, cleared a patch of counter space, and set about baking my first loaf of bread machine bread.

After some minor difficulties—I had to go to the store to buy yeast—I popped the ingredients into the pan in the prescribed order, pressed a few buttons, and a few hours later the apartment filled with the smell of fresh bread. The loaf that came out smelled nice and tasted fine, but it was nothing special. And I needed that counter space for other trinkets, so after another gentle wash, the bread machine went back into its little cardboard and styrofoam coffin.

Then we moved, and I am happy to tell you that the kitchen in our new apartment is an actual room, with cabinets and drawers and even enough space for a table and chairs. The bread machine got a spot on a counter all its own, and there it sat, mocking me. *Don't you want fresh bread?* it whispered. *I see you with that pre-sliced stuff.*

This time, before baking, I did some research, which is to say, I spent about an hour on the internet and then went to the store. I wanted to go whole grain, with a nutty flavor and chewy texture, and I bought whole wheat bread flour, all purpose unbleached bread flour, rye flour, toasted wheat germ, whole oats, and a bevy of other possible bread ingredients. I made a loaf of bread. It was pretty good, and we ate it up. I made another, with slightly different flours and proportions, and it was even better. Weeks later, I'm still tinkering, but I like the recipes I've developed.

I'm also starting to get ideas. The machine can make dough, which I could make into cinnamon buns. Or I could make homemade pita to go with my fresh hummus.

So why am I torn? Why do I shy away from this thing, even while I adore it? I never had any mixed feelings about the food processor: I welcomed that sweet baby into my kitchen with open arms, and now I can't imagine life without it.

Memory 1: Christmas

Here's the rub: when I was growing up, my mother used to bake bread by hand, herself, without any stinking machine. I have sense memories of this process: the soft flour, the strange rich smell of yeast, the risen belly of dough that looked and felt like skin, warm and elastic. And I have specific memories, of the nostalgia-inducing type. On Christmas mornings, my brother and I were allowed to get up early to open our stockings, but then we had to wait for mom and dad to wake up before we got to open the rest of the presents. My mother always had pans of cinnamon buns rising overnight on the back of the stove, over the faint heat of the pilot light. Once roused out of bed, mom put the rolls in the oven and dad fixed coffee, and then we ate fresh cinnamon rolls while we opened presents. Later in the day, we wrapped a plate of rolls for each neighbor and delivered them, each tied with a ribbon.

This is a good memory. The Christmases of childhood run together like sticky sugar icing, sinking into my psyche and filling me with longing. Was my childhood really like this, full of warmth and food and goodwill? Well, yes and no. These memories are true, but they're only part of the picture—a small part, really. Much of the rest was my mother's yelling and my father's deadly silence and the constant soul-eating strain of there never being enough money.

Memory 2: Boyfriend

I remember the first time I saw a bread machine. For high school, I got a scholarship to the snooty local boarding school, and even though I was a day student, living at home, many of my friends were boarders. My boyfriend was a boarding student: Tom, a sweet boy from Appleton, Wisconsin. He went home to Wisconsin for the summers, and one year we agreed that I would visit him for a week in July. I think that trip to Wisconsin was my second trip on a plane. He picked me up at the airport and drove me to the house he'd grown up in.

As soon as I walked in the door I knew I was in trouble. It was the nicest house I'd ever been in. Unlike my home—in every way unlike my home—there was no dust and no clutter and no cracks in the walls. There was a small stained glass window inset above the door—I didn't know you could have stained glass outside of a church. The kitchen counters were polished and cool to the touch, and there were an espresso machine and a bread machine—just sitting there!—as if they weren't the fanciest things ever. I had never heard of a bread machine before. It seemed like the height of bourgeois decadence to have a machine make bread.

At school, there wasn't much difference between me and Tom. His parents didn't spoil him, and I worked a few afternoons a week for spending money. While I always knew he was richer than I was, that information never mattered. But suddenly, standing in his cold kitchen, I understood something about money and about class that all the reading in the world couldn't make clear. I understood that I had grown up what was called lower class, and that Tom had not. And I understood that, through my education, if I continued to do well, I was transforming my social class. And somewhere deep inside me, I despised Tom for his unearned easy life, his money's family, the bread machine on his family's kitchen counter.

I wanted it, though, too. Being poor sucked. It was stressful. If the car broke down (and it always did, because it was always a very used car, bought for $50 or $100) it was a crisis. All our clothes came from thrift stores or from Woolworth's or Ames—two cheap department stores that have since gone under. And—this drove me crazy—my mother wouldn't buy a new sponge for washing the dishes until the old one fell apart. A sponge smells bad long before it disintegrates, and while I washed the dishes my hands would absorb that smell, which only time, not any amount of scrubbing, could get rid of. I hated those stinky sponges and the lack they represented.

I wanted a life with a car that ran and nice clothes and a stack of spare sponges. And a bread machine.

Memory 3: Illness

Around the time I was in Junior High, my mother got sick. She would have dizzy spells so bad she would have to crawl to get across a room, and her controlling personality became fragmented. Were these after-effects of a long ago car accident? Did she have an inner-ear disorder? Was she bipolar? There were only some of the possibilities suggested by the fleet of doctors my mother went to, one by one. To me, she irredeemably transformed from a strong, if intensely frustrating, person to someone who was fundamentally incapable. She became defined by her pain, by her unnamable illness, by what she could not do.

Given this, it's not surprising that I'm so attached to memories of her as a functional, capable being. Like memories of her baking bread.

What, after all, could be more primal than a mother baking bread? Mother, giver of sustenance and life, performing the alchemy that is baking: flour, salt, milk, butter, yeast and warm water, coming together, rising and falling, somehow transformed into a new element: bread.

Womanly Duties

But. Is this what it means to be a woman? Giver of sustenance and life, I wrote above. And, well, yes—on one level. Women do give birth, and then they suckle those small children. I may well someday do this, though I haven't yet. But I've spent my adulthood struggling against, struggling with, this limited biological definition of woman.

I don't want to be expected to bake bread. Yet here I am, expecting my mother to do so, missing her bread making, and—yes, here's a piece of the puzzle!—feeling guilty myself for not baking my bread from scratch, as she did.

But does my discomfort here stem from philosophy or psychology? What I really miss in my mother is her wellness, her being well and happy and functioning in the world. Fresh cinnamon rolls on Christmas morning are a sentimental example, one I can get a little teary over.

Memory 4: College

I learned to cook in college. I like good food, and I can't afford to pay other people to cook for me. The entirety of my very expensive college education was paid for with grants and loans—my parents couldn't afford to contribute. I worked part time to pay my rent and buy my groceries and for any spending money I might want. My big brother, bless him, dug me out of a couple of holes, but for the most part I took care of myself.

I turned necessity into opportunity and decided I wanted to learn to cook. My wonderful apartment mates and I tackled Italian and Indian cooking—I have no memory now of why we chose those two cuisines: possibly because of spontaneous cookbook purchases—and we graduated with a sizeable spice collection. In divvying up our collective possessions, I renounced all right to the dining table, chairs, and sectional couch in exchange for one gold silk-upholstered chair and the spices. My next apartment featured those, my desk, and far too many books to make moving easy—another lasting legacy of my education.

Womanly Duties 2

Baking bread isn't really the best use of my talents. I can be a cook, a baker, a doer of laundry and a cleaner of homes—and I am, frequently, all these things. Sometimes I even enjoy them. After all, they offer the great pleasure of achievable goals. Dinner can be made. The apartment can be clean. But these tasks can also be pure drudgery. They're time consuming and repetitive. Dinner will be eaten and resolve into dirty dishes—and then will need to be made all over again tomorrow. The apartment is not a static state—the coffee table will again fill up with unopened mail, umbrellas, and CD cases.

More than anything else, I am a thinking person. My job, both what I feel compelled to do and what I get paid for, is to read and to think, to write and to teach. I feel and act as well, of course, but thinking is what I'm really good at. It's what won me all those scholarships. It's what changed my social and economic class. It's what made me the person I am today, with this life, these particular joys and heartaches. Every once in a while, I need to take a break from that person, and then the solemn ritual of bread is perfect: the sleek flour on my hands as I knead, the slow patience of the rising. But for the greater part of my life, baking bread is not for me.

I love the dishwasher because it makes those eternally recurring dirty dishes go away. So why not love the bread machine that bakes my bread?

The Present

My spice collection has only grown in the years since I graduated from college. When we despaired of finding space for a large enough spice rack on the crowded kitchen walls, my brilliant husband mounted a single, narrow shelf along the seemingly useless foot of space between the counter and the cupboards. It's over seven feet long and crowded, allspice through vanilla.

Downstairs, the bread is done (it will be kept warm for up to two hours by that smart machine) and my husband is beginning to cook dinner. In our years together, he's become quite a good cook, too. We still don't have much money, so we don't eat out often, but we have a significantly higher income than my parents do. And thanks to our recent wedding, we have all these lovely, fancy presents.

Like the bread machine. That shiny, pretty box that performs magic, takes simple ingredients and poof! presto change-o! transforms them into leavened bread. In my mind it intersects with such weighty material: domesticity, gender, class, even family and memory. In the end, I think I'm okay with the bread machine, despite all my musing. It gives me the nice food I like, but without the effort. It connects me to my past with its evocative wafting scent, but without turning me a drudge or tying me to a gender role that just doesn't make sense for me.

Mother

And the truth is, I bought my mother a bread machine. She's doing better, by the way. Still not in top form, but better, for which I'm deeply thankful.

Her bread machine is a little less fancy than mine. I bought it second hand, from a graduate student who'd gotten a job in Cairo and was selling all his worldly goods. It's white and plastic and has fewer programmable settings, but that's probably good, because all those options can be intimidating. My bread machine claims that it can make jam, but I haven't tested it yet. My mother makes sourdough breads. She's experimenting with starters.

I don't know if her arms could handle kneading bread at this point. I'm glad she doesn't have to try. I'm glad she can have as much fresh bread as she wants without wondering that herself. And though she and my dad have been eating healthier, lately—low sugar, low carb—I'm glad that she can make cinnamon rolls whenever she wants.

Alia Yunis

Ramada in the Heartland
Fasting in the Midwest's Mideast

For Muslims across the world, all roads lead to Mecca. For Arab Americans, there is a short cut that leads to Dearborn, an inner suburb of Detroit and one of the best place this side of Beirut for decent baklava. Dearborn is strung together with strip malls and anchored by the famed Ford River Rouge Plant, a National Historic Landmark that by the mid-1920s was the largest manufacturing complex in the world. The factory was what brought Arabs—and others—here in the early 1900s. And they've kept coming ever since. Today, Arabic calligraphy forms the signs on many of Dearborn's stores, Middle Eastern pop music booms from the car stereos of teenagers cruising the main drags of Warren Avenue and Schaefer Road, hookah bars offering 52 different flavors of tobacco are busy well into the night, and the local MacDonald's proudly serves *halal* Chicken McNuggets, i.e. chicken slaughtered by merciful Islamic law before it is compressed, molded, and shipped here.

I was born in Chicago, but all my life I have heard stories of this Arab American promised land: considered by some estimates to be the largest Arab city outside of the Middle East, Detroit has been a sort of Midwest Ellis Island for Arab Americans ever since the first wave of Arabs, both Christian and Muslim, arrived here. They came from across the Middle East, from Yemen to Syria and Egypt, and each ensuing Middle East crisis has brought a new wave, the largest number being from Lebanon and the latest from Iraq.

I finally made it to Detroit one December afternoon on a work assignment. I headed straight for Dearborn. It was cold, icy and gray. And it was the end of Ramadan, the Muslim holy month of fasting. While I am someone who questions religion more than practices it, I do know the basic pillars of Islam, and fasting is one of them: so they understand sacrifice and empathize with the poor and hungry, Muslims cannot eat or drink from sunrise to sunset during the entire month of Ramadan. However, what I didn't know was how this was observed in an American neighborhood that has more Arabs than most villages in the Middle East. The person who helped me map that all out was my friend Rana Abbas, a 23-year old, cherub-faced Dearborn native whom you can't help but describe as bubbly and vivacious.

"Detroit is a big city, you know, but when it comes to the Arabs it's a small town," she said with her flat Michigan inflection as she highlighted the key shops of Dearborn on a map. "Everyone knows everyone's business, even if you don't want to."

Rana was right. With her homemade map, I took a walking tour of Dearborn, which involved answering several random and personal questions from chatty shopkeepers. My walk also revealed a bustling atmosphere that I quickly recognized from Ramadans spent in the Middle East—with a little slush and sleet thrown in for Midwest ambiance. Like in the Middle East, fasting shoppers, with surprising energy in their steps, scurried from store to store getting the final ingredients for the dishes they were preparing for *iftar*, the evening meal that breaks the fast. Crates of dates, the food traditionally eaten as fasting ends, were present in nearly every store, as was *jalab* (a raisin and rosewater julep), apricot juice, and tamarind juice, beverages that are often the first liquids sipped at *iftar*.

Rana fasts, as does her entire family. I don't so I was reluctant to go to her family's house—maybe some kind of Muslim guilt—until *Eid el-Fitr*, the day that marks the end of Ramadan. But first I had to make sure when it would be Eid. Ramadan is the ninth month of the Muslim lunar calendar, measured by the crescent of a new moon to the crescent of the next new moon. That's 30 days of fasting from sunrise to sunset.

Or 29. In Dearborn, it all depends on whom you ask. On the 29th day of Ramadan, during my walk, rumors started floating around the shops that Ramadan was going to be a day earlier than expected, that this could be the last day of fasting. At one grocery store, the owner had one idea, his workers another, and his customers were split. At 6 pm, I called the Islamic Center of America, Dearborn's largest mosque. I was told by an authoritative voice that tomorrow would be *Eid el-Fitr*. When I arrived at the mosque at 9:30 pm, I squeezed my way past throngs of exiting Ramadan worshippers, probably over 2,000, only to be told that there would be no *Eid* prayers tomorrow morning as it would, after all still be Ramadan. The mosque was indeed closed the next morning. But worshippers were arriving, ready to do Eid prayers. By their calculations, Ramadan was over. One frustrated man, who had brought his elderly mother for prayers, made a few calls on his cell phone. Soon, other cars formed a convoy behind him as he led them to a mosque that was celebrating *Eid* that morning. I could go into astronomy, the need to have two eyewitnesses to a crescent moon, and various Koranic interpretations, but to put it more simply this wouldn't happen in the Middle East, where most countries have some governmental department that announces the official end of Ramadan and the population follows suit. In the U.S., there is no official department.

I called Rana. Her family had decided it was Eid, although her office had decided it was not. She was at work but I headed over to her house anyway and found her mother, Fatima, already busy preparing dinner.

The Abbas home looks like all the other modest, post-World War II homes that line her block, most painted white with green or maroon trim. However, Rana may be from the most well known family in town, in large part because of their religious and civic accomplishments. She is the public affairs director at American Arab Anti-Discrimination Committee (ADC), a national grassroots organization founded by U.S. Senator James Abourezk in 1980. Her uncle, Haj Adnan Chirri, is the chairman of the board of trustees of the Islamic Center of America. The family's legacy really began in 1949, when Rana's grandfather, Imam Mohammad Jawad Chirri, was invited from Lebanon by the Muslim community to be its spiritual leader. He went on to spend years advocating Islamic unity among American Muslims.

"He was invited to the White House three times," boasted Fatima, who is his oldest daughter, as she walked back to the kitchen across Oriental carpets from Lebanon, pointing out the many pictures of her father that adorn the walls.

A dark-eyed woman with a deep, smoky voice that often breaks into robust giggles, Fatima continued to talk in the kitchen but her focus was on the Eid meal. She wasn't sure how many relatives she had invited, maybe 12, maybe 20. Hovering around her were Hana, Amanda, and Zeinab, her curly-haired nieces, all helping her wash parsley and peel garlic. They often hang out in her kitchen when they don't have school. With Arab Americans accounting for an estimated 60% of the Dearborn public school student body, the school board decided several years ago to make Eid an official two-day school holiday.

The girls began fasting half days when they were eight — their choice, they insist, not their parents' — and all three are proud to say they made it through all of Ramadan this year. After asking me if I loved hometown hero Eminem as much as they did and if I thought Justin Timberlake was cute, they told me that their aunt's cooking was so good she should open a restaurant.

"Oh, please," Fatima blushed, as she poured pan juices over three plump, paprika-brightened stuffed chickens browning in the oven. "Everyone says that...I was a little worried this morning that I wouldn't have enough food so I bought a leg of lamb at the butcher on my way back from my Eid prayers."

The lamb was roasting downstairs, in the family's equally well-stocked second kitchen. In addition to the leg of lamb and the stuffed chickens, Fatima was in the midst of making two other dishes: *fetee*, a layered dish of toasted pita bread, chickpeas, yogurt (she makes her own), meat, and pine nuts and *sheikh mashi*, eggplants stuffed with spiced ground beef and baked in a tomato and pomegranate. Meanwhile, the girls began washing dishes and Mohammad, the young man overseeing the prolonged construction of the house's new addition got chewed out by Fawziah, Fatima's frail 76-year old mother.

"God, I'm going to die before you finish," she shouted with the aid of her cane. He just smiled a beatific smile as Fatima laid out a plate of her homemade preserved olives and raised her eyebrows into a look torn between frustration and amusement.

Fatima wears a *hijab*, the white head scarf, in public. Rana lets her long curls hang loose, as do most of the females in the family. There are exceptions, like Haj Adnan's 21-year old daughter Vivian, named for Vivian Leigh, who began wearing the *hijab* last year, a choice many young Muslim women have opted for in recent years.

By late afternoon, Rana had come home and relatives began filing in, each carrying a gift box from Masri Sweets, a local landmark know for its rose and orange blossom-infused pastries. There were the exotically beautiful Randa and Majeda (the nieces' mothers, both devote Muslims and *People* magazine junkies), diminutive Rima (Fatima's daughter in medical school), Rima's husband, Randa's husband, Fatima's brother Ali, his kids, and someone's brother-in-law. I stopped keeping track. Two card tables were brought out to extend the dining room table. Plates in a mishmash of china patterns were added as people kept coming in and the nieces were sent off to wash more forks and knives for the table.

Talk shifted seamlessly between Arabic and English and between food and politics. Rana's eyes teared up when she talked about some of the hate mail and death threats they get at work. Her job at ADC is to deal with discrimination cases, and as the number of unwarranted firings and evictions has risen at such a sharp rate, it has taxed her personally, as well as the organization.

"But the truth is we've done really well here," Rana sighed, tossing a gargantuan bowl of *fetoush*, a pita bread, tomato, and greens salad traditional at Ramadan and *Eid*. "There are Arab American engineers at Ford whose fathers or grandfathers worked on the assembly line."

Rana's mood perked up when her husband Hicham came in. They got to know each other in Lebanon through a family set-up, on Rana's first trip overseas. They both reluctantly agreed to meet the other and fell in love at first sight. He moved to Dearborn to be with her and quickly become yet another helping hand in Fatima's kitchen.

While Rana and Hicham tried to keep their hungry guests entertained, in the downstairs kitchen, Fatima got the hummus started (her secret to getting the silky smooth texture of Middle Eastern restaurants is to keep the food processor running for 8 minutes) and went upstairs to do one of her five daily prayers. Meanwhile, Abbas, her husband and a salesman at the nearby Ford dealership, arrived home with some kid-friendly jokes in tow.

But senses of humor were running low, squashed by hunger. The nieces didn't want to hear jokes. They walked around carrying protest signs demanding to be fed. After all, for the last month, they had all been eating at sunset, at 5:30 p.m. It was now 7:30 p.m. On the day when they weren't fasting but rather holding out for Fatima's cooking, the family was starving. Back from her prayers, Fatima snatched a plate about to be filled with food by one of her sisters, demanding that everyone wait for Haj Adnan, also a salesman at the Ford dealership, as is another one of Rana's uncles.

Someone said there was no point in waiting—there wouldn't be enough room for Haj Adnan's family of five. They would have to eat on the second shift, when even more people were likely to show up. Still, Fatima insisted on waiting...until she noticed that her nieces were about to indulge in Hostess Cupcakes to ward off their hunger. This visibly frightened her. She told her sisters and daughters to start putting the dishes out. As the dishes filled the two tables, the guests quickly found seats for themselves. Fatima begged them to slow down, shooing hands away from serving spoons—although not a traditional part of an *Eid* dinner, she wanted to say a short prayer in her father's memory. Silence followed the prayer, but not devout silence. It was a silence tempered only by the quick swish of forks digging in for another mouthful. Arms reached across other arms as people filled their plates, sampling everything, and sending bowls up and down the dining room table and two adjoining card tables. When Majeda saw that I was too shy to fend for myself, she grabbed my fork and lopped creamy, garlicky *fete* on my plate, along with some *sheikh mashi*. The sweetly spiced eggplant was so tender it melted in my mouth, almost like cotton candy. Others kept coming into the house, bearing more boxes of sweets, not here for dinner, but rather to wish the family a happy *Eid*. Having already eaten dinner at their own homes, they talked amongst themselves as the family ate, declining Fatima's offer of a second dinner. And then the phone rang. Haj Adnan and his family were on their way. They would be there in another 20 minutes. The family intensified its eating, knowing that at least some of them would have to soon give up their seats and reset the table for Fatima's next round of guests.

Alia Yunis

❧ Jaj Mahshi
(Baked Stuffed Chicken)

Serves 10-12

Baharat is an Arabic seasoning mix containing anywhere from three to nine spices (the most popular versions have seven). Any seven-spice baharat will work here, as would a combination of allspice and cinnamon.

1½ cups long-grain rice
1 tbsp. vegetable oil
1½ lbs. ground beef or lamb
½ onion very finely chopped
¾ tsp. ground cinnamon
¾ tsp. baharat (Arabic spice mix, preferably seven-spice type)
Salt and freshly ground black pepper
2 lemons, halved
3 3½–4 lb. whole chickens, rinsed
6 pinches paprika

1. Put rice into a medium bowl, cover with warm water, and set aside to soak for 1 hour. Drain in a fine mesh strainer and set aside.

2. Preheat oven to 450°. Heat oil in a large skillet over medium-high heat. Fry onion until translucent. Add meat, cinnamon, Arabic spice mix, garlic salt, onion salt, and salt and pepper to taste and cook, breaking up meat with the back of a wooden spoon, until meat is no longer pink, 6-8 minutes. Add rice to meat mixture, reduce heat to medium-low, and

cook, stirring often, until rice absorbs juices, 6-8 minutes. Transfer stuffing to a large bowl, adjust seasonings, and set aside.

3. Squeeze lemon juice over chickens. Rub chickens inside and out with paprika and salt and pepper to taste. Fill chicken cavities with the stuffing, tie each pair of legs together with kitchen twine, then transfer chickens to a large deep roasting pan. Cover pan with heavy-duty foil and bake for 30 minutes. Reduce oven temperature to 350° and continue baking, basting chickens occasionally, until chickens are just cooked through, about 45 minutes. Remove foil and continue baking, basting often, until chickens are deep golden brown and completely cooked through, 30-45 minutes more. Remove chickens from oven and set aside to let rest for about 15 minutes. Discard kitchen twine and serve chickens and stuffing with pan juices.

Alia Yunis

❧ Fattee

Serves 4-6

The Arabic word fattee refers both to the breaking of toasted pita bread into pieces and to a variety of dishes involving broken pita, stock, and yogurt.

2 cloves garlic, crushed and peeled
Salt
2 cups labneh or other thickened plain yogurt
2 tsp. dried mint, optional
½ cup beef stock
1 15-oz. can chickpeas, drained
½ small yellow onion, peeled and sliced
Vegetable oil
2 5½" pitas, split open and cut into 1"-2" pieces
½ lb. ground beef
1 tbsp. butter
⅓ cup pine nuts
Leaves from 5 sprigs parsley, chopped

1. Crush garlic and ½ tsp. salt together with a mortar and pestle to a smooth paste. Transfer paste to a medium bowl, stir in yogurt and mint, if using, and set aside.

2. Put stock, chickpeas, and onions into a small pot, cover, and simmer over medium heat for 6-8 minutes. Strain chickpeas, discarding onions and all but 2 tbsp. of the stock, and set aside.

3. Pour oil into a large skillet to a depth of ¼" and heat over medium heat until hot but not smoking. Fry pita in batches until golden and crisp, about 1 minute per side. Transfer pita with a slotted spoon to paper towels to drain. Pour off oil and heat skillet over medium-high heat.

4. Add beef to hot skillet and cook, breaking up meat with back of slotted spoon, until browned, 8-10 minutes. Transfer meat with slotted spoon to a small bowl, season to taste with salt, and set aside.

5. Melt butter in a small skillet over medium heat. Toast pine nuts, stirring frequently, until golden, 4-5 minutes.

6. Put pita into a deep medium glass or ceramic dish in an even layer. Scatter chickpeas and stock over pita, spread yogurt over chickpeas and pita, then scatter meat on top. Garnish with parsley and pine nuts. Serve immediately.

Alia Yunis

❧ Shaikh Mahshi
(Eggplants Stuffed with Meat)

Serves 6-12

Stuffed vegetables are common dishes in many countries in the Middle East. This is one of Fatima Abbas's favorite versions.

12 small Japanese eggplants, trimmed and peeled
Vegetable oil
¾ lb. ground lamb or beef
1 small onion finely chopped
Salt and freshly ground black pepper
1 tbsp. butter
¼ cup pine nuts
2 cups tomato sauce
2 tsp. pomegranate molasses
1-2 pinches cayenne

1. Preheat oven to 350°. Cut each eggplant nearly in half lengthwise so that it opens up like a book; set aside. Pour oil into a large skillet to a depth of ½" and heat over medium-high heat until hot but not smoking. Working in batches, fry eggplants until lightly browned all over and beginning to soften, 4-6 minutes per batch. Drain eggplants on paper towels and set aside. Pour off oil and heat skillet over medium-high heat.

2. Fry onion in skillet until soft. Then add meat and salt and pepper to taste to hot oil in skillet and cook, breaking up meat with the back of

a slotted spoon and stirring often, until well browned, 8-10 minutes. Transfer meat mixture with the slotted spoon to a medium bowl and set aside. Adjust seasonings.

3. Melt butter in a small skillet over medium heat. Toast pine nuts, stirring frequently, until golden, 4-5 minutes. Add pine nuts to bowl with meat, mix well, and set filling aside.

4. Bring tomato sauce, pomegranate molasses, cayenne, ⅔ cup water, and salt and pepper to taste to a boil in a medium saucepan over medium-high heat. Transfer sauce to a large glass or ceramic baking dish and set aside. Stuff eggplants with equal amounts of the filling, then arrange eggplants, stuffed side up, in dish with sauce. Bake eggplants, basting with sauce occasionally, until very soft when pierced, about 45 minutes. Loosely cover eggplants with foil if browning too quickly. Serve warm or at room temperature.

Sharon Carter
Fish Market

Sandra Carpenter

Blessings, Blushes and Bruises
Grandma's Special Dinner

September's searing heat of a Mississippi morning melts the tar beneath my feet. The walk along Bessemer Boulevard reminds Grandma of the Devil reaching up from Hades to grab at her shoes. It is 1941 and I should have started school this week. But Daddy is a Naval Officer with a transfer to a battleship docked in Hawaii; he has a 30-day-leave first. He reminds us often that Pearl Harbor is a prime assignment, second only to remaining in California with mother and me.

We had taken a Southern Pacific train four days across the U.S.A. to Natchez, Mississippi, the home of my father's parents. His dad was the son of an Episcopalian minister; his mother had been Rebecca Marx from a prominent Jewish family of Biloxi. The scandal, on both sides, of this match made in the last year of the 19th century had died down by the time I arrived on the scene. Still, there were occasional cultural differences that made us all giggle. Or blush. Or bruise.

The one firmly fixed in my mind has to do with fish: her gefilte fish. On Thursday morning I shop with Grandma (she prefers *Bubbe*, but my grandfather said if he has to be a Grandpa then she is to be Grandma) and it becomes my honor to be chosen for this mission. We walk a few blocks to the store, a fascinating place with a tank holding large numbers of swimming fish. We study them for half an hour, then point to the one most preferred and the storekeeper tosses him out with a net on a long pole.

It isn't always a successful operation: fish don't wait to be caught, but swim swiftly. Often the man with the net catches the wrong fish. I enjoy this immensely, deciding Grandma is so smart—she never gets confused as to her selection, and always sticks by her first choice. Finally our flawless fish is caught, wrapped in layers of newspaper and tied with a string hanging from a metal cage near the ceiling. I wonder how the owner gets twine up there so high. We walk home triumphant, feeling clever at getting just the right one for us. The fish is unwrapped as the bathtub fills; he'll spend his last day in comfort, the least we can do.

Friday morning is special for me. In the kitchen, wrapped up in a canvas apron, Grandma begins with her potato latkes, her flour-white hair falling loose about her face. Those long, black hairpins spring from the wiry bun at the nape of her neck in any major effort. She'd never weighed more than 99 lbs. and at age 61 seems so old to me in her zippered, blue housedress, the one with the horseradish stain, only used for this purpose. Next she arms herself with a wooden mallet holding a huge, square head. To me it seems too big and unwieldy, but she handles it like Hercules, whacking the head of the fish over and over. I feel mystified that long after she says it is dead the tail of that fish twitches an uncomfortable number of times. This makes me uneasy but Grandpa hurls in the knowledge that nerve impulses make tails jump even after it is a goner. He always has answers for everything it seems to me.

Then the vital things start: the making of Gefilte Fish, the first course of her Sabbath meal, which Grandpa graciously allows—but in trade, Sunday, is his day for pork roast. Even if you had *nothing*, like their neighbors, the Kravitz', you saved all week to make it Shabbos. We could stare across the narrow street and see Dora Kravitz at her open kitchen window every Friday morning, with the same sounds coming from the metal chopper banging a wooden bowl. This is done for hours, long enough to make four or five pounds of fish into something resembling mashed potatoes, but it is white fish mixed with carp. The skin of the fish became pockets holding the choppings along with vegetables, special spices and herbs. Mr. Kravitz tells me he's supposed to turn up for the meal looking and feeling like a bridegroom, after a serious bath. Reminding me that their fish had so recently swam in that tub.

If you had no white tablecloth, you use a clean white bed sheet. If you ate coarse brown bread all week, you bake a glistening, golden loaf and put it on the table on a silver plate, if you had one. Best of all to Grandma, you put your worries and labors away. Your duty is to celebrate the best life has to offer. Grandma always forgave Grandpa his trespasses on Friday night, she told me. At age six, I could only guess what that meant. She had accepted the faith of her husband as the tenets of 19th century marriage demanded, had forsaken her heritage and family, never to see them again, drummed out like an army deserter. Yet the heart's core was a Hebrew one, no one could mistake that inner tradition.

Before the sun went down, Grandma lit the candlesticks, the same ones her mother secretly gave for her wedding present 40 years before. She put a golden silk shawl over her head, waving her hands over the candle flames, gathering blessings for our family. She half says and half sings: "May our home be consecrated, O God, by Thy light..." By then, Grandpa (who had been the city's newspaper editor as well as a journalism professor who should know better) is tiring of the whole ritual and says, "Good bread, good meat, Good God, Let's eat!"

My flustered mother, of the staunch Methodist upbringing, smirks, not knowing what else to do. Daddy swelters in the Mississippi evening, and the heat of old conflicts. Saying nothing, he adopts the intolerant expression of his dad. He is his adored mother's favorite; the second, feisty son, so much like her, while Gran's first-born, my Uncle David, has the reserved demeanor of the Episcopal minister he was born to be. Daddy adores her, yes, but she embarrasses him tonight, that much is clear.

Then Grandpa's hand hits the lace-draped table with a swat that sends the silver dish an inch into the air, "Becca, enough already!" His tone unmistakable: he is hungry. But Grandma won't let him get away with it, picking up the cup of sweet Kosher wine to chant the blessing. I have a teaspoon of the wine in a glass, feeling quite grown up. Serenely she completes her singsongs, hand reaching for mine. I rise to stand beside her and the silky, faded yellow shawl slides over my blonde hair. Abruptly, my father stands, taking her arm and mine in a trinity of joined generations. Her sparkling brown eyes meet my youthful blue ones in an intent smile and I realize my small, tan hand resting on her work-worn one was cut from the same ancient cloth.

She had taught the head of her household, Grandpa, under great duress, to cut off the end of the loaf, break off a small piece and pass it, hand to hand, to each one at the table. It wasn't ever offered on a plate, but handed about while Grandma softly sang her dedication. Now her Shabbos is official.

The gefilte fish is tasty, the horseradish is lethal, those potato latkes oven-crisp and prize-winning at a long ago Hanukkah contest. Chicken soup is richly saffron, full of huge drops of oil, perhaps the cholesterol that ended up killing them both with early heart attacks. The only item never mentioned, certainly never praised, is the chicken itself. It cooked from 7am to 7pm and lay dry as a desert. Still, her matzo balls are like feathers, light as air. Carrots, cabbage, spinach and beets melted in a savory soup. We have half-sour pickles and half-sour tomatoes—garlicky, crunchy, delectable. Her special dessert is a combination of prunes, sweet potatoes, carrots, butter, brown sugar, lemon juice and golden raisins baked until honey soft. None is left over. Grandpa sees to that with licks of the huge, golden serving spoon.

Tea is the meal's crowning touch at the end. Everyone wants a different kind, but my choice became *Swetouchney Te*, which arrives in a metal box painted red and gold with a lid swinging back on heavy hinges. I'd been a good helper, so I had a teaspoon of cherry preserves in the bottom of my glass. Grandma put a lump of sugar between her teeth, sipping her tea through it. I learned much later that most others drank tea from cups. Yet they had metal-framed glasses with fancy, rose-carved handles which had been clandestine wedding gifts from her family's rabbi, to be treasured always. And she had.

They were a noisy, debating, loving family who taught me that diversity could be delicious. I'd always remember that—with every taste of tea, with every sniff of fish.

Sandra Carpenter

❧ Oven-Crisp Potato Latkes

2 large russet potatoes shredded
1 white onion shredded
2 shallots, minced
1 teaspoon salt
1 lg. egg beaten
2 matzo, broken small
½ teaspoon Pepper
3 tablespoons olive oil

Toss shredded potato, onion, shallots, salt in bowl, transfer to strainer to drain for 15 min. Squeeze a handful at a time over bowl to dry out, leaving some moisture in mix, move to a large bowl. Pour off liquid in first bowl, leaving the white starchy sediment. Add starch to potato mixture, add egg. In a zip-close plastic bag, crush matzos into coarse crumbs. Sprinkle crumbs and pepper over the potato mix and toss to combine. Cover, then refrigerate until matzo softens, half an hour.

Preheat oven, 425 degrees; coat baking sheet with Pam. In a large skillet heat 1 tblspn. oil. Stir potato mix, scoop ¼ cup into pan, pressing with spatula, repeat to flatten 4 cakes. Fry until crisp and golden, about 3 minutes each side. Transfer latkes to baking sheet, repeat with remaining mix, adding tablespoon of oil to each batch. With all (12) latkes on baking sheet, bake at 425° until heated through, about 10 minutes.

Ella deCastro Baron

Café du Monde

Papa was right when I told him I was going to visit New Orleans. I thought he was paranoid when he told me that I wouldn't feel comfortable in the South. Why did I ignore him when he said they don't serve him and his Filipino Navy "buddies" in restaurants in Alabama or Georgia on their stationed leaves? And this has been true for over twenty-five years since he's been in the military? The last time, they told him they don't serve "brown folk his kind" in a restaurant somewhere in Louisiana.

11 July 1993 — Café du Monde, New Orleans

I can't believe I'm only two hours away, here in this metropolis of ideas and cultures, from Hell. Shaun took me to meet his cousins on his mom's side so that I could meet some of his family before we get married next year. It wasn't a big deal to me that two of his second cousins married each other; first and second cousins marry each other all the time in the Philippines to keep the money in the family so I thought, what's the big deal?

When we got there, his cousin Annette was cooking food for us. She made no eye contact with me, but I didn't think it was because she couldn't stand my color. Shit. Can you believe it? I went to the bathroom, and while there I could hear them talking, interrogating Shaun.

I could hear Joseph, Annette's cousin-husband, talking in his Looser-ana drawl.

"So Shaun, what is she? I never seen anyone like that before." I heard nothing from Shaun. "I mean, she ain't one of us, that's for sure, but she ain't no nigger either."

I heard Annette say from the kitchen's direction, "Maybe she's more like one of those **sand** niggers. They come in all different looks."

I opened the door to step out, and they stopped talking. Shaun was speechless; I could tell by his face. I know he wanted to defend me, but he wasn't prepared for this. He finally said, as we sat down to home-cooked red beans and rice (that Annette bowled out from a big, industrial pot with a two-foot long hambone sticking out) "Ella's a Filipino."

I corrected Shaun, "Filipina-American. American." I don't know why I added that.

I tried my best to drown the entire event, to hover over the situation like I used to pretend to do when I heard mom and papa fighting, threatening to leave each other, and I had to sit there trying not to cry while swallowing broccoli beef and rice.

Joseph noticed I was spacing and said, "You never been to a real farm before, huh?"

At least he's talking to me, I thought desperately. "No, it's such a large piece of land. How do you get to the supermarket or the store when you need something?" I didn't want to hear an answer; I just wanted the meal to end so I could run out of there.

He sat up, suddenly acting interested. "One thing we like to do — I forgot to tell you this Shaun for when you come hunting for deer with us in Georgia — is that, when our shells get old — we don't like to keep rifle shells for more'n a year because then some of 'em don't work when we try to shoot'em — we take the shells, and I mean boxes and boxes of 'em, the boys and me, to some of the nigger neighborhoods and drop 'em on the street out the windows of our trucks."

Shaun and I were visibly perplexed, but I was more stunned by his nonchalant use of the "N" word. I couldn't speak. Shaun asked for us, "Why do you do that?"

Joseph shoveled a large spoonful of beans into his mouth, answering while he chewed, "We figger if we can't out and out shoot'em dead, maybe they'll find our shells and kill each other!"

He laughed with his mouth hanging open, punching Shaun in the shoulder while his beans and rice oozed molten from the corners of his mouth. Annette got up to fill his plate with more slop.

While this happened, Shaun was pursing his lips, and I was trying to scream for help from behind my eyes, my teeth, my skin. Then, in a glitch, Joseph stopped smiling and laughing, leaned forward as if he recognized something in me—maybe my horror I thought, so I grabbed Shaun's hand under the table—and he rested his chin on his elbow-propped hand. I could see the motor oil stains on his curled fingers. I felt I might vomit.

He kept staring quietly now, and as Annette returned to the table, he winked at me and said, "Ohhh, now I know who **you** are. I remember **'Nam.**"

I don't know the next thing that happened except we were driving back down from Thibodaux to New Orleans. I was in so much shock I couldn't react, certain that my spirit was savagely raw, mutilated around the edges, open.

And there they were. The holes, exposing the thing, that Thing I couldn't name but suspected was in me: dark, hot, better left uncultivated.

Ella deCastro Baron

ࠫ Arroz Caldo

This is a Filipino "rice stew," as we kids called it growing up. It literally translates, "hot rice" and is found simmering on stove tops during family gatherings. Our family never ate it alone; it mostly fed the dozens of kids buzzing around the house and yard while our parents played blackjack or mahjong until two or three in the morning (who knows if they ate at all).

2 to 3 lb. cubed chicken — preferably dark meat, but use the breast if
 you like
3 tbsp. vegetable or corn oil — olive oil if you want to be healthier
2 tbsp. minced garlic
¼ cup chopped onion
½ inch ginger finely diced (you can simply slice it if you like, but kids
 hate biting into a chunk of ginger when their brains are thinking,
 "Mmm, chicken")

NOTE: you can use standard measurements, or you can use my relatives and stepdad's measuring tool: use your thumb to point to different digits on your forefinger. For example, a ½ inch of ginger is the distance from the finger tip to the first joint your thumb reaches. Two tablespoons of garlic is equivalent to the thumb pointing to the middle knuckle.

6 cups water
2 cups uncooked short-grain rice
¼ cup chopped scallion
salt or patis (fish sauce) to taste (you can get patis in most metropolitan supermarkets)
¼ tsp. freshly ground pepper

Heat oil, brown garlic, and sauté onion and ginger. Add chicken and salt or patis. Simmer approximately five minutes. Add water and rice. Simmer over low heat for 20 minutes or until rice and chicken are tender. Stir often to prevent sticking.

Scoop into bowls. Garnish with fresh pepper and chopped scallion. (Let the kids decide if they want the scallions; they have enough to contend with avoiding the ginger!)

ৰ্ক

Interesting Thoughts I Have When Making This Dish:

#1 – The first Filipinos to come to the United States came to Louisiana swamps, escaping the Manilla Galleon Trade, as early as the late 1700s. They stayed discreet, but they have left their mark on Louisiana's history. Some of them even fought for the famed Jean Baptiste Lafitte under Andrew Jackson in the Battle of New Orleans, War of 1812.

#2 – A circulated point of pride is that Filipinos gave the word, "boondock" to Louisianans and the South. The Filipino (Tagalog) word for "mountain" is "bondoc" (pronounced *buhn-DOK,* short 'o' sound in second syllable).

#3 – Rice is an import from Asia. How different in purpose (comfort food) and at family gatherings (easy to stretch sparse ingredients to feed many) is *Arroz Caldo* from *Red Beans and Rice*?

The Blessings of Dirty Work

Janet R. Kirchheimer

Gardening with My Father

Staring at the rain and wind, the remains
of Hurricane Charley on its way through New England,
my father paces the house, restless to be in his garden.
I am more content, left to my knitting.

Knit one, purl two. Knit one, purl two.
My mother and I knit afghans for soldiers.
Ten boys have requested them. We are down to nine.
One killed in action last week. The more I knit,

the fewer boys will die.
I am happy to be away from the dirt today.
Two days later the rain stops. My father and I
go out to see the damage. Some of the Big Boy

tomatoes have been split open. Zucchini
squash lies in the dirt and explodes at our touch.
A few blossoms have been knocked off the pole beans.
Now over six feet tall, the stalks are strong and

can survive the rain. In the late August heat,
my father picks beans on one side of the fence
as I work the other side. We rifle through
the leaves that camouflage the beans to find all

the hidden ones. I finish picking and start
to thin out the carrots. I hate this job. I
want them all to survive, but my father keeps
on making me do it, again and again.

They can't all grow to maturity. I throw
the small ones back in the dirt as fertilizer.
I return to my knitting, restless, knitting
as fast as I can.

Dan Brook
The Harvest

Corie Feiner
Burdock

> ...black from dust but still alive and red in the
> center...It makes me want to write. It asserts life to
> the end, and alone in the midst of the whole field,
> somehow or other had asserted it.
> — *Tolstoy*

I want to be that stubborn root,
limbs interlocked with soil and rock.

To be that long muddy weed
of clingy burrs.

To be tenacious and ugly.

I want to smell of sulfur, bug rot, and salt.

I want to cling to your cuffs,
hitchhike on your heels.

Call me Gypsy Rhubarb, Beggars Button,
Gobo, or Burr.

I want to grow alongside your quiet street
and in your tailored garden,

I want you to pull me from your compost
and rock, dislocate your shoulder,

I am buried deep within the earth.

Mary Chang

Delivery

All the ingredients in a dish should enhance the flavor of the main ingredient. This is why asparagus or bamboo shoots are often cooked with chicken, duck, and fish: the blandness of these vegetables enhances the light, delicate character of the meat. Similarly, the blandness of shark's fins and sea cucumbers (beche-de-mer, sea slug) can be offset by cooking them with Chinese ham, chicken, or pork, or in a highly flavored stock.

—*Xue Yuan*

A large white truck pulls up in front of Blessings II Go. One of the delivery men from New York unloads bags of bean sprouts and boxes of other vegetables from the back of the truck while another carries the boxes to the back door of the building. After the men finish, one comes in with clipboard in hand to find Chi Wai, 22, the Chinese take-out manager. As Chi Wai signs the paper, he tells me there are about 50 suppliers in New York City that make the two and half hour trip up to New Haven. They stop here, then head down State Street to other take-outs. He could go with more local suppliers, but says he sticks to the companies he was introduced to by his father's friend two years ago when Chi Wai's family, newly arrived from Hong Kong, opened the restaurant not just because they are Chinese-run, the folks easy to communicate with because they speak the same language, but because they've got better prices.

Soon it is the afternoon rush and Chi Wai, who is in charge of the counter and takes orders, wipes the sweat from his forehead. One customer fiddles with the container of wooden chopsticks, but Chi Wai doesn't seem to notice. A steady stream of customers—drop-ins, call-ins—warrant his attention. Unfazed by the heat, Chi Wai doesn't stop moving.

Chi Wai packs cartons of dishes into two plastic bags, each with a paper bag as lining, and just before stapling the orders to the tops, he throws in a handful of plastic forks and spoons. He grabs the bags and swings out from behind the counter. Chi Wai is on delivery duty today, along with pitching in behind the counter, loading soda and restocking sauces. The driver said he needed a day off although it is not his usual day. Chi Wai lets his thirteen-year-old brother take care of the counter.

"I've got to go do some deliveries. Want to come?" he asks me while he grabs his keys.

I live in the neighborhood and had passed by their storefront weekly on my way to do laundry. I worked at a non-profit since coming back from traveling in China, and missed the frenetic energy of the streets. I had stopped by the take-out a few months ago and asked if I could write about Chi Wai and his family. He said yes, and I had been visiting regularly since then to speak with him, but this was the first time he asked me to go on a delivery.

I jump into the front seat. Chi Wai starts the engine, turns the air conditioner on high, and we're off.

To be outside and on the road feels liberating, sort of. It's so hot today that Chi Wai's grandfather had earlier pulled a chair from his usual corner table inside the restaurant and set it underneath a nearby tree where he sat looking at the road.

Today there were phone troubles, and Chi Wai had to repeatedly contact the telephone company. He worried about losing calls from customers. He has just ordered DSL and wondered if that was part of the problem. But the phone company finally determined the wire needed to be replaced. And Chi Wai would have to pay for it.

It's nice to get away. We swoosh under Interstate 91, and Chi Wai's grandfather comments softly and points to busy Fair Haven Park, full of kids playing basketball. The road beneath the highway is wide but the sidewalks under the highway alongside it are glum, strewn with broken glass. Interstate 95 connects New York City to the wealthy suburbs of Connecticut and the casinos. Just east of New Haven, it crosses Interstate 95, fragmenting the city. "They kill the neighborhoods they go through," Vincent Scully a local professor said of the highways built through many towns in the 60s, an era of urban renewal. "Follow the development of these roads and see how they devastated communities. See how they separate people from each other, from their churches, their schools."

The Fair Haven Park is close to where I live, but I've never thought of going there to toss the Frisbee around. I'd hop on my bike and take Orange Street down to East Rock Park instead of crossing underneath the highway. In New Haven, the highways also cut the city off from its coast. It's easy to forget that it's even there, although on some nights, when the wind blows a certain way, you can smell sea-salted air. But the highways don't affect Chi Wai who breezes under them as if they don't exist.

"I go to work, I come home, but I live so close to where I work — I feel local, like my life is small," I say to Chi Wai. "I've lived here for two years in the same neighborhood as Blessings, and hardly know the city."

"Me too," he says. "I go to many places to do drop-offs, but I don't know what is beyond these buildings, what is happening inside these places that I pass by. I'm too busy normally; it's work." With him, I see the city from a new perspective, see life and potential in all the places I've just passed by before.

Fair Haven, though just on the other side of the interstate from State Street feels like a whole different neighborhood. Doors are open, kids are out on the stoops, people out in the street. Lots of sunlight and lots of cars on the road. Chi Wai knows the city streets well. He has to.

"You don't have time to consult maps when you've got ten orders to deliver," he says.

The two-bag order goes to a Polish woman in the heart of Fair Haven. She orders big once every couple of months and tips well, says Chi Wai. I walk up to the door with him. She smiles when she sees us and asks him to put the food on her small kitchen table. Not much is said, but her thank you as we step out the door is quite warm.

"Forty dollars for a thirty-six dollar order," Chi Wai exclaims in a way that says 'that's a huge tip,' as he closes the gate to her garden, which is filled with yellow flowers, and other late-summer blooms.

Chi Wai looks paler than usual, and yawns repeatedly, rubbing his red eyes now and then. He's exhausted, not only because it's been a busy day, but also because he got only four hours of sleep after attending a business associate's wedding in New York City's Chinatown last night.

He left New York at two in the morning and got home at four. He went as the representative of the family. "I had to go. If you don't go to something like this, it is like saying that you are cutting off relations with them. It's the Chinese business culture; one must participate in it if one wants to do business with them. To get anything done, people will ask everyone who knows you about you — friends, family. You've got to have a good reputation for someone to sell you a place or to help you out at all. It's like in China, people don't follow the laws so much there, but they do have rules, a different sort — that of the group you are a part of. There is much pressure to follow them."

Chi Wai sighs, "The weddings are all the same, though, the same program. Dancing, singing, speeches from the parents and friends, dinner, and a magic show while dinner happens. About two hundred of us last night. You have to pay a company something like twenty thousand dollars for a wedding like that. They'll do all the set up. If you have only ten thousand, then you'll get something similar but less. Why go through this? Because if you don't, people will say you're cheap. Reputation counts. When you are going to do business with someone, you ask around. If the person is not giving money to his parents, you think of the person as being selfish. This makes for a bad reputation. You wouldn't want to affiliate with him."

He says to me, "It's good that you know a bit about Chinese culture because you are Chinese American."

As we pull into the Blessings driveway, Chi Wai turns off the engine and savors the cold air, this moment of peace. He shuts his eyes and rests his head on the steering wheel briefly. The tiredness falls around his shoulders.

The pace has been non-stop. We've just been down Artizan Street, Main Street, and through West Haven.

The afternoon passes quickly. Soon, we are out the door and on the street again. This time, we drive to the west side of town and pass by Ivy Noodle, a Chinese noodle shop that is known for the surliness of its all-Chinese staff, but that has nonetheless done extremely well since opening a few years ago. The counter and tables that run the length of the place are always nearly filled. It is great for lunch because one can order something simple, and it's convenient for dinner because it also offers stir-fried dishes. The atmosphere may be a key part of its success, I think. Though busy, it has an open kitchen, and enough space to chat with friends, giving it a casual feel.

"Noodles are cheap, plus they've got a good location," Chi Wai says. They're located on Broadway, just across the street from chain clothing stores and near student residence halls.

"I've always thought a fresh-made dumpling store would do well in this town," I say. "People who work in my building eat lunch out every day." Dumplings would be easy to make, and can come in so many varieties, I think. I remember visiting a dumpling house in Beijing that offered thirty different kinds, all freshly made and hand-wrapped. They're healthy. People can season as they want with soy sauce, vinegar and sesame oil. One bowl always makes a great meal.

Chi Wai shakes his head as if to rein in his musings about possible evolutions of the restaurant, and says he feels he can't afford to take risks.

I ask why so many Chinese restaurants and take-outs are similar. He says, "One guy tried it this way and it worked, so others just want to do the same. They are all in the same mold. We make what Americans want to eat." In general, Chinese restaurants and take-outs are organized like any chain, often using the same suppliers so that there is a kind of uniformity in presentation. They not only buy the same kinds of food, packets of sauces, disposable kuai zi (chopsticks) and napkins, but also have the same type of outside signage, along with menus and recipes for dishes that "Americans like." Hubs in New York, which help connect workers with restaurants also serves to list restaurants for sale. Potential buyers and owners are linked up. Special scouts seek out potential new restaurant locations in every part of the country and keep an eye out for any going-out-of-business properties. The scouts purchase them to sell later to a Chinese buyer who also promises they will use the suppliers that the scouts suggest. There's a whole network set up for the Chinese restaurant take-out business.

I think back to the white truck from earlier, how the suppliers in some ways defined what could be served. It made sense for them to keep everything as simple as possible. On their supply trips, at their many stops to take-outs all over New Haven, they dropped off the same things although in varying amounts. If there was as much reluctance to try different suppliers in other take-outs as there seemed to be at Blessings, the suppliers had quite a committed clientele. A chain of Chinese take-outs existed, but without any central control. There is no CEO of a corporation or board making decisions from the top; there instead is a kind of decentralized system of families trying to make a living, taking part in a system that was evolving, but somewhat rigid. Suddenly I saw how learning about how one take-out worked was like getting a glimpse into thousands nation- even worldwide. Individual families were the shareholders, and it was a system they willingly participated in.

Chi Wai seems reflective, then says, "Chinese are not risk-takers." Why not? There's the family to think about, he says. "They depend on me for survival. Things are stable now." It's a safe way to make a living. He had left college when the family business in Hong Kong collapsed in order to help make money to support the family.

Late afternoon, it's still hot and traffic is heavy. Chi Wai hands me a couple of bags for delivery, as we slip into his car I ask, "Do you take delivery orders even if they are far away?"

"Sometimes, someone will call and it will take us forty-five minutes to drive out for a ten-dollar order. It's not worth it, but we have to go.

Sometimes if it's really busy, I tell them they'll have to wait for an hour, and usually they'll just go somewhere else."

We pass under 91 again, and this time drive to Wooster Square, the old Italian part of town where two famous pizza places reside that give our neighborhood pizza joint the most competition, and where many buildings were saved from being razed in the 60s. It's now one of the most beautiful parts of town.

"You can try it this time," he says as he hands me the order.

I approach No. 85 in a row of townhouses. The door is open. I peer into the dark kitchen and see a man with his feet up on the table, his back to me, and a phone pressed to one ear.

I knock lightly. He doesn't hear me. He's laughing at something the person on the phone said. I knock louder. He turns his head slightly to me.

"Delivery?" I lift up the white plastic bag.

He goes on with his conversation and rises from his chair, then disappears into another room. Two girls come to the door. They both take wads of crumpled money out of their pockets.

"How much is it?" one says gruffly.

"Twelve dollars and nineteen cents," I say, checking the receipt stapled to the top of the bag.

They squinch up their noses, their looks somewhere between pain and disgust.

"So expensive!" the other girl says.

I show them the receipt and shrug. The bag feels heavy. They must have ordered a couple of things. The comment quells my elation at making my first delivery. I feel myself becoming defensive, wanting to have some quick comeback. But I don't say anything.

Chi Wai later tells me his drivers argue with each other about who gets to deliver to the big tippers. When there are many orders, it concerns him that they go to the big tippers first, because Chi Wai feels all of his customers should be getting the same good service.

"Not much of a tip, right?" Chi Wai says as I get back in the car. I'm embarrassed that they didn't pay enough — nineteen cents short. I hadn't thought of it until I stepped away with the one five and seven ones in hand. I don't know how he knew—perhaps he could see the looks they gave me or recognized their slowness to pay. I remind myself to slip some money into the tip jar to make up for the money I didn't get. I find that I am gaining a steady respect for the difficulty of his work.

It's quiet. I remember a thought I had once when I passed by Blessings II Go and saw Chi Wai and his grandfather sitting together at one of the tables, laughing. How nice it must be to be part of a family business, the different generations working together—the trust, the closeness. Something works here, but there is so much that I don't know. I feel badly for chiding him about cutting down his hours and taking a day off every week. Perhaps it's not so much of a choice. Tired as he is, he'll be doing this late into the night tonight. I think of how I've invited him over for dinner a couple of times with my husband and I, and how his answer has always been the same, "No time."

The sun is setting as we head back to Blessings. I point out the orange glow on the brick buildings, how alive it makes everything look, how warm. Chi Wai tells me he has a dream of buying a "car with a home on the back." His family thought him silly, he says. But he still likes the idea. He could take it around on vacation. When he wasn't using it, he could allow some of his workers to live in it.

He asks me what my future plan is.

"I don't know." It's an honest answer. When I first thought about interviewing him and his family, I had thought of my own life experience as being quite different from theirs in part because the outlines looked different. Although I was born and raised in America, my family moved around a great deal; we weren't part of any Chinese community and as a family we didn't work together. To visit Blessings II Go and find out about life here meant I'd see another perspective of Asian American living, a glimpse into a corner of the world of my neighborhood. I had thought I'd feel like visiting the restaurant was a kind of traveling. But now I realize the distance that I had thought so wide, wasn't. Our families in some ways are more similar than what I had first thought.

When my parents first came to America, my father was in graduate school. I was born during their first year here. I remember how my mother told me my father worked nights, washing dishes at a local restaurant to make money for the family because graduate student teaching paid so little. My mother remembers how he'd come home with sore feet. He'd soak them in warm water, put them up high on a chair, and lean back with his eyes closed. She would tell us that he did this for us. When I was older, whenever my father was angry, he'd say, "Look at how hard I've got to work to support all of you. I have a job today, but who knows about tomorrow." My mother gave up pursuing a career to raise the children, to give my siblings and me a stable life. As a child, I knew she was capable of doing so much more, but didn't, for the family.

Visiting and writing about Chi Wai and his family is like traveling in one sense—I've found that going some place else, being somewhere new, often helps me see the place from where I came from better, more crisply, by giving me a different angle on my own life. From being here, I realize I'm a product of the family centered system in some ways, although I chose a different path, went off on my own, defied parental expectations. Instead of going into engineering or becoming a doctor as they had hoped, I had gone traveling, pursued photography and writing. Now here I was, trying to figure things out, figure out what's next. By rejecting the path my parents had set out for me, I was left on my own.

Chi Wai seems to intuitively understand this. We are quiet for a moment.

"If you ever need a job, you can work here," he says.

I look at Chi Wai and say quietly, "thank you. Thank you."

He had said it almost as if in passing, but I knew he meant it, and that it was a generous offer. If I needed a place, help, a job, I could come here, because we were friends now. Chi Wai had said before that being a boss of anything was better than working for someone else. I think of how it's true in ways I hadn't realized. I realized the power of a place such as this, a family-run business, where there was room for people, even strays like me. Although you'd have to play by the rules, there was space.

Elizabeth Schott

The Weird Vegetarian Poem

Here is how it works:
you stop eating everything
that seems to be sentient,
everything that can run away,
have fear, or feel pain.

You go on for several months this way,
and you begin to notice things.
The animals in your dreams are different;
they no longer hide from you
or fight you for their lives.
Your own animal body
no longer wrestles the protein
into your stomach.
You no longer stand guard
over the tissue of the now-dead.
You feel a clearness and a lightness
that you had not known you were missing,
a quietness, like you can hear the vegetables humming,
and they sound happy.

Only then, you listen a little closer,
thinking you will overhear some quaint, tribal song,
not realizing that the natives are getting restless.
You read about the one-celled devouring each other
before the plants had arisen, evolutionarily speaking.
Which means that plants are,
in a sense, descended from animals.
They could be thought of as animals
who have given up defending themselves

in exchange for not having to take it mortally
every time they lose a limb.
You start to think differently about pruning,
about pulling things up by the roots.
You begin to wonder if carrots
will hear the prayers for absolution
we no longer dare say over a cod.

Perhaps it comes down to learning
to pray in another, vegetable
language. Think of this:
You pick apples one morning,
and each time you grasp one,
you pull gently enough
to make it a question, not a demand.
Feeling how the fruits give way gladly,
you shake the tree and watch your breakfast
drop to the ground all around you,
the big plant laughing.

Mary Makofske

Children, Growing in a Vacant Lot

Nothing listens to them.
Not young men whose hats
hair bands or jackets
tell their tribe
not crack glazing
neighbors' eyes
not knives or clubs
not snub-nosed pistols
baby Uzis, .45s
not bullets homing
through walls like robot
bees to their hives
not rats or roaches
not paint flaking its poison
not cold or the cold drip
of time, not hunger.
So what do they expect
when they poke seeds
in ground they've cleared
of broken glass and crack vials?
Nothing. And when sprouts
spear through earth, open
their first pair of leaves
like hands palm up
offering the light,
what do they expect?
Not much.
But when green leafs up in hearts
to shade white blooms that tongue
out beans no longer than

an eyelash, when beans
stretch, fatten, dangle
plump goodness into hands
and give themselves up
to snap under teeth and fill
paper bags and bellies,
the children don't know
what to expect.

Barbara Kingsolver

The Blessings of Dirty Work

In my neighborhood of Southwest Virginia, backyard gardens are as common as satellite dishes. Now is the time of year for husking corn and breaking beans. Jars bobble quietly in water-bath canners on our stoves: tomatoes, allspice pickles, whatever the garden has overproduced today. If we don't have our own, we can buy bushels from our neighbors' trucks at the Saturday market, because farmers have plenty right now, and what they grow is our sustenance.

Elsewhere that connection may be a stretch of the imagination; here it's not. We move to the same impulse that makes squirrels hoard their nuts, rising at dawn to pick, returning in the evening to pick more. We freeze, we preserve, we give away excess. It's the gardener's World Series — an all-consuming hoopla at the end of the season. We will finish with full larders, our chest freezers overstuffed like suitcases lugged home from the duty-free zone.

I face this work each year with satisfaction, but not without self-consciousness. I come from a line of folks with some dirt on our jeans who've watched the long exodus from the land that seems inevitable to our species. As a popular World War I song asked, "How ya gonna keep 'em down on the farm after they've seen Par-ee?"

Paris I have seen, and places beyond, where many different languages assign similar scorn with the phrase "dirty work." My generation has absorbed an implicit hierarchy of values in which working the soil is poor people's toil. Apparently we're now meant to rise above even touching the stuff those people grow. The real labors of keeping a family fed (as opposed to the widely used metaphor) are presumed tedious and irrelevant. A woman confided to me at a New York dinner party, "Honestly, who has time to cook anymore? My daughter will probably grow up wondering what a kitchen is used for." The lament had the predictable blend of weariness and braggadocio, unremarkable except for this woman's post at the helm of one of the nation's major homemaking magazines.

This is modern thinking. Even keeping house does not dirty its hands with food production. Sorry, but we have *work* to do, the stuff that happens in an office or agency or retail outlet—waiting tables, for instance. Clicking a cash register at the speed of light. Driving a truck on a long-distance haul. We have risen above the muddy business of an agrarian society, heaven be praised. People in China and India do that for us now.

On the other side of the world from that New York dinner party, another influential woman gave me an opposite perspective on leaving behind the labor and culture of food: that it's impossible. We only transform the tasks, she claims—and not necessarily for the better.

Vandana Shiva, director of the Research Foundation for Science, Technology and Natural Resource Policy, is an elegant scientist in her silk sari, with a red bindi on her forehead like an accent mark over her broad smile. She was trained as a physicist but is best known for her work for farmers' rights. The soil of her country, India, is home to one-quarter of all the world's farmers. Increasingly they grow commodities for export rather than traditional, locally adapted foods for their own communities. This strategy was laid out by the technological Green Revolution, as it was called in the 1970s (when "green" was not the word it is today), which promised that one farmer with the right tools and chemicals could feed hundreds, freeing the rest of us for cleaner work.

It sounds good unless you're that one guy on a tractor in Nebraska, and the price of soybeans won't quite refuel your tank and pay for your fertilizer. Elsewhere, it's worse. In India, Shiva says, 150,000 farmers have committed suicide—often by drinking pesticide, to underscore the point—after being bankrupted by costly chemicals in a cycle of debt created by ties to corporate agriculture. Centralized food production requires constant inputs—fertilizers, pesticides and irrigation—that in some settings are impossible to sustain, and chemical-based farming virtually always damages the soil over time, whether in India or Nebraska.

Traditional farming retains soil structure, but intensive modern agriculture does not: Since the 1970s, while global grain production has tripled, an estimated 30 percent of the world's farmland has become too damaged to use. Also shrinking are the fossil fuel reserves for a system that requires petroleum to run the farm machines, serve as the chemical base of fertilizers, fuel the milling and processing plants and drive the food to widely dispersed consumers. Shiva puts it this way: "The new modified crops brought to us by the Green Revolution were described as 'green oil of the future.' Ironically, that has turned out to be correct in a way, as the Green Revolution makes a renewable resource—food—into a nonrenewable one, just like petroleum."

Farmers come to Shiva's farm-based institute in Derha Dun to learn how to free themselves from chemicals, indebtedness and landlessness. Shiva's research has shown that returning to more traditional multi-crop food farms can offer them higher, more consistent incomes than modern single-crop fields of export commodities. She identifies the extinction of traditional seed varieties as the principal threat to food security here; to name an important example, South Asian farmers once grew about 50,000 varieties of rice, a number that has dropped to around 5,000 as a globalized seeds-and-chemicals industry displaces tradition, sometimes with coercion from the Indian government.

The institute, called Navdanya, is a small, green Eden framed against the startling blue backdrop of the Himalayas. On the morning of my visit last December, birds sang from the fruit trees as we ate our breakfast of millet porridge with fruit and nuts, lemon pickle and tea, all grown on the farm's intensively planted organic acres. Sixteen years earlier, with no funds beyond her small savings, Shiva and her acolytes had bought this piece of ruined land, which neighboring farmers advised her would never grow anything at all.

Her devoted team has built the soil with compost and careful crop rotation to its present lushness. After a tour through the fields, we took off our shoes to enter the seed bank room, a precious library of germ plasm collected in labeled jars and baskets: oilseeds, mustard greens, wheats and barleys, 380 varieties of rice. Other farmers throughout the country are building different seed banks of locally appropriate varieties, all replanted in the fields each year as a living catalogue. "This is the basis of Indian farmers' sovereignty," Shiva said. "Our traditional crops."

Navdanya now hosts what Shiva calls the Grandmothers' University, a series of cooking festivals to help connect the conservation of traditional crops with the practical skills of cooking and eating them. Clearly, traditional farming and time-honored food customs are mutually dependent.

Less clear is whether this country could lose its powerful food culture—what is more important to an Indian girl's education than perfecting the art of making her mother's daal? But Shiva warns that even here, the consumption of packaged foods is on the rise. "The nutrition transition is driven by economic changes that coerce people into jobs that give them no time for food culture," she said. "Tech jobs, telephone industry jobs here are mostly held by kids who may have very few other employment prospects. They are making great money by local standards, but they are sometimes working 20 hours per day! In a life like that, there is no time for your mother's daal."

Industrial farming—however destructive to the land and our nutrition—has held out as its main selling point the allure of freedom: Two percent of the population would be able to feed everyone. The rest could do as we pleased. Shiva sees straight through that promise. "Most of those who have moved off of farms are still working in the industry of creating food and bringing it to consumers: as cashiers, truck drivers, even the oil-rig workers who generate the fuels to run the trucks. Those jobs are all necessary to a travel-dependent, highly mechanized food system. And many of those jobs are menial, life-taking work, instead of the life-giving work of farming on the land. The analyses we have done show that no matter what, whether the system is highly technological or much more simple, about 50 to 60 percent of a population has to be involved in the work of feeding that population. Industrial agriculture did not 'save' anyone from that work, it only shifted people into other forms of food service."

Waiting tables, for instance, or driving a truck full of lettuce, or spending 70 hours a week in an office overseeing a magazine full of glossy ads selling food products. Surprise: There is no free lunch. No animal can really escape the work of feeding itself. We're just the only one with fancy clothes and big enough brains to make up a story like that: Hooray, we are far from the soil, and that has set us free.

I'm not convinced. When I consider my own employment history, I can see how much of it was somehow tied to feeding my species. My first writing job was in the public relations office of a university College of Agriculture; I was prouder of the "office" than the "aggie" part of my title. As a 20-something with a paycheck and benefits, I had risen above my rural roots and thought myself quite the professional gal. I wore stockings and pumps to do important interviews. I can still remember how my feet felt at the end of a day when I kicked them off.

These days when I finally kick off my shoes, they are apt to be muddy. Then I can see myself for what I am: an animal that hasn't quite escaped from the land that feeds me. Heaven be praised.

Olivia Chin
A Day at the Market
Phnom Penh, Cambodia

Kim Addonizio
Served

Isn't it lovely when your love brings you coffee
in bed, along with the section of the paper
you always want first, and when you finally get up
your mother-in-law is sliding her spatula
under the cheese blintzes, the potato blintzes,
the special made-with-lemon-zest blintzes
and the sour cream to spoon over the blintzes
that keep emerging from the pan,
the small bagels she ordered special,
have the lox, have the whitefish,
go on she's serving and can't seem to stop;
and after the visit, there's the long airplane aisle
down which the attendants drag the heavy silver cart,
while you snack and drink and recline
your seat completely back. At home
you're too tired to cook, so it's out to the restaurant
with its booths and dim lights, the silent busboy
delivering bread, keeping your water glass filled,
the waitress introducing herself and saying
what a pleasure it is to bring you wine and lamb,
reciting the list of delicious desserts, smiling as though
it truly is her pleasure, until you begin to feel
you deserve it every day, and start to think
this must be your true purpose on earth,
to just sit back and let the others work,
to slip your thumb into your mouth
the way you used to, with no one to slap it away.

Donna Isaac
Thursday Dinner

A boy named Charley once gave me the gift of venison
perhaps because his father had threatened to shoot me
if I trespassed on his property.

A peace offering, the meat lay red and rich beneath white paper,
and the bones, the bones were slight and delicate,
not like shanks and haunches or racks of meat

filling a roaster, all gelatinous hanks and gristle.
I was afraid to eat such nimble flesh pinned together
with a *y* of white, thin like the handle on my mother's teacup,

but I thought about him, poor dumb boy, who shot
his own foot cleaning a gun one day, and about the deer he got
and knew it must have been all about destiny.

I fried it in a pan with butter and ate the sacrificial steak
with a glass of red wine, toasting the boy who hated school
but loved the mountain and the crush of leaves beneath his boots.

Kim Jensen

Long Shelf Life

We became accustomed to a world
without water

We grew at home in a world
without gardens

We raised our children on the prospects
of cardboard

and more wars

Our daily bread
was leavened with the excretion

of combustion engines
and enriched with residue

of uranium.

For eighteen years we lectured
on the merits of public schools

but lived and died
beneath a cloud of human ash.

and often drove past
men with gangrenous lesions

hobbling through
well-lit avenues

but we were accustomed
to the sins of omission

and came to believe
that there was no difference

between past and present
hell and heaven.

Donna Watson

Makin' Groceries

Nan's hands are pecan brown. Not green like the giant's. She say he ain't nuttin' noway 'cep' a figment of corprate 'mericas 'magination. *Don't no green man in tights have nuttin to do with makin' groceries so ya'll betta get out here and learn to grow your own.* So we do. Me and my friend Rachel who came for a weekend in the country. That's the place Nan grew up. She say clean air and sunshine's good for you. We sleep where Nan slept when she was little until Daddy Slim (my great-grand pop) say "Rise and Shine you coal black mines…they'll be no strike today." Then Nan'd throw on overalls, tee shirt, brush her teeth, pour cereal and hope the milk don't have cream on top (which she cain't stand) or taste like grass 'cause it wasn't past your eyes. Her and her sister Kat, big brother Dave, little brother Donnie pickin' rocks out the field and Daddy Slim drivin' the one-ton GMC down the rows in front of 'em. She din't understand then, but she do now cuz she older and done come into her wisdom.

Nan say rocks, *geologically speaking*, come from the earth's insides. Like a woman havin' a baby squattin' under a Poplar tree, pushin' from deep down where everythangs bubbly like applesauce boilin' in the stockpot on back Lil' Bit's wood stove. She my great grandmamma who I barely knew. Nan say Lil' Bit'd mash up the Grannysmiths, strain skins from the meat in a sieve, add sugar and boil down the sweetness. She'd pick apples from the tree or ground (they's called drops and you get 'em cheaper at the Farmer's market) and boil Mason jars, puttin' wax on top to keep the good stuff in and bad stuff what cha don't want no way out.

Lil' Bit had safety pins pinned all over her shirt just in case sumpin' happin' cuz sumpin's bound to happin' like the night after school when them boys pinned me 'gainst the car like a butterfly and tried to you know what me right in the parkin' lot outside B-11.

That's the apartment me, mamma and Dada live. Dada ain't really my real dad. My real dad's inprisoned, (just like I was that night) for selling drugs like a lot of brothas from Baltimore do, carryin' on and makin' the spot hot. If he wasn't before, Dada sho' was my daddy that night when he heard me hollerin' like Nan told me to if I ever get into a pickle.

I'm big for my age, but not big enough to get a whuppin', which is what mamma promised when she marched me upstairs. *Just get up...I done tol' you...y'all know better...* And soon's we in the door, Nan give us the third degree. She mindin' her bizness, workin' on her research project, which is nothing like the Marshall Square projects in North Philly where we live. *Why was y'all out so late...why you din't call me?*

Rachel's face breaks into a zillion pieces. I open my mouth, but Nan gives me one of those *if looks could kill* looks so I hush like I got what's left of the good cents God gave me. Nan say *it don't matter* cuz she and Mamma workin' they ass off makin' dough, *not the kind you knead but the kind you need*, stackin' cheese so we can move on up and out (like the Jeffersons) of 'merica's nightmare, which is how black folks is livin', 'specially in north Philly near the Richard Allen projects where Unca John grew up.

I say "Nan...you ain't spozed to curse." She say *sometimes you got to baby, but sparing like salt in the stew.* Nan say there's a time and place for everythang and that's why we went to the country 'cause she say what happened to Mamma when she was little ain't neva gon' happen to me.

Later that night Rachel whispers *sorry.* I whisper back *ain't no thang but a chicken wing.* It's important to give the benefit of the doubt if I'm gon' be a judge when I grow up, which I am. Not like Judge Judy—like Judge Imani (which is my name). Then them boys betta watch out. I roll over and go to sleep cuz I been to the country and sometime Nan jokes but she don't play cuz Daddy Slim made a hustler outta her even though she really din't wannabe.

It's April and the last frost just passed. Nan say *you don't need no alma-nac if you mind the sky.* Aunt Carole say *it's a shame to have all this land and no garden.* Some things gotta be planted in hills like pumpkins and squash, and string beans, peppers and collards gotta be planted in rows. Nan say she ain't never planted "Kentucky Wonders" cuz they pole beans and the vines curl 'round like a double heal licks. Unca Dave found bamboo sticks in the garage and Nan say, *these'll work fine.* But before we plant, me, Rachel and Niara (my four year old cousin) gotta pick rocks out the ground just like Nan did.

She gets the wheelbarrow and brings gloves so our hands won't get ruint. Niara's hands are tiny, but Nan puts them on anyways. Unca Chap say Nan's crazy cuz when harvest time come in August she gon' back to California with the suits and panny-hose and ain't gone get no food no way.

Leave them girls 'lone, Unca John yells from the John Deer mower, and Unca Chap start laughin' like some crazy ol' June bug. Unca John turns the mower east toward Haycock mountain. He cain't walk so good count of his hip replacement, but he gets around good for eighty sump-thin'. He been lovin' him some Aunt Carole for the last forty years and him and Nan's born on the same fine October day. She say her and Unca John's cut from the same country cloth, which mean they's family beyond what the dictionary say.

Nan keeps hoein' payin' Unca Chap no never mind. He been messin' with her ever since she ran behind him down Oak Lane when she was five years old. He *say* he skipped a stone on accident, but Nan got a scar on her forehead testifyin' different. Unca Chap's mad at the world cuz no matter how hard he try, he cain't turn white.

I wave at Unca John and on the sly lick my tongue at Unca Chap walkin' down the Old House for his constitution. I say *Nan...why Unca Chap so mean?* And Rachel say *yeah Nan* (even though she ain't her real Grandmama, we's extended family) *why he actin' all greedy?* Nan points to a hawk huntin' mice dartin' in and out the hay.

He's scared.

"Scared a what?" Niara pipes in as she drops another rock in the wheelbarrow.

These days people depend on someone else makin' groceries. Even when their belly's full they're scared of being hungry.

Nan say growin' your own food is a miraculous metafive, which is higher then a metafour (where you say one thing but mean another like the 'ministrators at her job). She say African women *been farmin', planting rice, yams and cassava,* all kinds a provisions like the lovely ladies in the Caribbean. That's why *the green giant's a fallacy.* If anythang he was vented by some slave master *workin' folks to death like in South Carolina and the Sea Coast islands. Then Denmark Vesey* (a carpenter and preacher) *and Gullah Jack* (an Angola shaman but folks call him a hoodoo man) *organized the people and planted a rebellion.*

"How you plant a rebellion?" Niara asks.

Africans outnumbered whites ten to one and could a took over Charleston like Toussaint did Haiti if it wasn't for the haters.

I say "Nan…what you know 'bout haters?" Me and Rachel bust out laughin' and Niara's eyes twinkle as a smile creeps over her baby teeth.

Nan pulls out a seed pack, and reads the flipside to make sure the science matches what she 'bout to drop. *I know what the shadow knows.* She points to the far side where her shadow stretches across the garden. *Pumpkins gonna come last so we'll plant a patch in the corner.* Niara claps her hands cuz she cain't wait to go trick-a-treatin'. *We'll plant zucchini in hills cuz they need room to spread like y'all.*

Nan gives us three seeds each. *There's reason's to seasons and you got to regulate what goes where.*

I say "Nan…what you know 'bout regulatin'?" She wipes sweat with a blue kerchief Aunt Carole got from the clothing bank. *Land got spirits too.*

"It does?" Rachel asks, pattin' a hill.

What you think happens when they bury people?

I look at Rachel. She looks at me and we don't say nuttin'. Nan's flashin' (that means she gone through the men o pause) and wipes her face again. *Lil' Bit was an agriculturalist.*

"An Agri-who?"

A farmer who knew how to put food on the table.

"Oh."

She'd roll out string, tie sticks on the ends to measure rows.

"How she learn all that?" Rachel asks.

She only went to ninth grade 'fore a man named Levi twisted her in shapes she never knew before. But her lack of book learnin' didn't matter cuz she knew geometry without calling it that.

Me and Rachel stop, but Niara keeps right 'longside Nan, puttin' out her hand to get more seeds. *Eleven children and four men later, I watch her work the sky, tastin' it with her finger, listenin' to the wind whisperin' when to plant, water, fertilize and cultivate.*

I lick my pointy finger and test the sky.

She had a garden for plantin' and a garden for paintin'.

"She tagged the ground?" Rachel asks.

She planted flowers but was really paintin' ground signs like her fore-mamas when they needed help from the ancestors.

"What's ground signs?" Niara asks. Nan starts drawin' what look like pictures in her research books. *The ground was her canvas, the flowers her paint.*

"What kin' a flowers?" Niara's asks.

Purple hyacinths…blue flags. Nan bends down like she makin' salat and whispers what don't sound like nobody's English. *Tiger lilies and pansies had a mind of their own when it come to color.* Niara blinks as a grasshopper drops in Nan's lap.

She don't flinch when it crawl down her arm and into her palm. *Daddy Slim told us bout Ant and Grasshopper* Nan say.

Sister worked hard, stackin' cheese, and all Grasshopper did was what he pleased. Sisters on her grind, night and day, preparin' for the' seasons come what may. Autumn arrives, turnin' leaves. Grasshopper pluckin' on his banjo strings.

Not a care, or a curse or a kitten kaboo

Sing a jump so song just for me and you…

Turned up his flask, took a swig, sang his heart, danced a two-step jig.

Kept on jiggin' til the days grew nigh, and Ol' man winter heaved a chilly sigh.
Now G was down, but never faded, draggin' his banjo all about the place.
He soon come upon Sister's door, swallowed his pride. Softly implored.
To his dismay there was no response. So he sang and played with ambience.

I'm a troubadour, a gent of leisure,
   but I ain't got a window or pot to pee in,
   No morsel, a chedda, no slow hand to feed
   No gravy to sop where fat meets greasy

Sister's in her parlor with her family chillin', restin' weary bones by the fireside grillin'. Heard a knock at her vestibule. Grasshopper steady actin' a fool.
   Ain't got no place to lay my head,
   Feel like butter scraped over too much bread
Sister pulled her shawl round her shoulders, opened the door and this is what she told him:
   You's a troubadour, a gentleman renown. But here's my advice and you can take it or bounce...
   You danced summer away all day on the street
   while I slaved away to make ends meet
   as soon as the sun met the top o' the line
   you sat there croonin' all jiggyfied
   it sounded so lovely, so bittersweet...
   now go dance winter away up on easy street

Then Grasshopper spread his wings and flew over the fence. Nan smiles so wide you can see the gap in her front teeth. Then she whispers like Horton talking to Who folk floatin' on a dandy-lion. "What cha doin Nan?" I say (tryin' to get her tension and hope she ain't really gone crazy like Unca Chap say). *Come have a look-see.* So we do. Tip-toein' over to

Nan, which is no easy task in tennis shoes on ground that's shaky and newly hoed.

Niara trips and falls face first. I brush her off as she spits dirt. She inherited the Eczema from Lil' Bit and sometime her skin looks like alligator shoes. Rachel starts screaming cuz baby spiders is crawling on Niara's legs. Nan brushes them off cuz she don't believe in killin' spiders unless it's on accident. *They're bringing stories from the other side.*

"Other side a what?" I ask. Rachel's breathin' hard cause she never seed spiders spilling out the ground. *"Where they come from?"* Niara asks still spittin' dirt. *Other side where the bush ghosts live,* Nan say, gettin' a seed pack out her fatigues. *Zucchini grows fast. When you pick it the next day there's another one hanging on the vine.* We know (without showin') what to do. Nan leans against the fence and starts telling us another one of Daddy Slim's stories.

Once there was no food to be found in the palace, in the village or even the town. It hadn't rained in a month of Sundays. To make matters worse, the spider webs were empty. Only dreams they was catching was the bush ghosts' hakilele. Resonating when the wind cried ahwwoo-ooo between delicate fibers and silvery threads. A dry spell swept the vast savannah and the sky God forgot to send down manna.

Mama spider began to cry. Oh Dada dear what shall we do? The children's starving and the pot's so cold its black bone blue. No matter how clever a web I weave, nothing's captured, nothing retrieved. Anansi looked up from his corner cot, said it's time to pay a visit to Grandfather's spot. He'll know what to do. Give me a sign or some kind of spell to relax your mind.

Went to the island just off shore, dove in and swam 'til he spied the web above grandfather's door. He knockity-knocked and the door swung open. Grandfather sat with his corncob smokin'. 'Pull up a chair,' grandfather nodded, gave him a Kola nut and said 'to what do I owe this distinguished honor?' Anansi chewed the Kola and began to relate the untimely story of his village's fate. Grandfather listened with earnest ears, nodded his head, said 'have no fear'. Went to the fire, retrieved a vessel, gave it to Anansi, with this whatsay: As long as you're never afraid to share, it'll never run out of pepper stew.

Anansi thanked grandfather, finished his Kola, bowed low and swam to the ocean's surface. Home in his village, in his tiny hut, he put the pot on the fire to heat it up. He was happy the village would have lots to eat, but his heart turned cold, and his spirit weak. Instead of sharing like grandfather said, he hid the pot underneath his bed. Days went by and Anansi grew, while his wife and children barely made do.

One night when he fell asleep, his wife looked under Anansi's sheets. She spied the pot, pulled it out, put it on the fire and it started to spout. The children ate to their heart's content and spirit told her what to do next. She took the pot to the village square. Told the people to gather together there. Off came the lid. Then she dished up stew and the people ate their belly's full. The pot overflowed. It wouldn't stop. Then it cracked into pieces right on the spot.

The noise woke Anansi, and he screamed "Woman…what chu done done to me?"

Why you din't tell me 'bout the luckypot?

Why you so selfish, such a greedy-got?

Anansi didn't answer cuz he was vexed. Ran back to the ocean, dove in and swam. Again he knocked on grandfather's door. Door swung open and Grandfather roared, "I told you before. I'll tell you again. It's fear brought you to this fateful end. It's greed made you afraid to see—there's more than enough for the whole world's need. Then he picked up a stick and spoke a dyamsay and the stick beat Anansi around the way. All the next day stick continued to beat him, til he vanished and was never heard from again. Some say they hear him in the night, running on eight legs for his very life. Others say that they been told, he's where the bush ghosts hakilele on the famished road.

I don't know what all that mean, but Nan say you got to read between the rows. She say language roots on your tongue like the seeds we plantin' and blossoms no matter how many times your people's uprooted, or cast to the wind.

The sun paints the sky blood-orange. Nan tells me to get the hose so we can water. And I do. She leaves tomato plants for tomorrow. We gotta get up early and beat the sun. I turn on the spigot and Nan puts her thumb in to make an arc. The water shoots high then falls to the ground. She squirts. We run, scream, then come back for more cuz it feels good on your skin. Nan waters us, then the garden, then us again til our shadows stretch 'round her legs. And after awhile you cain't tell anymore where the earth stops and where we begin.

Terrie Relf
Borrowing Breath

A crew lost in space
knows sympathy will not
refill their oxygen tanks,
replenish fuel,
or guide their
cartographer to familiar

star systems. So they gather
in the ship's greenhouse,
exchange their last
breaths with pomegranates
hanging thick from
hydroponic limbs,

pomegranates that
offer themselves as
hope until at last they
find peace in stasis tea,
rocked to sleep
within robotic arms

where what dreams
still linger are a sacrament
taken beneath an
untoward bliss of moons.

Flavia Tamayo
The Lesson

My husband wants summers
back, when he was boy, when he
slept in hammocks or on rooftops
under the Bahia desert moon,
the Sea of Cortez whispering
at his back. He wants bonfires
on the beach, his father making
them blaze up, flash, then darken.
It was the place where he learned
to trap and skin a rabbit, watched
women cook the meat and tortillas
on the hoods of abandoned cars.
The place where a father taught
a son how to bait and gut fish,
where he learned the slaughtering
of pigs, the bloodletting of cows,
knives slashing necks, hands
cupping and drinking blood,
the impermanence of things.

Lisa Gavin
Bringing Home Dinner

Chris Baron

The Last Table
An Entry from a Waiter's Journal

Cioppino cooked right

1 lb skinless red snapper or halibut fillets, cut into 1½-inch pieces
1 lb large shrimp (16 to 20), shelled (tails and bottom segment of shells
    left intact) and de-veined
¾ lb sea scallops, tough muscle removed from side of each if neces-
    sary
½ cup olive oil
1½ cups chopped onion (1 large onion)
1 cup chopped green bell pepper (1 large green bell pepper)
3 coves garlic, minced
1 teaspoon salt
1 28-ounce can tomatoes
Broth from the mollusks
2 cups red wine
2 cups tomato juice
2 cups fish or shellfish stock
An herb bouquet of bay leaf, parsley, and basil wrapped in a layer of
    cheesecloth and secured with kitchen string
Salt and pepper to taste
½ cup minced parsley for garnish
love   hate

Just when I had finished topping off my salt and pepper shakers, refilled
the last packets of sugar and sweet-and-low alongside an equal number

of puffy packages of granulated pure sugar and the brown paper-bag shapes of sugar in the raw. Just when I had finished folding my pile of napkins for the next morning's shift. Just when I had topped off the coffee beans in both the regular and the decaf. Just when I had finished stocking the hot tea stash, and the lemon wedges, and the side plates, they sat me a four-top. An older couple with what appeared to be their two sons. As a "closer" I had no choice but to take the table. I looked into the bar where my co-workers recapped the night over Sapporo and left over sushi, their aprons folded in their laps. It was my night to be on late, and though I hated it, I put down the all-purpose cleaner, washed my hands, and started in.

I reluctantly cut their bread overcompensating with extra slices so that I wouldn't have to keep bringing them more. I poured them water even though it went against my own philosophy. I had argued many times with the other servers about how water is a finite resource, and we have to be careful to only pour water for the guests on request. I asked them to imagine the number of wasted gallons if they poured water for every customer every time. Here I was pouring four waters for the new table because when it comes right down to it I guess I am as slothful as everyone else.

At the table I heard them speaking another language, German maybe, or Dutch, and this was normally a red flag in the tipping department because of the variance of customs from culture to culture. In some countries it just isn't customary to tip. In some it was included in the salary of the server. I had reconciled this some time ago. I understood that tips were an added bonus for a job well done, but now, right around closing time, the last thing a server on the verge of checkout wants to hear, is broken English of any kind. The father looked at me and smiled, "Beer?"

"Oh, you'd like a beer" I replied. "What kind would you like?" He looked around at everyone, puzzled, as if I had said something so mystifying, so perplexing that I thought the dictionaries would fly from the satchels draped on the backs of their chairs. Finally one of the sons smiled and said, "Would it be possible to get four Budweiser?"

A clean step I thought. "Of course."

I brought their beer in record time, and they were ready to order when I returned. I suggested a few things: pasta, salads, other dishes that were quick to make and eat, tried to make them sound appetizing, but they had already made decisions. The concierge at their hotel must have given them a recommendation because almost simultaneously their fingers danced to a specific menu item. In the late hours of the darkening restaurant, when the last tables have squeezed their way in to the last round of seating, and the chefs are midway through cleaning the kitchen, and even the tomatoes are wrapped and put away, one word cracks the restaurant like an earthquake, a word that could virtually send the building into complete disruption. The word — Cioppino. Cioppino is the bane of late-night eating. It is a crockpot stuffed with every kind of shellfish from cockles to mussels, calamari rings, bay scallops, prawns, and finfish, all sautéed in fresh marinara sauce. In the center, nestled in a bed of linguini, there is a giant spread of Dungeness crab legs so succulent and invincible that the meat is almost unattainable. Cioppino was ordered, four of them. I smiled my way through, but when I reached the side station I dropped the other closer a look of defeat. She smiled and continued to refill the coffee beans. The other servers sitting at the tables in the back of the house doing their checkouts and napkin folding shot me looks of ridicule and compassion.

Not only did it take a good portion of the evening just to eat an order of cioppino once it was served, but the preparation for the cooks was endless. It would take them a solid fifteen minutes to prepare the stew. I ordered it. I waited. Other tables paid their way, had coffee, left the building to stare at the water lights on the harbor. My table had another round of Bud, another round of bread and butter, and then another.

The cooks muttered their way through the cooking while unwrapping the butter and the marinara. I muttered with them in my broken Spanish trying to connect, trying to let them know that I felt their same pain, that in some way if I could cook the food I would have. By the time I brought the four cioppinos to the table most of the restaurant was empty. Usually I could carry three plates at a time, but the service for the cioppinos was more challenging—giant silver crockpots with garlic bread, crab-crackers, bibs, lemon wedges and special forks—a sight to behold. They seemed excited when I set down the food. They told me they had everything they needed, but as soon as I left to hustle to the back to see if there was any more leftover sushi, I saw one of their hands go up. They ran me. First it was more beer, and then when I returned with more beer, it was more butter, and then it was more cheese, and more ice, and more bread, and then coffee. They never looked up, the sons mystified by the crab legs, a beer in one hand, a loop of calamari hovering on in the other, the father wiping marinara from his chin. I served and waited. Didn't they have any compassion; couldn't they see that the night was over, that my side work was finished, that I had beer in my fridge at home? It wasn't fair I thought, and I did everything I could to speed up their meal.

Still, they were my table, my responsibility, even if I did despise them. So over and over again I recommitted. This time there wasn't even a polite hand raise. I had my back to the table, and I had begun to refill all the salt and pepper shakers in my station when I heard one of them say, in a low creaky voice with a mouthful of food, "Water!" I filled a pitcher, which had been long since cleaned and emptied, turned the corner from the side station, and with a scowl made my way, but the situation had transformed.

There was a baseball cap knocked to the ground. The younger son was sitting there, his head down, his hands gripping the solid oak table like he might snap it in two. The mother was right behind him in an instant, his head shook violently, but the more it shook the stronger she held it, his shoulders swayed without control, and she embraced him with a supernatural strength. The others watched, as if for them it was common practice. I was frozen, and by the time the manager got there the spasms had stopped. The mother took a red napkin and dipped it in the *almost* empty water glass. She wiped his chin and spoke to him, and even though I couldn't understand the language, I could feel what she was saying to him. It was the language of a mother speaking to her son. It was a language more beautiful, more real than any other.

"Ep-i-leps-y." She whispered to us in her best broken English. While the Father and the other son took their last bites. The mother rocked her now quieted son back and forth, rubbing his head gently, whispering in his ear. He might have been awake, but he stayed perfect in his mother's arms.

After a few moments I asked them if they needed anything else, they asked "Would it be possible to get the bill?" Of course I said. I brought it; the father dropped some cash on the tip tray. It dropped like a heavy weight, the coins spinning along the edges. They rose slowly and exited, smiling, the full grown man a little boy nestled against his mother's shoulder. I couldn't help but look at them. It was as if time itself had abandoned the restaurant, and I couldn't see the bar anymore, my coworkers drinking and laughing, my absurd desire to sit washed away. I wanted only for them to have stayed and eaten their cioppino.

How can something be two things at the same time? How can perspective feel like concrete but then suddenly wash away into fine sand in an instant? This had never been about me or *my* time at all. For them every moment of freedom is precious, every spoonful of garlic and bay leaf is new, every attempt at a crab leg worthwhile. I walked to the table, picked up the cash they had left as a tip, and as I went to clear the last plates of the evening I noticed that two of the cioppinos had been eaten all the way through. The other two were left, untouched.

Song

Marilyn Chin

After Enlightenment, There is Yam Gruel

When Buddha woke up hungry the animals offered him their favorite food. The baby sea lion offered him day old fish bits that her mother regurgitated. The jackal offered a piece of smelly rotting meat infested with maggots. The squirrel monkey offered a handful of bruised bananas, veiled with gnats. The hare was the most selfless of all. She went into the forest and gathered an armload of wood, lit it on fire and placed herself in the center as sacrifice. Mrs. Wong, exhausted from long hours at the restaurant, was not impressed with the feast. She handed Buddha a broom and said, "Old man, sweep the back porch first, then, the filthy hallway," and went to the kitchen and heated up last night's yam gruel.

Ilya Kaminsky
from Musica Humana

I am reading aloud the book of my life on earth
and confess, I loved grapefruit.
In a kitchen: sausages; tasting vodka,
the men raise their cups.
A boy in a white shirt, I dip my finger
into sweetness. Mother washes
behind my ears. And we speak of everything
that does not come true,
which is to say: it was August.
August! the light in the trees, full of fury. August
filling hands with language that tastes like smoke.
Now, memory, pour some beer,
salt the rim of the glass; you
who are writing me, have what you want:
a golden coin, my tongue to put it under.

Karen Rigby
Song for the Onion

Let me love the onion worn
by the thumb's touch—
sulfur and sugar a scent Egyptians believed
could ferry the dead home
from their sleep.

Let me flay the double-heart
that stings or melts
to caramel depending on time, temperature, weather.
Let me taste the pure, explosive signature.
Let the lioness outshine her sisters,
the shallot and the leek.

Let the field bury crystalline skins.
Let the roots drive the green hands skyward
in spite of the earth.
Let me remember the primitive,
underground birth, and the kingdom
of sleepers. Let me consider

the lily's doppelgänger.
Let the onion telescope
multiple selves. Let me admire
her reckless theatre.
Let nothing else weep on behalf of the blade.
Let me praise the onion's sacrifice:
a trapezist blooming in release.

Carlos Reyes
Piute

for Rich Blevins

He has been to Rush Creek
near Mono Lake

gathering food
in the traditional way

for the old people
the *Ku-za-de-ka*:

the larvae eaters.

He shows me: *Ku-za-vi*,
fly larvae skimmed
from the lake
(grainy, chewy, with
resiny aftertaste),

Piaghi, dried moth caterpillars
captured from the Jeffrey Pines,

Tu-ba-a, piñon nuts
ground into meal
into a metate.

He says, you try it,
sometime.

The next day I find a note
tu-ca, to eat, i.e. eat
(to encourage me).

That evening
more instructions:

Before you eat, say something
good, like a little prayer.

Say, this *ku-za-vi* will be good for me,
something good will happen
if I eat this *piaghi,* etc.

I hesitate—
He pauses, laughs
his own full laugh
then says:

You can say it in English.

Krista Madsen

Air Wasn't Air

based on a true story

1. Birdbrain

When I come to, there is a hand, a human hand, cradling me in its palm, my head between two fingers. A mouth so close to my beak I think I may about to be eaten, but there is a cooing and gentle rocking and I can calm my twittering heart and brain — *Birdbrain*, was his nickname for me — in the knowledge that I am safe. At first I am in the dark, then in a small oblong box with an oval cut-out and I can gather information but my body's too stunned to act on it so I just listen, piece together what I can about what happened to me, to us. I hear more than I can bear but I bear it the way we were built to bear, and I sneak a glance to the window, trying to decipher from the smear-stains which one might be his.

I met him in May and heard him declared dead in February, when what looked like air wasn't air. When we pelted like a slanted hailstorm (to use her word) against the glass, and fell. Dead upon impact, no trace of any external injury, I hope at least it happened instantly, while some like me hadn't achieved such speeds and were just stunned into temporary paralysis. I like to imagine he fell near me in the cold grass, as if I was his idea of heaven, or home.

I want to believe he had no time to register the reflection of himself in the glass before it knocked him senseless. Just replete with berries, impossibly happy with color and juice. Better this way surely, leaving me when there were still so many things too good to be true. Before the dissolution that would surely set in, bitterness, regret, onto-the-next-bird, secret hurt. We counted our love by more berries than your average couple, more months.

May to February, as quick as that, but longer than our kind can usually lay claim to, when the fledglings disperse and the practical union has run its course. In the beginning, in the spring mating dance, we hopped back and forth, passing our berries between our beaks. Soon I squeezed our five eggs from my body into the nest we made. He perched on a branch overlooking this position I was stuck in, incubating for two weeks, and fed me the berries we love most, along with flower petals, beetles, weevils, ants, cicadas, caterpillars. There were young ones to feed and we caught insects at first, then onto berries by the second day. In a month's time, our babies were gone, unlikely to return again, perhaps we'd recognize a note or a feather someday and feel a tinge but never be sure. He could have left then too, all duties done, but I begged him to do better than that, could we not surpass our biological clocks, I asked with my buzzing trill, he called it. Begging. His face that black mask we all have, particularly hard to read, particularly at times like this. *Pecker*, my ladybird friends called him, *he only cares about one thing and it's not you*. But my memory of him is all crimson and fluttery and haloed in the sun's corona. My memory of him is all tied up with that word *love*. *Come with me to the Carolinas*, I said. *Let's go south.*

It's a gregarious flock, I would have seen him regardless, moving in on next year's mate, and I would have had to admire the orange striped tail of the male in front of me just to spite him, but instead—and I could have never dreamt for this—he stayed by my side as we flew ahead of the coming snow. He hinted that he knew a place for us to summer in, a veritable paradise of berries.

You and your berries, I joked, trying to seem light and humorous when tangible waves of adoration and relief rolled through me and I had to flap even harder to steady myself in the formation.

Other couples only had berries on time for the children, the whole mating thing timed so the berries are ripe for the babies. But we always had berries, nine months of fruit, an abundance of berries. And the way he used to serve them to me, beak to beak, like passing bits of his red heart, until I suppose there was none left to pass.

2. Fed Up

I am all eyes, all nose, all taste. I can sense the berries before any of them, far off in the inscrutable distance, in the future, in the past. And the desire for the fruit becomes larger than anything, engulfs the world, until the sun itself, all burnt in the winter afternoon, looks like the best and biggest berry of all, and we fly closer and closer, and I lead them. Until we burn too.

We burn on the inside. But it burns in a way that reminds you which organ is which and where and how inside you are *insides*, not just this idea of self, soft and soulful, but real, blood and guts, acid, churn. All else recedes. The hunger is insatiable, impossible, overpowering, simplistic, until suddenly there is fullness beyond repair, and no recollection of how you let it go this far. There was no set path between not-enough and too-much, no markers, no stopping mechanisms. Our species, if I can blame it on the species, should be fat or extinct, but we're *birds*, and whatever piggishness we have is somehow accounted for in the formulas and the hyperactive digestive patterns and the way it all just *is*. So we consume, we are engines of consumption, and when presented with a field of berries, we will continue eating them until the supply is exhausted. If the berries are late in the season and softened by a few too many frosts and temperature increases, they will be fermented but we will eat them all the same. Until we fall drunk off the branches with whole berries clogging our throats, our entire systems steeped in this toxic ambrosia, falling to the grass until we groggily retrieve our bearings and do it again. Or we will have the fuzzy confidence to think we're fine and stagger off toward wherever it is we think we need to go, only we will go about it clumsily. Being always in a flock and never just isolated incidents unto ourselves, others will follow, until before we know it, we smash against whatever it is we're smashing against and just that snapping sensation of something breaking inside and the clarity for a second in which all one can think is how clearly they seem to be thinking and then: nothing.

I led us to this, we, she and I, all of us. I knew from a few states away that the berries weren't right, that the buildings surrounding this courtyard of holly bushes were dangerously close with their panes and panes of illusionary glass. Glass is always a problematic material for us, whether transparent or reflective. Turns out these were reflective, so we just saw more berries ahead of us in every direction. Holly berries, a rare treat, not particularly desirable to most species, but how could they not be. The red is so vibrant it shows through my eyelids when I blink, when I sleep. The fruit is female, pollinated by the male, and I desire her. There is one black slightly protruding dot on each round globe of red as if an all-seeing eye. Looking at me looking at it. Unblinking. The skin breaks in the mouth, there is no lust like this, washing the pallet with this bittersweet rush, sour and sugary, and the one impulse is more, more, more. It's not just me, the more takes over us all. The more threatening the fruit, the more rancid, the greater the tangled pull, the more the more, and it becomes an addiction, all we need. She is a glutton for it as much as I. The more I fed her from the first moments of our early courtship, the more it justified my own habits, the more it disguised the truth of the matter, that berries are all to me. All to all of us, like it or not. And I'm tired of the hope and delusion of something greater than this, the imposition of meanings and feelings and words on what is only smell, taste, sight. I am tired too of the reality of the smell, taste, sight. The inevitable pressures of patterns beyond our control and how we so falsely believe, must believe, we can control. The only way I could fly outside of the cycle was by stopping the cycle. I knew the ends. I led us all to this, a few of them my own children even, former mates. We are only eyes and beaks and bellies full of berries. En route to our images in the glass, we will be dead already. The evolutionary success of flight among our kind has not yet responded to threats posed by manmade structures, so I knew they wouldn't recognize windows as windows, that there would be no association, no alerts, no outcry, no fear.

But I saw her in the reflection for a second, reduced to grazing cow, as I led my intoxicated army elsewhere. Too drunk to even join us, and I hated her for that.

3. Heaven or Home

A hailstorm, I told them. That was my first thought when I heard this rat-a-tat-tat on the windowpanes adjacent to my desk. With the global warming the weather has been so up and down and all around these days, I wasn't too surprised to hear it going sideways, firing the glass with pellets of ice. February can be cruel, seasonally confused by day, back to winter business by night, one hardly knows what to wear. But then I pulled my head out of the drawer and saw the culprits, not colorless ice but bold feathered things turning into instant taxidermy before my eyes and I made my second assessment: bird flu. I'd heard the stories of birds just dropping dead out of the sky in Armageddon fashion due to the new strain of disease hitting some parts of the country. Now it had come to our courtyard, a conflagration turning our ordinary berries into a last supper. Does the flu make a bird crazy? How would one measure crazy in a bird? To a bird, I might have looked crazy at this moment, jumping on my side of the windows, flapping my arms around as if I too was trying to fly, knowing that they couldn't see me anyway as you can see out but not in. They kept coming and coming, rapid succession of hits, like corn kernels popping at peak heat, and I was crying, shouting, flapping for dear life. I hurried to make hurricane Xs on the glass with masking tape (again more to busy myself than for their benefit), calling for help from Lucy in the adjacent cubicle but she was on her lunch break, as was everyone else it seemed. Because of my recent promotion from assistant to office manager, I was working through lunch, sorting out the neglected supply cabinet, labeling my hanging file folders, committing to a new diet of green things in Tupperware. I'm a notorious yo-yo-er when it comes to dieting, usually tipping the scales on the side of Yodels, but so far so good this year: ten pounds off, eight pounds on, five pounds off, three pounds on, and so on and off, but minutely

more off than on. Along with the keys to the supply closet kingdom of
sticky notes, pens, legal pads, correction fluid, is my unlimited access
to cases and cases of diet sodas which I drink nonstop to add oomph to
granny apple slices, wilted spinach, slaw, peas, celery sticks and sprouts.
So because of my diet and my promotion (also involving a coveted move
to window status), the work and the diet got pushed aside as I took on
the role of witness. I had my fifteen minutes today, telling the report-
ers what I saw, providing sufficient shocked/saddened expressions when
the camera lights cut through the shadows. Fifteen minutes extended
into an hour as more television network vans arrived with their excess
of equipment and self-generated electricity, and again I said "hailstorm!
bird flu!" on cue. Still wearing my rubber finger protector but now outside without my coat, I pointed to them in the courtyard grass, sprinkled
like bacon bits on a salad. Soon my amateur theories were amended
by these Audubon folks with medical gloves and clipboards gathering
them up, distinguishing the fifty or so living from the fifty or so dead.
One professor-voiced man I overheard was telling an anchorwoman in
a purple suit that it was the berries in fact, the birds got drunk—*drunk!*
In the hubbub as the humming lights turned from me to him, I was able
to snatch one up for myself.

Cedar waxwings, he said, cranial hemorrhage, internal bleeding. I
have ten cats at home, two parakeets, a gimpy-legged mutt of unknown
origins, a turtle named Shelly, and a few bird feeders I position myself
in front of with identification books and binoculars, so Lucy, when she
returned from lunch, was gracious enough to pass me her box of tissues
to cry into. I found myself retelling her what the expert told me, how
before the World Trade Center towers fell, maintenance workers collected some thirty-two window-interrupted birds a year off the plaza,
which doesn't account for the many more believed to have been stolen
already by rats and cats, how it made me think of the other thwarted
flights there, the planes hitting, the bodies jumping, how far away it felt
to be in South Carolina at the time, safe and guilty, coupon-clipping and
laundering. But he was onto more numbers, the annual bird death toll
in the U.S. due to windows, nearly a billion. Add all these rotten berries

at such close proximity and you've got guaranteed disaster. This time closer to home.

Today the everyday has turned bleak, the courtyard become a grave-yard, this tissue box a coffin when I replace all but the bottommost tissues with my bird, and I can't help but think that the tape Xs look like tilted crosses all in a row, nothing but morbid decorations. Berries are illicit substances, windows are assassins. I stroke its belly, listening to the tinier rat-a-tat-tat of Lucy on the other side of the partition back to typing emails from the tips of her fake pink nails, deleting the spam, keeping up. I try to apply the expert's information about these birds, combined with what I'd read in my guidebooks, to the creature before me. He continued talking, giving them their due specificity upon death, but it was too much to hold the reporter's (and by proxy, the viewers') interest so he turned to me, my own bird hidden for the moment in my pocket. Whether male or female, the cedar waxwings have the same bold mark-ings, rare, it seems, for the bird kingdom. So it's impossible to tell what I have before me, a mother or father, son or daughter. It seems male with its regal, svelte body of satiny finish, taut as the pre-pubescent school-boys playing soccer in the fields near our building. I fantasize about what I would eat if I too were blessed with a digestive system as fast, or how decadent it must be to go on an annual food tour from Canada to Costa Rica. They can strip a field of its fruit in minutes, he said using the word frugivorous, which I had to look up. I wonder if I, volunteering perhaps to take on the added responsibility of courtyard manager, should gather next year's berries before the birds arrive. Sieve the seeds, spice the pulp, sweeten the pot into some kind of jam for my coworkers on bagel day. But they are inedible to humans, I remember, my father telling me once when I tried to find out for myself and he restrained my chubby hands. There was a lot of holding of hands back then, I would have dented the perfect surface of every birthday cake if given the chance, and while I loved animals I had no qualms eating them too. I don't know whether to pray over it in the tradition of the religion I was raised in, or eat it pagan-style. What a shame to let such a pristine creature go to waste. Perhaps I could tailor a quail recipe to suit its proportions. Stiff and light, with its small bones perhaps it would taste of frog and rabbit.

Upon further inspection, I notice a bit of berry stain under its stubborn beak, or is that blood. Did it blink at me? Turn its head? I suppose it could very well be alive but still stunned, perhaps the awake state proved too treacherous and it's weighing the options, gathering its avian forces into something resembling a decision. If the bird expert returns I'd like to ask him to define "windows." Seems to me they should categorize a different sort of disaster, that windows that don't open and only reflect are not actually windows at all but mirrors.

Amy Paul
Sacred Fruit

Brandel France de Bravo

Lace

> Children must not eat chicken feet or else the girl's
> knitting and the boy's lasso will snarl.
> —*Belief among the Chamula people, Mexico*

She flopped on the boat's bottom among the mackerel
and sardines, her tail withering before the fishermen's eyes
until suddenly the wind carried it away, revealing
two legs, pink and new as the skin beneath a blister.
Having seen enough, the fishermen dove overboard,
swimming as fast and far as they could.
The startled mermaid sat up, lifted the fishing net
to her mouth, and gnawed off a section the size of a scarf.
Then summoning a squid she dipped the swathe
of crude lace in an inky cloud and draped it over her face.
The water dead to her now, the sea's widow rowed ashore
to walk into her new life, touch her feet to the sand,
mussel shells, dune grasses, and hot asphalt.

A Mayan cowboy on his pinto spotted her
wandering naked at the edge of the pine forest.
He grabbed his lasso, threw it round her
like a wedding band, and reeled her in.
He walked home with her on one side and his horse
on the other, a rope in each calloused hand.
When he got there he tied up his horse and freed
the woman with matted hair the color of kelp
in a room which he left and latched shut.
He knew he could not keep her this way
so he went to the *curandera* who told him
the dishes to prepare to ensnare the siren,
elicit the love he longed for.

The mermaid drank the tea brewed from fern roots,
and then throwing aside her veil, ate with gusto
the stew of nightingale tongues,
tamales filled with hummingbird hearts,
and cake made from flour that the cowboy had dusted,
like talcum after a shower, over his sweat-covered body.
After this meal, the cowboy's desire for her stopped being a noose
and became a hammock that held and rocked her
like her first lover, and she knew she would have his children.

The day her water broke and the pains began
the cowboy ran from room to room, unscrewing every jar
with butterfly hands, opening all the doors and drawers.
Outside, he uncovered the well, loosened a knot in the clothesline.
A boy and girl were born and the mermaid put one to each breast
where they spent drunken days and drowsy months.
No sooner had she weaned them from her milk,
which tasted like pearls, when the cowboy came home
to find her feeding the children with her own fingers
from a plate of chicken feet, crisp and golden.
"What are you doing?" he shouted. "Now our son's lasso
will tangle and he will never wrangle a wife the way I did you.
And our daughter's yarn will always snarl.
How will she weave her wedding *huipil*?
How will she make the time pass when her husband leaves
for a year, maybe more, to work on the other side?"

The mermaid tenderly wiped each child's mouth
before turning to face her husband:
These are my two shoes.
With this food, I am tying the laces tight
so that we may walk together always.

Rochelle Mass
Celebrating Humus

In Acre, by the sea, Yusuf makes it coarse with cracked kernels
crispy as pecans.

A man called Kobi serves it to me smooth as velvet in the
last row of the Tiberias souk.

On the highway, near the number 80 Army Camp they fill the center
with tehini, lace it with olive oil.

The Ahmed brothers, in Afula, run a place with a kosher stamp,
a Rabbi sits at a table near the kitchen inspecting what goes in and out.

The brothers pile whole buds in the center, add bits of parsley
big enough so I recognize the shape of the leaf.

Just past the memorial to fallen fighters, at the Golani junction
hot fava beans to fill the middle, paprika sprinkled till the surface glows.

On Yermiyahu street in Tel Aviv, it arrives *ashkarah style*
with a full radish, green onion stalk, an egg boiled brown.

No matter the recipe or the service, humus is to be wiped. I tear
pita quickly, twist firmly into the taupe mass, reach for

cracked syrian olives and diced salads that parade the humus
till the table swoons in peppery sharpness

till pickled aromas challenge the minted tea
till my celebration ends.

Al Zolynas
A Political Poem

At the corner cafe
where I sometimes eat
I ordered a raw egg
broken into a cup
no toast no coffee.
I tossed that egg down
my throat like a Cossack
taking vodka.
I did it for shock
value, for the value of the shock.
I did it for the waitress
for my mother for the sunny siders
and hard boilers the over easys.
I did it for those hopelessly
scrambled by America.

Leon Stokesbury
The Legacy
for Erin

Just so, when they come demanding,
you might possess some grasp of facts—
just in case motivations at some point
        might appear unclear—just
            to insure with certainty

you will recall later on: take
one peeled cucumber now and grate it
finely as you can. Swirl this and the juice
        of two lemons with one pint
            of yogurt, setting it

aside somewhere, cold. So
there will remain some record, cube
three pounds of lamb, then sauté it
        lightly floured, in a skillet
            with one stick of butter, dice

one large onion, then combine
the meat and onion in a stew pot
under water enough to cover all. To this
        mixture add three bay leaves, add
            three cloves of garlic

crushed. Add one tablespoon
of pepper, then one teaspoon of salt. Into that you sprinkle cumin: three
        teaspoonfuls, and then to make
            it strange, two heaping

teaspoonfuls of powdered
cardamom, a grayish beige in its dry
state (but it will turn the water green),
    and then you cover this and cook it
        for three hours on low heat: stir

    the soup occasionally, but
do not let the liquor boil away. Remember:
when they come in the night, screaming
    with their torches, beseeching
        you, fingers of torchlight

    warping their wan faces
in that dark, your front porch flickering
unearthly, remember then what
    I say now: after the lamb
        has simmered for three hours,

    in a separate saucepan
cook two cups of rice. While the rice
is cooking, peel, then slice in white
    inch-thick circles, three large
        eggplants. Fry each slice

    in liquid Crisco cooking oil
in a skillet until browned and heavy, then
place the eggplant out on paper
    towels to soak some oil away —
        (by now the cardamom

    has drenched your house
in incense: massive hints of orient,
odalisque, Babylon and Berber,
    Bedouin and myrrh) just
        so I will know you

    know, layer in a casserole
first the lamb, then the eggplant, then
rice on top of that: lamb again, egg-
    plant, rice, until the dish
        is almost full — then

pour the chartreuse
juice into the casserole: bake it covered
for an hour, in an oven, at three hundred
    eighty-five degrees—but whatever
        else, do not forget

        they will be coming, certain
as the glacier's pain, wrapped in cowls,
in their injunctions, screws and ropes,
    racks and chains, insisting
        you confess

        your sickness, producing writs
commanding you disclose what sources
taught you to concoct such venom,
    declaring all your actions
        darkness, everything you live for

        bane. Child, do not listen,
do not answer. Deny them. Lie to them
at every path (a thick, green, good,
    sweet pungency for hours
        will have lacquered

        every wall, satiated, smeared
the air, redolent, ancient, tang
of loam or salt or sea) but remember
    when the dish comes from the oven
        you must serve it

        right away. In the middle
of a large, hot, black plate, stack
a steaming mountain of the lamb—
    then along its peak, pile
        three dollops of the yogurt

mixture—late spring snows
melting from the sun, cascading off
the milky mountainside in rivulets,
    tiny runny tributaries
        winding out to sea. And

        at this point in time, when
the heat and cold conjoin, you must
call forth your beloved. You must sit
    your beloved down. You must ask
        of your beloved

        if he wants for any thing,
placing there before him, then, this plate
you have prepared, permitting him to sample
    (always know they will be coming!
        they carry metal rams to batter

        in your door!) your creation,
daughter, and when he lifts it to his tongue—
O, at that precise moment, daughter,
    from all previous moorings then
        his heart will be set free.

Sylvia Levinson

Spoon

for Sally

Slender silver spoon
delicate handle, swirl
of jonquil, tapered oval
which I now dip into
narrow-mouthed jars
olives, capers.
This same tiny spoon
dipped into strained carrots,
introduced first foods
to my first born, this
daughter of mine
her eager mouth
sucking the sweetness,
I, carefully catching
the spills, wiping
the cleft of her infant chin.
O spoon, this child
you nourished, learned
her lessons well: she welcomes
life with open mouth
taking in the world
from savor of first tastes
she grew voracious
to devour life.
To sip the garnet wine
of Cotes du Rhone,
color of her birthstone,
dine on succulent green-lipped
mussels from New Zealand

waters, a sprig of mint
from her own herb garden,
foods ordinary or exotic.
She travels,
treks steep paths
the Cinque Terre
above the Mediterranean,
in the swelter of August
sits in silent respite,
in Assisi, the cool damp
crypt of St. Francis.
Sucks the marrow
of knowledge, studies
language, literature, law.
O spoon,
you served this child
well. This woman
lives *con brio*,
open eyes, open heart.
She feeds me.

Heather Grange

Cookery Book

I wonder how many people still have theirs. I brought mine at St. George's Anglican Christmas Bazaar when I lived in Paris more than 30 years ago. The 1954 edition of Good Housekeeping's Basic Cookery in Pictures was written for 'a young housewife or a daughter-at-home called upon to produce a meal in time of domestic crisis.' Black and white and coloured photos illustrate how to make porridge, steam fish, boil eggs and serve coffee through muslin into earthenware jars. How those bright greens and oranges of vegetables and salads, those yellow mayonnaise and pink and red dressed crab and juicy steaks must have added a sparkle to those grey post War days!

There are chapters on the treatment of fish, meat and poultry, there are pages on fluffy dumplings, Irish Stew, Steak and Kidney Puddings, Rabbit Pieces, Stuffed Hearts as well as cooking times (an ox heart: 2-3 hours, sheep, lambs' or calves' hearts: 1½ - 2 hours). Our grandmothers would have been proud of our Yorkshire puddings! For garlic and raw onions, it reads, it is: 'sufficient to rub a clove of garlic round the salad bowl' and 'herbs are best used singly and not mixed.' Parsley, mint dill and tarragon, the most popular, can be grown successfully in window boxes or flower pots—advice which was carried down through the decades. I remember admiring my friend's herbal display in her window box on the sixth floor overlooking the Paris rooftops.

Soups were made from bone stock: 2lb of uncooked bones in a pan with pieces of vegetable, such as carrot, onion and celery, a bunch of herbs and 1tsp of salt covered with cold water simmered with the lid on for 2-3 hours. The Jam Roly-Poly, Adam and Eve Pudding and Victoria Sandwich look as though they are ready to be put in the window of a cake shop.

The book gives the reader an insight into the frugality, optimism, class structure and manners of post-War Britain: food rationing and the unavailability of fresh green plants meant opening tins, most house-wives would have saved dripping and eaten it on toast, they would have known how to clarify it for pure fat for pastry making or frying, to make fruit in jelly, trifle and sage and onion stuffing and nothing was wasted. There are detailed instructions on creaming fat and sugar, when to mix with a fork, how to use a palette knife for icing and the care of cooking equipment, eg. cleaning aluminum pans with soapless detergent and a nylon mesh sponge.

Foreign-sounding phrases: purée, roux, sauté, crème brulée, chaud-froid sauce or French dressing would have appealed to the more sophis-ticated and well-traveled. The wisdom of "wanting to get best value for money and dealing with reliable trades people," and "a false economy of buying inferior goods to save a few pence," however, would have been universally acknowledged. "Most of the electric ovens are fitted with a thermometer and standardized thermostats on gas ovens are not yet uni-versal," it claims. Some of the brand names have been lost: Bridal Icing Sugar, Sutton's Pickled Capers and Kraft grated parmesan cheese but Sainsbury's Plain Flour, Bird's Custard Power and Tate and Lyle Sugar have survived. An elegant model poses in a modern kitchen surrounded by adverts for Nescafé coffee, Cadbury's and prestige fine housewares, Mirroware and Tempo. 'Smart women are reading Good Housekeeping at only 2s a month' the caption reads.

The company also prided itself on its care and service, welcoming tele-phone calls to Sloane 4591 or letters to 30 Grosvenor Gardens, London, SW1. I wonder how many people wrote in.

Language students could make good use of this textbook. Words like "wholesome, by no means essential, if desired, to facilitate, nourishing, steam fish readily digested and particularly suitable for children and invalids, counteract the richness of, and general speaking" would give them an insight into an England that was paternal and still had an Empire.

Was the book's first owner an expatriate, a career diplomat with his last posting at the British Embassy, or was she a nanny or au pair? Perhaps they worked in a bookshop and went back in the evenings to heat something on a solitary electric ring under the Haussmann eaves or, perhaps, they patronised a local bistro until their family finally despaired and gave them the cookery book as a Christmas present. Did they invite their friends round to home-made scones, fruit cake and cucumber sandwiches? Did the pictures of the 1950s housewives in gingham aprons, clean surfaces, Formica tops, tureens and doilies make them feel nostalgic for home? This is a world of elasticized metal watch straps, small watch faces, unvarnished nails, short-sleeved jumpers and tweed skirts, small pearl earrings, washing machines with wringers, black telephones, gingham curtains, Venetian blinds, straw hampers, blue china tea cups, wooden chopping boards, oven-to-table glassware, decorated plates, red check tablecloths and linen tea towels, pictures, even now, to drool over.

My edition has hardly been used. I wonder where it gathered dust. No pages automatically fall open at favourite recipes, nor are there are any thumb prints, so whose stains those on pages 38 and 100 for beef stew and flaky pasty?

Andrea Potos
To the Coffee Shop

Praise to the early riser who unlock
the doors at 4 a.m., create
lemon blueberry crumble,
orange raisin scones dunked
headfirst in sugar,
oatmeal cookies stuffed
with cranberries and pecans.
Praise to the splash and sizzle
on the grill, smells rising
from childhood's deep cache,
when you entered the kitchen rubbing your eyes
and your father kissed you
over the top of his *Times*,
and your big sister looked ridiculous
with her milk moustache.
Your mother turned to greet you
as if you alone were the sun
while eggs burbled in her pan —
praise to the succulent yellow yolks
that were not yet broken.

Sharon Carter
Always Hungry

Barry Seiler

Hot Dog with Mustard and Sauerkraut

You eat it waiting out a storm in a train station
in a small mountain town, the kind where a few shivering pigeons
lean from the rafters crying softly like hungry, vagrant ghosts.
A few passengers sit on the hard benches, clutching their baggage;
the ticket taker chews his pencil over a crossword puzzle.
The dog approaches your mouth like a train entering a tunnel.
a drop of mustard, solitary light, flickering on the tail.

Susan Rich

The Dead Eat Blueberry Scones for Breakfast

with a touch of butter and sweet cream,
a cup of black coffee to reenact the morning;

some food, some drink, soon opens
awakening to a new place. One swan

keening as he circles our silvered lake.

The dead skim the headlines of the *Irish Times,*
re-imagine the aroma of eggs on toast;

they mime the domesticity we simply
breathe in and then just as recklessly let go —

our every action alive with their echo.

They hover at our shoulder
as we buy blood oranges

off the back of the young man's truck;
waving good-bye as he leaves

so suddenly. This evening the dead keep singing,

She is the belle of Belfast City,
then finger the jug of red wine

lingering near a woman's arms
alive in this careless air.

Katharyn Howd Machan
The Beets Poem

Beets: now there's a subject.
Dark red, rounded, hard as—
well, hard as beets.

I know a woman
who grew a garden last summer,
planted it with nothing
but lettuce and beets.
The lettuce didn't grow
but she had plenty of slugs
and beets, plenty of beets.
Now whenever anyone visits her
she takes them down cellar,
says, "See my beets?"
And there they are, pickled,
row after row of dark red jars
no one will ever open.

Someone else I know
always asks for beets, no matter
what kind of restaurant we're in.
Even at the beach
he'll go up to the hot dog stand.
"Got any beets?" he'll say.
And when the man at the grill
just stares at him, he sighs
and turns away, and spends
half an hour just gazing at the waves.

I know what you're thinking.
Why don't I introduce these friends,

have them both to dinner
one night, serve vegetarian?
It's not so easy.
Remember, beets is our subject,
and beets is what I hate about them both.

My Body Knows

Kim Addonizio
Affair

God it's sexual, opening a beer when you swore you wouldn't drink tonight,
taking the first deep gulp, the foam backing up in the long amber neck
of the Pacifico bottle as you set it on the counter, the head spilling over
so you bend to fit your mouth against the cold lip
and drink, because what you are, aren't you, is a drinker—maybe not a lush,
not an alcoholic, not yet anyway, but don't you want
a glass of something most nights, don't you need the gesture
of reaching for it, raising it high and swallowing down and savoring
the sweetness, or the scalding, knowing you're going to give yourself to it
like a lover, whether or not he fills up the leaky balloon of your heart—
don't you believe in trying to fill it, no matter what the odds,
don't you believe it still might happen, aren't you that kind of woman?

Kim Addonizio

❧ Two Quick & Dirty Drink Recipes to Get You Quickly Dirty

The E-tini

Into a glass, flask, juice jar, paper cup, hollowed coconut shell, or other suitable container such as cupped hands (having a partner for this last will prove to be useful), pour:

⅓ Absolut Vanilla vodka, fresh from the freezer
⅓ cold orange juice
⅓ cold pineapple juice

Top with a floater of the Absolut. Do not stir. Drink immediately.

The E-tini tastes like a Dreamsicle and was invented by my friend Elizabeth Sanderson. It's simple, refreshing and full of sugar, but you can feel good that you are drinking two kinds of juice. If you wish to bypass feeling good and go straight to feeling fucked up, try the K-tini.

The K-tini

1) Open freezer and remove any hard alcoholic beverage.
2) Unscrew cap.
3) Open mouth and apply to bottle.
4) Swallow as many times as possible on a single inhale.

Wine from the refrigerator or cupboard may be substituted for step one; in that case, however, the characteristic and oft-mentioned "kick" of the K-tini can't be experienced. Wine is for wannabes. The K-tini is the drink for those in the know, those who are sick with thirst, those whose demons are swarming. Your demons snicker at wine, at lite beer, at bitters and soda. Give them what they clamor for: give them K-tinis.

Enjoy!

Alison Stone

Starving for God

Twelve years old and always happy,
I am fortified by the religion of control.
Although fat follows me
like a retarded twin, I will remove
these hips and tempting breasts.
Already I am healed.
I have stopped the blood.

The others are jealous,
fail to praise
the sculpture I am making.
They do not see
it is their way, not mine,
that leads to death.

I am stronger than that.
Hunger is a prayer
for the time when I will have no flesh
with which to sin.

I see perfection
and am almost thin enough
to slip through the door.
I run, I burn, I am blessed.
I will not stop until I touch
the pure ivory bones of my temple.

Trissy McGhee

Suicide

for Gerald

In the hours after the call comes, my body becomes a dumb thing to be led to the toilet. To be walked. To be showered, its legs shaved for the service. To be fed and watered, though everything turns to ash in my throat. At your parents' house we gather, our faces made of torn paper, burnt holes for eyes. Spines sag into the couch. We go to the store for Coke, fruit, water. Someone brings a lasagna. I make Gram's shortbread: three sticks of butter kneaded into rice flour on your mom's table. More flowers come. I press beads of butter between my fingers. At the viewing, I touch your arm plumped with Perfect-tone. Your body no longer needs anything, just some time and a place to dissolve. By your casket we eat the shortbread, chased with a burning dram of Glenmorangie. Follow the crumbs as we unspool back to Las Vegas, Portland, San Diego. Come. I'll make you a cup of tea. We won't have to talk.

Trissy McGhee

❧ Selina's Shortbread

3 cubes of butter, softened
¾ cup fine sugar
4½ cups flour
¾ cup white rice flour

Cream butter, sugar together. Add plain flour, mix until crumbly. Turn out onto table and gradually add rice flour. Knead until rice flour disappears. Knead, knead, knead. Half and put into 9" round pans. Flatten with a round tipped knife, then prick with a fork all over. Put into 400 degree oven. Bake until golden. Sprinkle with fine sugar. Cool just slightly and cut into pie shapes with a sharp knife. To eat: take a bite and then sip a bit of whiskey or tea. Repeat.

NOTE: My grandmother said the best way to make this shortbread is with your hands, though you can use a food processor as well.

Steve Kowit

Alpha Centauri

We were down at the Hungry Hunter's
after a peace march, when Danny,
whose passions are social justice
& roast Cornish hen,
starts whipping himself into a frenzy
over the President's lies,
multinational greed,
the Pentagon's homicidal agenda.
"The exploitation of anyone,"
Danny says, lifting that small bird's body
in both of his hands
& tearing a wing off,
"oppresses us all!"
& with that he starts in on the rape of the Congo,
slavery in Cape Town,
torture in Turkey,
El Salvador,
Poland,
Afghanistan,
Alpha Centauri...
Ripping the last bit of flesh with his teeth,
Danny says there are millions of corpses
under our noses
that nobody sees.
& when everyone else at the table agrees,
he shakes his head as much as to say
it's beyond comprehension,
& wipes a trickle of grease from his chin,
& crumples his napkin onto a plate
full of bones & pieces of skin
& left-over peas.

Pamela Annas

Seventh Month

November is when I'll deliver you, a slick brown envelope fat with promise, like those letters from my grandmother filled with news clippings, packs of juicyfruit, dollars for hair ribbons; like packages from my mother bulging with Texas pecans and boxes of lime jello. I feel you pushing against my waist, or where my waist used to be in wide belts tight over swirling skirts or harem pants when I swung to "In the Mood," hustled to "pink Cadillac," swayed to a country waltz—"Could I have this dance for the rest of my life"—which led to you ballooning below my breasts so when I talk on the phone long distance to my former lover who is glad for me, yes, my breath comes faster. It would anyway, to hear her furry Louisiana drawl that still can brush my skin like the cotton sheet that's enough for sultry Southern nights. I wasn't ready then. In my forties I'm easy as a ripe peach. My mother, my sister and I climb up on ladders and reach for peaches the size of baseballs, fill buckets and paper sacks. The fallen ones drip juice on baked Texas grass in the possessive purr of bees. Evenings we peel the peaches, freshen the family gossip, put them up to freeze. All winter and spring we'll serve peaches on pound cake, peaches on vanilla ice cream, peach pies and cobblers, sliced peaches for breakfast. Jam is too much trouble. It was too much trouble to have a baby in my teens, twenties, thirties. I had to make a living, find some ground to stand on. I would have said no. I said no. Then no slid into yes and here you are pressing up against my diaphragm, making me breathless as you metamorphose from a blue flutter of wings through weeks of silken swimming in your private pool to something brown and wild leaping from branch to branch.

Susan Luzzaro

Meditations on Mother's Milk

When my mother was hospitalized due to alcohol she lost her mind for about a week. Sometimes her hands were tied across the front of her white gown. During one visit, however, her hands were free and restless. They hopped around the bed snatching at imaginary things. Then she lifted her nightgown and offered me her flattened, aged breasts. "Pies," she said as she smiled sweetly, "pies."

For many years I was angry with her for this gesture. My anger was a twisted affair. The child in me remarked bitterly to itself, *she never nursed me, why is she offering me her breasts now?* I was 37, did I want to be nursed? Of course, the base of my anger was her alcoholism and much deeper than alcoholism, her abdication of life. Yes, I wanted to be nursed.

Memory is kaleidoscopic. The little colored pieces always falling into new arrangements. Only yesterday, twenty years after my mother's death, I thought to myself, that when she offered me her breasts, it was really the deepest offering she could make. Now her gesture says to me, "Here, love, you will need sustenance." No doubt on my deathbed, I will revise the story again, will remember the sweet taste of her milk.

The mystery of mother's milk is that, like the fishes and loaves of the Biblical tale, the more that is needed the more that is created. With my first child I was not as successful in nursing as I would have wished. I was caught between child-rearing doctrines. I had inherited from my mother and Dr. Spock, the punitive idea that a baby must wait 4 hours between feedings. Any crying in-between would only serve to build character. I thought that by the end of the 4 hours I would bring my breasts freighted with milk to my son. But the reverse was true. Feeding on schedule diminished my milk and by the sixth week or so when my son had only gained a little weight, I was persuaded to quit nursing him. I was wiser with my daughter. I fed her whenever she was hungry and my milk was plenteous.

Primal in nature, breast milk is on a metaphorical par with *what came first the chicken or the egg?* Yet, how odd the world turns. In developing countries there has long been a controversy regarding the aggressive marketing of infant formulas. It is well supported that mother's milk offers an infant many advantages and that formulas have caused malnutrition and even death. Equally ironic, in the United States, in Canada, and in Australia programs have been launched, taxes paid to teach women how to breast feed and to encourage them to do it for longer periods of time. My mother did not nurse any of her six children. None of my aunts nursed their children either. Shortly after WW II and around the time that my parents began having children the formula market exploded in the United States under the guise of progress, even science. My father believed in airplanes, my mother in formula. They were, in their way, on the cutting edge.

When I had my children, child-rearing doctrines reflected the then conflicting ethos of the late 60s and early 70s. I felt as I sometimes do standing between two weather patterns — the Santa Ana winds from the desert and the onshore flow from the Pacific. Breast-feeding in friends' houses or vegetarian restaurants was personal and political. The air was thick with theory. To bare your breast and feed your baby was to say *a la* Marcuse: *The body is natural, breast milk is natural, repression is bad and part of the way we are controlled.* Not so simple when I took out my breast in my in-laws' house. Once Uncle Nino and Aunt Alberta traveled from New Jersey, among other reasons to see the new baby. I reasoned, badly, that because they were Italian American they somehow would be less repressed than my Irish German parents. When I discreetly lifted my blouse I was hurried from the room with a towel thrown over my breast and my baby. I heard Aunt Alberta say from the bedroom, "That Nino should see such a thing."

During that same time, I was attending Southwestern Community College. One of the professors brought her baby to campus, not to class, and in the course of time apparently nursed in a public setting. Finally, the school board got in such a dither that they actually forbade the professor to bring her baby on campus. Motherhood is apparently only sacred in the home. Ultimately, the courts, distanced from the offending breasts and crying baby, overruled the board's decision. Still, there is a great deal of legislation surrounding this mundane act. Nursing is circumscribed by laws that vary from state to state and country to country and a woman still doesn't know when she will be asked to leave the room.

Who does the breast belong to? When I was nursing, I was aware that everything I ate or drank entered my milk. I worried about balancing green and orange and eating from the sacred food pyramid. I abstained from drugs and alcohol, except, mercifully, dark beer, which was said to increase your milk. My body was separate from me, a bit like a factory, my milk a commodity. And time was a painful leash. If I was away too long, my breasts would leak through my t-shirt and my baby would be fussy and unappeased. My parents, my in-laws, my doctor all discussed how long I should nurse, as if the decision were objective, belonged to them. This alienation occurred more with my first baby because I was only 19. With my second baby, I was more in control, nursed until she was talking, until she lifted my blouse and demanded *Milk*.

Men are wont to believe that the breasts belong to them. With both my children, I was immersed in my own cycle of pleasure and concern. I never surprised a look of envy on my husband's face, but I rarely looked up. My whole being was focused on the well being of the baby. Perhaps, too, I was reluctant to look up because I didn't want to share the strong sensual feeling that happened when the baby suckled and milk poured through my ducts. A triangle is bound to exist. Since then, more than once I have seen a displaced look on a man's face, a mixture of envy, longing...and even disgust. Long ago I read in a La Leche book that men in tribal situations could lactate given enough stimulation. Grandmothers, too, and, by extension, adoptive parents. It might be a solution to jealousy, more nutritious than formula. But on *YouTube* I watched a young father stimulate his breasts to produce milk. In the brief video, he never achieved lactation but he does get his child to suckle sweetly at his breast. In the background, the mother looks on with what I perceive to be envy, longing and a little disgust.

Mother's milk is said to be the perfect food, starting with the antibodies all the way through to the perfect balance of fat and protein. Perhaps a breast-feeding foody TV series is in order. At first there might be less glamour, less to sell—the striated engorged breasts, the babies drowning in the first flood of the milk. There would be no use for cutlery or Tuscan-colored plates, though something colorful might be done with napkins and shiny pendants against bare skin. As these shows rarely comment on the dangers of e-coli or the carcinogenic potential of barbecued food, it would also not serve the beauty of a breast milk series to discuss the harmful ingredients in mothers' milk. When I nursed my children, DDT was the particular concern as the use of this poison had just been discontinued. Breast milk is in large part manufactured from the fat in the body, where DDT is also deposited. Progress being what it is, the concern in 2007 is the explosive found in rocket fuel, perchlorate. A Center for Disease Control/Boston University study showed that infants in the Boston area were ingesting more than twice the amount of this rocket fuel component than the Environmental Protection Agency considers safe. Perchlorate has leaked from military bases and defense and aerospace contractor's plants in 22 states. (Environmental Working Group website).

At first glance you would think this intimate scene, this mother and child *pieta,* would be a closed circle. Yet, there is a whole world in-between. Just a few nights ago, on what passes for the local news, a newborn was found dead in a recycling center. Somewhere a woman's breasts are filling with milk.

Nadia Mandilawi

Keeping Up Appearances

You, in the hospital like
a cold slab of meat. Pink,
body puffed.
Me, finally doing everything I've put off.
Dyeing my hair.
Catching that movie,
instead of going to the hospital.
Your mother, screaming,
because you were speeding, no seatbelt.
Hitting her head against
the waiting room wall. Trying to wake-up.

We had plans—like last New Year.
Stuck at some shabby
hotel party with our parents.
The self-proclaimed
Excellent International Disco DJ in his shiny orange suit.
Rings of sweat exposed
when he lifts his arms.
Revolting American tracks,
even worse Arabic music blaring
out of half-blown speakers.
International DJ
leading party in conga line.
"I'm not 23 and really *here* on New Year's,
right," you said,
between dirty martinis and tabouli.
Plastered,
you dared me to smoke a cigarette,
the biggest thrill of the night.

"Have you ever smoked in a stall?"
You asked, as you threw your hair back,
flirtatious.
"No." I replied,
fidgety and damn cold in my skirt.
You're flawless in your shimmery red dress,
shoulders and back showing.
Skin shining,
black liquid liner perfect on your lid.
You couldn't just watch, had to have one too,
and we were back to back in the same stall,
laughing,
trying to blow circles,
hiding,
standing on the toilet.
On top of the world for a second,
swearing we'd be somewhere else
next year.

Your insurance lady came with pictures of the car.
Front seat pushed through the back window.
Two-door car
crushed to one.
"It's a miracle really," the lady kept saying,
"She would have died if her seatbelt was on."
Yeah, a miracle, have you seen her?
She doesn't have any teeth, lady,
24, and no teeth.
I'm upset like this all the time.
I'm upset with you,
at our parents.
Putting your mistakes out on a platter,
letting everyone
pick at them with toothpicks,
like pieces of smoked salmon.
Letting so-called friends come and see you like this.
Half naked.
Split in the face, pelvis and body broken.
All the whispered questions,
"Do you think she can hear me?"

Not that they care.
These are the same people
who used to say you dressed like a slut.
Too much make-up.
I wish you could see them now,
fresh from the office or gym.
In the same vests and
stale running suits.
Their fat faces
wet
and crying
over you.

Sara Irene

Deserted

Burning Man: It is an annual counterculture festival that takes place in the Black Rock Desert of Nevada the week of Labor Day. Burning Man is a lesson in experimental community in which a city rises and falls in a single week. People are encouraged to participate and not just "see." The festival is marked by artistic expression including installations placed all over the desert, theme camps and costumes. There is no commerce other than ice and coffee sales with the proceeds going to the school at the Indian Reservation 30 miles away. Participants must confront their own survival and bring everything they need to survive a week in the desert including extreme heat, cold and high speed wind storms.

❧

I'd been waiting at the Reno Airport for over an hour when my cell phone finally rang.

"Sara, it's Sara, I'm here!" my overenthusiastic friend squealed. "I'm here! Meet me at baggage!"

I'd in fact been waiting there since my flight had arrived. Sara and some other friends had persuaded me to come. Who knew when we'd be on the same side of the country again? I actually really didn't care, but I was in Reno out of obligation. I was apprehensive about this whole trip. It had been a year since we'd seen each other and, as she emerged from the terminal, I wondered if this person rushing toward me was in fact my friend. Somehow that year had made her look like a crack whore slithering through the airport in a silky evening gown that she had clearly been wearing for days. "I know, I know," she explained, "I look like shit. I went to the tanning booth and I'm all burned and this is the only thing I can wear that doesn't hurt!"

I know I was supposed to feel better about this news, but the truth was it made me more upset. She had gone to the tanning booth and I was going to be paler than vanilla ice cream. I'd only been pretending that I wanted to be here; I didn't want to disappoint her and all the other friends I was meeting. This was supposed to change my life, but I just didn't see how a trip to the desert was going to change anything.

We walked out of the airport and got into Marie's truck. Our friend Marie had already been out in the desert for a week and she came back to Reno to get us at the airport and to pick up more supplies. We babbled through our two-hour drive east until I could see lights way off in the distance. The moment I had been dreading for days had arrived; I was at Burning Man.

It should have been the dead of night, but this temporary city never sleeps. The entrance gate was crowded. Sara and I were "virgins" and we had to be hazed in before we were allowed on to the "playa". This ritual involved climbing onto a fake toilet, ringing a bell and being spanked with a plastic glow worm toy and then we were off to find Marie's camp. The way in was lined with signs with all sorts of catchy phrases involving leaving the real world behind. I swore I would remember them, but of course I don't.

Marie was anxious to show us this world she loved so much. We grabbed our coats and water bottles and wandered through a maze of camps and people until we arrived on the Esplanade. Lights were everywhere, blinking, glaring and beckoning us to places we could not have imagined existed. I knew the basics of Burning Man; "tent" city, created and destroyed in a week's time, don't be a spectator, wear fancy costumes, find the nearest hallucinogen, and simply just be. *The problem was I could never just be. On the inside I was miserable, scared and lonely, on the outside I was a cheerful pushover.*

Back at camp it was time for bed. My cot and tent had come up with some other friends and we still hadn't found them. I slept on the floor of Marie's tent and nearly froze in my single sleeping bag. The ground was hard and the party going on outside never stopped. It was a very rough night. I have no idea what time we woke up in the morning. I quickly learned that time, while of the essence, is also nonexistent on the playa. Our friend Kellee had come to visit from her camp several streets away. "Gooooood Mooooooooorning!" she sang. "Get your asses dressed and out of the tent!"

I really hadn't done much with the costume situation. My costume wardrobe consisted of a few pairs of drawstring pants with silly prints and a few pieces of sparkly fabric, nothing all that inspired. Most girls wear sexy lingerie, revealing costumes or even go topless. I wasn't that brave or secure about my body. In fact, I weighed nearly three hundred pounds. My weight had been the major issue keeping me from Burning Man. Burning Man was supposedly an all inclusive situation. Everyone was supposed to be welcome, and though I hoped that for once this would actually be true, I had a suspicion that I would be ignored as I always was. I was almost certain that Burning Man was for the beautiful, sexy and brave and I was none of those things. While some of the reasons for my insecurity were manufactured inside my own head, many of them were painfully obvious. Men were not attracted to me because of my size and other women made snide comments loud enough for me to hear. I didn't matter to most people and Burning Man amplified my fears one thousand-fold. Yes, I had a lot of friends, but I didn't feel close to most of them. They were there to keep me busy, but I couldn't let them really get to know me.

Navigating the labyrinth in daylight proved to be a very different experience than our brief venture of the night before. My first well-lit glimpse revealed a gorgeous scene; mountains molded the area into a bowl of desert, to the East there was a vast expanse of open land as far as the eye could see. The desert floor was packed hard with random cracks in the surface. The dichotomy of truly being in the middle of nowhere yet surrounded by so much creative effort stunned me.

Early morning is the quiet time of the playa. At 8 AM most people have only been in bed for a few hours and those that are awake are going about their morning routines preparing breakfast and opening their camps up to the community. I've always been a solitary person, almost a hermit, and the idea of just walking into someone's home, even a temporary campsite, made me very nervous. I barely even knew my neighbors in my apartment building! As Kellee, Marie, Sara and I rounded a corner onto the Esplanade a naked man popped out from behind a tarp and asked us if we wanted some coffee. I was ready to run away but Kellee and Marie were sitting in his camp before my fight-or-flight response had even kicked in. I declined a beverage and sat silently while the other girls chatted away.

With coffee finished our expedition began again. The camp wasn't open yet so we ventured out to the Man. The Man is really the whole point, hence the name Burning Man. The city is shaped in a circle with a two mile radius. The man stands in the center of this circle and the first street, the esplanade is a quarter mile from the man in either direction. There are seven streets after the esplanade, all circular. The Man was a three story stick figure with a triangular head sitting on top of a two-story lighthouse structure. During the week, the man was visible from anywhere on the playa. The Man served as a navigation tool during much of the festival but is burned down on Saturday night as an effigy of release and renewal.

I was in sensory overload. There was art and images everywhere that challenged my imagination and the structure of what I thought could exist. Sculptures, performance art and technological art were sprinkled all over. Camps had interactive projects and activities and conceptualized vehicles roamed the playa. A giant, 20-foot red bubble gum machine drove past with people bouncing like gumballs inside the clear bubble top. A pirate ship cruised past with swashbucklers yelling obscenities at the people who got in the way. A group of bicyclists wearing only colored paint nearly crashed into us. It could only be described as surreal.

I was going through a personal crisis. I couldn't be my usual upset and angry self because this whole new world confused me. Art was everywhere. People were being creative and expressing themselves. I wanted to express myself too, but I didn't know who to express. I usually stay silent and soak it all up and let others tell their personal truths. I internalize and digest the world, just as I ingested the food I was addicted to. And somehow I found myself in this place where shoulds and musts are not even a part of the vocabulary. It was only a world of want and be. And I wasn't ready to admit that I wanted to be anything.

Sara was there at my side and I grew increasingly annoyed at her. We were an interesting match, brought together through loneliness and the hope of finding sameness in this world. She'd hurt me, thrilled me and disappointed me, but I still loved her like a piece of myself. We were, after all, the "Sara Sandwich." I began to hate her that morning. I was jealous, extremely jealous. We had the same name, some of the same favorites, but she was adventurous and free where I was cautious and closed off. She was thin and cute; I was humongous and ugly. I'd thought we were the same and suddenly against the backdrop of a giant penis sculpture I realized we were not the same at all. She had only been an idea of what I'd hoped to be someday and having the same name had allowed me to believe that she was a mirror image when she really wasn't.

I needed to escape her somehow. And as Burning Man is known to do, it produced exactly what I needed at exactly the time I needed it. We'd arrived at the camp of some different friends of mine, that none of my others friends really knew. Amy and Dave appeared to me like an apparition of Jesus. I was saved. Before I had even arrived at Burning Man I had built an escape route for myself. I had told Marie and Sara that I might be camping with Amy and Dave, though I had neglected to really inform them of this fact. As Amy was showing me the dome shaped disco of the camp, I asked her if they had room for one more tent. She felt certain the other members wouldn't mind if I stayed there.

We left Kellee at her own camp and found our way back to Marie's camp. Marie had a "date" and promised she would return in the early afternoon to drive me over to Christine's to get my camping gear and then take me to my new camp. I was really worried about having to spend time with Sara but I just couldn't bring myself to explore on my own. I was certain that people would take one look at me and know that I was the fat girl without any friends. Fortunately, Evan and Shonda came to the camp and we all hung out on the carpet and told crazy stories. I wasn't adjusting to the climate all that well and I had a horrible headache to match my horrible mood. I tried to act like I was okay but I think it was pretty obvious I wasn't. Shonda suggested that she and the others should go exploring and I could just stay at camp and rest. I wanted to try to feel better somehow and decided that a shower might just do the trick.

Showering at Burning Man is a lot of effort. Our shower consisted of a large plastic shower bag with a nozzle hung over the driver's side mirror of Shonda's truck. Beneath the shower bag was a wood palate on top of a large piece of black plastic to catch the water and aid in evaporation. That's it, no curtain, no water pressure, just me and a bag of water. I gathered all my shower supplies and glanced around to check if anyone would be able to see me. All the neighbors appeared to be out. I put on a long, black dress and began washing my legs, then my arms, and my hair until the only parts left to wash were covered by my dress. Looking around again, I quickly removed my dress and started washing the rest of my body. Suddenly I heard voices, "Sara, hey do you know where Shonda and Zach are?"

It was Eddie and his boyfriend Rob dressed, appropriately, as pirates. There I was, standing naked and they had chosen this exact moment to stop by camp. *Stay calm. They don't even realize you are naked and fat. They must realize you are naked. They don't care. Act like you don't care and they won't know that you care. They have no idea you are freaking out. You're fooling them. If they don't care, you don't care.*

"So, do you know where they are?" Eddie asked again. With the argument going on in my head, I had completely forgotten I was technically having a conversation with people, and that I was showering. I had been standing naked in front of two of my friends for at least three minutes, and they weren't even sick or throwing up!

"Um yah," I stammered. "I think they went out to the big Duck with the casino in it, but they were going to try to make it to see the Lily Pond too."

"Okay, I think we are going to try to find them. Do you want us to wait for you?"

I definitely did not want them to wait for me. I wanted them to instantly teleport to the Duck right now. I shook my head and gestured toward the shower.

"Naw, I am trying to get cleaned up before I move to another camp when Marie gets back."

Eddie and Rob said goodbye and I had peace at last. I finished my shower at world record pace and covered up as quickly as possible. As I sank into the pile of pillows we had in our chill space it occurred to me that I had just, for the first time in my life, surrendered to the moment. I had a conversation with people while I was unclothed and we all survived. I had no intention of repeating the experience but I felt okay with it. I wasn't worried that Eddie and Rob were going to run back to their camp with a detailed horror story of seeing me naked. My shower had just been a brief stop along their day and quite frankly, my naked body, no matter how many fat rolls it had, could not compete with the freak show around us.

Later in the afternoon, Marie returned to take me to my new camp. It was beginning to get dark and my tent still had to be put up. She motioned for a few of the guys, camp mates I had not even met yet, and directed them in assembling my tent. I was embarrassed by this. I could put my tent up by myself and I didn't want my new camp mates to think I was rude. The guys were all really nice about it and made quick work of it, and then introduced themselves to me.

My new camp was filled with really great people. Most of them had known each other since high school and although they were all very kind, I felt very much like an outsider. I hadn't considered this when I had decided to move, but I had felt like an outsider with my own friends anyway. They were all getting ready to "go out." I hadn't really been invited. I didn't know if I should just go with them because they were all going or if I should stay behind. I decided to feign exhaustion and just stay at camp. I didn't want them to hate me already. As it turned out, Cade was tired after being awake for almost two days and he decided to stay behind as well.

We sat quietly in our camp chairs. I was afraid to speak to him since I had just met him that night. Cade was very tall and he was wearing a dress. For some reason I have always found men in dresses to be quite sexy. He instantly made me nervous.

The night was cold and I started to shiver. Cade asked me if I wanted to go hang out in the back of the rented U-Haul so that we could warm up. I followed him to the truck and was surprised to find the inside furnished with carpet and blowup furniture. We sat on the floor and began talking. It turned out that we had another friend in common who lived in New York. We talked about her, and what we did for work and about his past years at Burning Man. I felt a chemistry with him that scared me though I was certain that the attraction wasn't mutual because I was sure that no one could possibly be attracted to me as large as I was. I had sworn off romance long ago after an abusive relationship. It was an easy thing to do since no one wanted me anyway.

The generator ran out of gas and the truck was enveloped in darkness. Cade began to touch my face and I was confused. I understood what face caressing would mean if it was between two beautiful people, that sort of thing didn't happen to people like me. But it was happening, and it was happening so quickly that I was going to miss it. He leaned over and kissed me. I hadn't been kissed in a long time. It was so soft and warm. A mouth was on mine, a beautiful mouth that belonged to an even more beautiful man and I was completely floored. How could this be happening to me? How could I be sitting in the back of a rented U-Haul and have this fantasy come true. But I was there and it was real and most importantly he was real. His body was pressed against mine and I could feel him, a live human boy. But I didn't deserve this; I didn't deserve love, no matter how fleeting. *Did he feel sorry for me? Was he bored? Was he crazy? Was he on drugs? Was this actually real? Was I on drugs? What did it mean? What could it mean?* It didn't matter because he kept kissing me and I stopped thinking.

We kissed for what seemed like hours. During that time I was floating. My body didn't matter. I forgot that I was fat, hadn't even considered I was disgusting. I got to be beautiful for a moment that I had forced myself to believe I was never going to get to have. As quickly as it began, it ended with the words, "Sara, I um have a girlfriend. We don't have to stop, but this can't go any further."

It did have to stop. I wasn't that kind of girl and he wasn't really that kind of guy. He'd forgotten reality as much as I had and as soon as it came rushing back we had to return to being the Sara and Cade we were just before the lights had gone out. I can't say that I was happy about it, but I knew what the right thing was. He pulled me close to him and we cuddled for a while and fell asleep.

We eventually woke up and he walked me to my tent and kissed me on my cheek. I was mostly confused about the night. I felt in love or at least enamored. I hadn't considered the possibility of what love had to offer to someone like me. We could never have had a happily ever after but our moment served its purpose. It left me shaken.

The Man burned a few days later. Cade and I sat next to each other in uncomfortable silence watching the Man fall to the ground. We were strangers once again, trying to pretend our night didn't happen, keeping it a secret from the rest of the camp. I'd purposely sat next to him, hoping to create a tidy, happy memory that I could bring home with me to sentimentally ponder in the months to come. That didn't happen. He barely looked at me. This event was supposed to be the culmination of the week, and I didn't want it to end that way.

Back at camp I asked Cade to take a walk with me. The city had a different tone now. People had stolen street signs as mementos and it was difficult to find our way in the dark. Burn night is like Christmas morning, but I was still hoping to take a few presents home. We ambled through the city and talked. I don't remember what we said but it mattered to me that we weren't going to part as enemies.

Heather Eudy
Post-Nicotrol

I've got a pattern down for this routine
of shelling seeds at night. They break beneath
my hungry hands and teeth replacing smoke
with dusty food. Substitute flower meat
for cigarettes. Supplant grandmother's scotch.
Here all I need is mouth and sound, a seed
that opens willingly and dries my tongue.
A paper plate receives the shells I've emptied
spread out like scabs, like fingernails. Disgust.
Temptation. Both attract a habit's birth.
I touch myself and dig into the bag,
but dirt slips through my hands of muddy earth.
I draft my right leg's shape then zig and zag
across a length of thigh an alphabet
inscribed in denim, drawn by thumb and nail.
Though numb and motionless, I'm newly wet,
out of breath. I cup a fallen entrails
and slide it to the floor with the same hands
that stiffen at my crotch, that arch for more.
My toes pick the seeds out of carpet strands
a little sticky, flecked with white and blue.
I reach into the bag and break the home,
the hard skin of a body eaten through.

Jennifer Cost
Garlic

Cali Linfor

My Body Knows the Four Colors of Corn

My hair is red
Indian clay
and I am as Irish
as soap carved out
in the summer heat
of Oklahoma porches
by my great-grandfather's knife
while you shell peas
and hide half
under an apron
for your reservation cousins.

My skin is white
watermelon rind
eaten back
to the green
of the garden
you plant
with my grandmother
four times a year
and sing each time
for the corn
to come early.

My lips are yellow
with the corn bread
and honey butter
you were caught

sneaking to a man
two shades darker
than the dirt
and your hair
in the starlight
stretch between
the house and the barn
where your husband
tried to kill you
for staining his sons
in Cherokee blood.

Jeanne Bryner

Berthie Stiles Searches for Answers:
Winter the Cow Died, Crossroads, West Virginia, 1918

Snow drifts clear to my waist
13 children wild as starved cats
prowling, snotty with colds.
Not enough grease to fix bub sop.
No man, no sack flower for biscuits
in the pantry. No dried beans
nor apples on a string.
Three half rotted onions
and no deer meet hung
in the smokehouse. When
our cow took sick and died
I knew we mustn't eat her.
I have brung in clean snow
played like its ice cream
four days now, but their black
looks are hell's thirteen circles.
Jesus says, *In heaven
there's a bountiful table.*
Well, we can't cinch our belts
back one more notch.
In the barn maybe there's mice
if not, there's a rope.

Karen Greenbaum-Maya
Pumpkins & Squash en Clair et en Obscur

Sydney Brown

The Difference Between a Horror Film and a Scary Movie

My boyfriend the film buff and I are on our way to see a scary movie because they're making a comeback. I keep track of the signals we encounter: yellow, red, green then green again. "You know," he says, "there's a difference between a true horror film and a scary movie." Red light.

"Psycho—classic horror film, stylized—Hitchcock at his best." He stops and grabs a parking ticket from a small white machine and I'm amazed at how little he has to reach to make the connection. As he tosses the ticket onto the dash, I'm reminded of how I have to open my car door and place my foot on the ground, stretch to the point of discomfort to accomplish the same task.

"Scary," he says, "scary is fun—makes you scream like someone jumpin' out from behind a bush, but it won't keep you up at night. Horror, true horror, pushes you beyond the scream, makes you pull your collar up around your neck, look under the bed. It can mess your shit up for life."

At Denny's, after the movie, he speaks passionately about "the blonde with the big fake tits who got crunched by the electric garage door." He tells me there's a part two, "funnier, gorier—already in production." I order the sampler basket: fried cheese, fried onions, fried potatoes, and fried zucchini. "Part two," he continues, peeling open an Equal packet for no apparent reason, "has three times the murders—some totally hot supermodel-chick gets decapitated."

He blows sugar substitute from the table as I wonder if the onion rings will burn my throat, if the mozzarella will lodge in my esophagus and make me choke, if the green of the zucchini will be the only vibrant color in the bowl. Or, if by some grace, it will return gently like baby food: a warm, blander version than it was the first time. Our meals arrive and I ask for milk and water.

He is annoyed that I want to sleep in my own bed when we are minutes from his. I tell him I had a long day, unzip his pants, take him in my mouth for the ride home. I know he will not ask to enter this way—when he comes in my mouth I am at my doorstep waving goodbye, watching his pick-up disappear into blur—row after row of green lights like trees. I do not know why I wait until his car is beyond the visible signals to enter my home, but I do, then I enter and slide the bolt behind me.

Alone, I turn on the bathroom sink, drink warm water from my cupped hands and leave it running. I remove my mascara with a cotton ball, pull my hair back, grab a towel from behind the door and fold it neatly, place it on the ground before the toilet. I tell myself *five heaves, maybe six*, then kneel, push my left hand into my stomach, right index and middle finger down my throat.

Some women leave the water running to drown out the retching and coughing; I leave it on because once, when I was five, I was ill and had to take a urine test. I couldn't go. My mother turned on the sink, called it magic, the bright yellow leaking into a paper cup. This is the image: Mother holding the cup and laughing at me laughing at the magic; urine running down her steady hand, tears rolling down my soft-feverish skin.

When there is nothing left but bile and tears I lay back on the floor, curl-up in a loose ball, pillow the towel beneath my head and think about nothing. Sometimes it takes awhile to reenter a world where I do not know what my own scream sounds like.

Jennifer Chapis
First Christmas Single

The kitchen is heat and garlic, rosemary and snoozing dogs.
Roses smell like carrots in her hands. Organic mathematics:
the sun times the moon equals the white onion.

In the driveway, couples trudge through snow, parmesan, love
together. Holiday bells, hot broth, baked goods in Tupperware.
But I'm hungry for more than bread and spice, a stuffed bird.

That's when
the dogs start to look good — fur tight and attached, bony chests rising,
falling....

Urgency is vision and no discomfort is insignificant, no boundary or myth.
No bra:

The sharp ice of her hand runs up the length of each sleeve (doorbell ringing)
bra straps undone. She tears at the tiny binding clips
under the tight weight of too many layers.

Her breasts spill from their warm pockets. Guests bloom
through the doorway in pairs — parkas suntan-red, creamsicle-colored.
My nipples stand like two hairs from a wool sweater.

I have peeled virtually
into halves.

Window in the snowy floor?

Kitchen, all but outside,
a white-cold.

Jeff Crouch
Pear Able Less

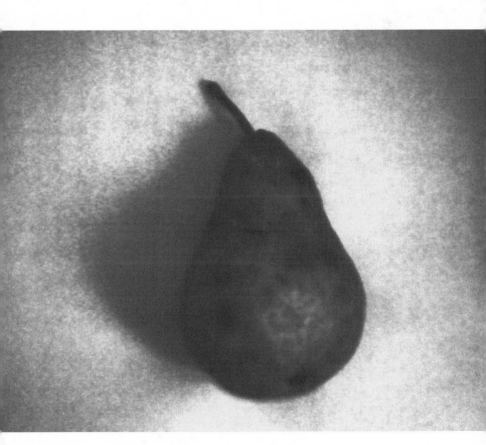

Li-Young Lee

The Cleaving

He gossips like my grandmother, this man
with my face, and I could stand
amused all afternoon
in the Hon Kee Grocery,
amid hanging meats he
chops: roast pork cut
from a hog hung
by nose and shoulders,
her entire skin burnt
crisp, flesh I know
to be sweet,
her shining
face grinning
up at the ducks
dangling single file,
each pierced by black
hooks through breast, bill,
and streaming from a hole
stitched shut at the ass.
I step to the counter, recite,
and he, without even slightly
varying the rhythm of his current confession or harangue,
scribbles my order on a greasy receipt, and chops it up quick.

Such a sorrowful Chinese face,
nomad, Gobi, Northern
in its boniness
clear from the high
warlike forehead
to the sheer edge of the jaw.

He could be my brother, but finer,
and, except for his left forearm, which is engorged,
sinewy from his daily grip and
wield of a two-pound tool,
he's delicate, narrow-
waisted, his frame
so slight a lover, some
rough other
might break it down
its smooth, oily length.
In his light-handed calligraphy
on receipts and in his
moodiness, he is
a Southerner from a river-province;
suited for scholarship, his face poised
above an open book, he'd mumble
his favorite passages.
He could be my grandfather;
come to America to get a Western education
in 1917, but too homesick to study,
he sits in the park all day, reading poems
and writing letters to his mother.

He lops the head off, chops
the neck of the duck
into six, slits
the body
open, groin
to breast, and drains
the scalding juices,
then quarters the carcass
with two fast hacks of the cleaver,
old blade that has worn
into the surface of the round
foot-thick chop-block
a scoop that cradles precisely the curved steel.

The head, flung from the body, opens
down the middle where the butcher
cleanly halved it between

the eyes, and I
see, foetal-crouched
inside the skull, the homunculus,
gray brain grainy
to eat.
Did this animal, after all, at the moment
its neck broke,
image the way its executioner
shrinks from his own death?
Is this how
I, too, recoil from my day?
See how this shape
hordes itself, see how
little it is.
See its grease on the blade.
Is this how I'll be found
when judgement is passed, when names
are called, when crimes are tallied?
This is also how I looked before I tore my mother open.
Is this how I presided over my century, is this how
I regarded the murders?
This is also how I prayed.
Was it me in the Other
I prayed to when I prayed?
This too was how I slept, clutching my wife.
Was it me in the other I loved
when I loved another?
The butcher sees me eye this delicacy.
With a finger, he picks it
out of the skull-cradle
and offers it to me.
I take it gingerly between my fingers
and suck it down.
I eat my man.

The noise the body makes
when the body meets
the soul over the soul's ocean and penumbra
is the old sound of up-and-down, in-and-out,
a lump of muscle chug-chugging blood

into the ear; a lover's
heart-shaped tongue;
flesh rocking flesh until flesh comes;
the butcher working
at his block and blade to marry their shapes
by violence and time;
an engine crossing,
re-crossing salt water, hauling
immigrants and the junk
of the poor. These
are the faces I love, the bodies
and scents of bodies
for which I long
in various ways, at various times,
thirteen gathered around the redwood,
happy, talkative, voracious
at day's end,
eager to eat
four kinds of meat
prepared four different ways,
numerous plates and bowls of rice and vegetables,
each made by distinct affections
and brought to table by many hands.

Brothers and sisters by blood and design,
who sit in separate bodies of varied shapes,
we constitute a many-numbered
body of love.
In a world of shapes
of my desires, each one here
is a shape of one of my desires, and each
is known to me and dear by virtue
of each one's unique corruption
of those texts, the face, the body;
that jut jaw
to gnash tendon;
that wide nose to meet the blows
a face like that invites;
those long eyes closing on the seen;
those thick lips

to suck the meat of animals
or recite 300 poems of the T'ang;
these teeth to bite my monosyllables;
these cheekbones to make
those syllables sing the soul.
Puffed or sunken
according to the life,
dark or light according
to the birth, straight
or humped, whole, manqué, quasi, each pleases, verging
on utter grotesquery.
all are beautiful by variety.
The soul too
is a debasement
of a text, but, thus, it
acquires salience, although a
human salience, but
inimitable, and, hence, memorable.
God is the text.
The soul is a corruption
and a mnemonic.

A bright moment,
I hold up an old head
from the sea and admire the haughty
down-curved mouth
that seems to disdain
all the eyes are blind to,
including me, the eater.
Whole unto itself, complete
without me, yet its
shape complements the shape of my mind.
I take it as text and evidence
of the world's love for me,
and I feel urged to utterance,
urged to read the body of the world, urged
to say it
in human terms,
my reading a kind of eating, my eating
a kind of reading,

my saying a diminishment, my noise
a love-in-answer.
What is it in me would
devour the world to utter it?
What is it in me will not let
the world be, would eat
not just this fish,
but the one who killed it,
the butcher who cleaned it.
I would eat the way he
squats, the way he
reaches into the plastic tubs
and pulls out a fish, clubs it, takes it
to the sink, guts it, drops it on the weighing pan.
I would eat that thrash
and plunge of the watery body
in the water, that liquid violence
between the man's hands,
I would eat
the gutless twitching on the scales,
three pounds of dumb
nerve and pulse, I would eat it all
to utter it.
The deaths at the sinks, those bodies prepared
for eating, I would eat,
and the standing deaths
at the counters, in the aisles,
the walking deaths in the streets,
the death-far-from-home, the death-
in-a-strange-land, these Chinatown
deaths, these American deaths.
I would devour this race to sing it,
this race that according to Emerson
managed to preserve to a hair
for three or four thousand years
the ugliest features in the world.
I would eat these features, eat
the last three of four thousand years, every hair.
And I would eat Emerson, his transparent soul, his
soporific transcendence.

I would eat this head, glazed in pepper-speckled sauce,
the cooked eyes opaque in their sockets.
I would bring it to my mouth and—
the way I was taught, the way I've watched
others before me do—
with a stiff tongue lick out
the cheek-meat and the meat
over the armored jaw, my eating,
in sensual, salient nowness,
punctuating the void
from which such hunger springs and to which it proceeds.

And what
is this
I excavate
with my mouth?
What is this
plated, ribbed, hinged
architecture, this *carp head*,
but one more
articulation of a single nothing
severally manifested?
What is my eating,
rapt as it is,
but another
shape of going,
my immaculate expiration?

O, nothing is so
steadfast it won't go
the way the body goes.
The body goes.
The body's grave,
so serious
in its dying,
arduous as martyrs
in that task and as
glorious. It goes
empty always
and announces its going

by spasms and groans, farts and sweats.
What I thought were the arms
aching *cleave*, were the knees trembling leave.
What I thought were the muscles
insisting *resist, persist, exist,*
were the pores
hissing *mist* and *waste*.
What I thought was the body humming *reside, reside,*
was the body sighing *revise, revise.*
O, the murderous deletions, the keening
down to nothing, the cleaving.
All of the body's revisions end
in death.
All of the body's revisions end.

Bodies eating bodies, heads eating heads,
we are nothing eating nothing,
and though we feast,
are filled, overfilled,
we go famished.
We gang the doors of death.
That is, our deaths are fed
that we may continue our daily dying,
our bodies going
down, while plates-soon-empty
are passed around, that true
direction of our true prayers,
while the butcher spells
his message, manifold,
in the mortal air.
He coaxes, cleaves, brings change
before our very eyes, and at every
moment of our being.
As we eat we're eaten.
Else what is this
violence, this salt, this
passion, this heaven?

I thought the soul an airy thing.
I did not know the soul

is cleaved so that the soul might be restored.
Live wood hewn,
its sap springs from a sticky wound.
No seed, no egg has he
whose business calls for an axe.
In the trade of my soul's shaping,
he traffics in hews and hacks.

No easy thing, violence.
One of its names? Change. Change
resides in the embrace
of the effaced and the effacer,
in the covenant of the opened and the opener;
the axe accomplishes it on the soul's axis.
What then may I do
but cleave to what cleaves me.
I kiss the blade and eat my meat.
I thank the wielder and receive,
while terror spirits
my change, sorrow, also.
The terror the butcher
scripts in the unhealed
air, the sorrow of his Shang
dynasty face,
African face with slit eyes. He is
my sister, this
beautiful Bedouin, this Shulamite,
keeper of Sabbaths, diviner
of holy texts, this dark
dancer, this Jew, this Asian, this one
with the Cambodian face, Vietnamese face, this Chinese
I daily face,
this immigrant,
this man with my own face.

Susan Richardson

Wendigo

after Ted Hughes

What am I? Stumping along past
the bear-kills-caribou tree past the swallowing-place
that I love the suck of the ground that also loves me
What am I to make this shiver-walk? Why don't I want
this snow bunting to nest in my hair? What
shall I be called? I know ice-speak I can feel
how deep the lake is through the soles
of my feet wherever I go I leave the crunch
and spit of winter and now I am inside
the snow I am in a hunger-hole I have stripped
all the moss from the bog I have ripped up
six willows and one birch but my black lips
are still searching searching If I don't unearth
more food I'll blow snow-snakes
to make this whole place storm-confused
and is this why people don't like
me? Where should I move now so they won't
find me? They throw ducks with beaks full
of summer at my chest they send weasels down
my throat to end my heart-freeze Is this freedom
this need to keep ahead of the melt-season? Why
do I dread the moment when the ice fractures
into floes when the saxifrage blooms
and makes a sizzle in the cold? This is not freedom no
but I will not stop trying will not stop turning
the fox's fur to white though I might have only
these wolf tracks in the snow to eat I'll
still keep striding

Ronda Broatch

Hunger

In the middle night
I forage for food to steal
the edge of sleep.

            Moon is an eggshell
        above migrating cloud, a glow
      by which the banished bear roves.

Chickens have turned to stone,
dogs are mad with barking.
I wait on the other side of glass

            dry bread in hand
      and water to sustain me.
        Sometimes the bear

is God moving
in and through my life.
Ravenous he breaks me

            open like fruit,
        consumes me wholly.
      I climb through the night window

his name burning my throat
like wine, hunger
connecting us

            wind searching
        for something it has
         not yet touched.

A Little Poison Along with the Sweetness

Josh Baxt

Vons

It wasn't a real argument. The real ones were emotionally bloody, with all past grievances grandfathered in. This was just spit-spatting at each other, nurturing those angry thoughts for later. Why'd you go this way? How was I supposed to know that was important to you? Can you pass this truck already?

We were going to a party empty-handed.

"I thought you were picking up chips and salsa?"

"Why is that my responsibility?"

I made a sudden right into the Vons parking lot. The car rocked as I barreled up the driveway.

"Ea-sy!" she said. I grabbed the first available space and powered out of the car before she could unlatch her belt.

"Don't get those weird, blue chips you like," she said. "Think of someone else." I took the keys and carefully slammed the door.

It was early evening and the store was crowded. They had the blue chips on the end cap. I got both kinds. The store was relentlessly bright. Someone had dropped a bottle of cranberry juice, gumming up one of the aisles. I picked up guac and salsa and then some hummus, just for kicks.

I headed for the express checkout, one of three people converging on the same spot in line. I let the other two go first. A woman fell in behind me with just a cantaloupe. I let her go too.

I felt comfortable in line. Everyone was friendly. The cashier was busy but not rushed. She chatted affably with the regulars and scanned each item in a slow, steady motion.

Small, happy reunions were taking place all around me. A group of women shared a laugh with the clerk at the bakery counter. The line moved forward, but I felt no need to follow. I let two more go ahead.

I read all the tabloid covers. *Barbara Streisand Drives Off Space Invaders With Alien Death Song!* Bald, genderless, space beings recoiled from Barbara's wide-open maw. I laughed out loud and waved three more in front of me. No one seemed to notice what I was doing; they were just happy to move on. I heard my Honda's tinny horn in the parking lot and thought; I'll just say they were writing checks. People never fill out the date and payee information ahead of time. They all had 16 items too.

Nancy Cary
The Promise of Trout
—for L. T.D.

I give my dad credit for taking us fishing,
the rented rowboat, the sure wave to mom.
He seemed endlessly patient with hooks,
swivels, and five kids' tangled lines.
He'd have on a gray sweatshirt and kneel
in the same old Sears pants he'd wear for mowing.
Bent over his tackle box, he'd rustle through
metal trays for leaders and lead weights.
The son of a failed farmer, my dad
was no mechanic but wanted to be a doctor.
He threaded line through the swivel's eye,
the silver hook dangled and danced.
He talked of tension and the wait for the fight—
a tug on the line, the gasping mouth
and hook we'd rip deep from the trout's throat.
Years later I'd hold his patient's hand,
not turn from the scalpel blade that cuts flesh
but watch and remember the slit gut, the entrails
scooped onto newspaper, the pan-fried trout,
its crisp skin, salty on my tongue.
Like iridescent sequins, scales freckled our hands
gracing our lives all through the night.

Nancy Cary

❧ Pan-Fried Trout

Fresh trout, gutted and split
1 c. flour or cornmeal
½ stick butter or ¼ c oil
½ tsp paprika
Salt and pepper

Clean and dry the trout. Dredge in flour. Sprinkle with paprika, salt, and pepper. Melt butter in a cast iron frying pan over medium heat. Cook trout on one side 3-5 minutes until skin is brown and crispy. Cook on other side 3-4 minutes. Enjoy—crispy skin and all.

Fancy: in melted butter, lightly brown almonds and pour over trout.

WARNING: watch out for fish bones. One vacation at a Northern California lake cabin, my dad swallowed a fish bone. With needle nose pliers, he pulled it from his tonsil.

Mike Ferrill

Cooking for Life

There is a callous on the inside surface my right index finger, near the point where the digit connects to the hand. It is hard and fleshy, the way most calluses are I suppose. It has been formed over many years from constant rubbing against the handle of a variety of kitchen knives, the primary tools of my profession. It has changed in size depending on the amount of cutting I do in the kitchen, but it has been there so long that I consider it like an old friend. During the years I spent not cooking it faded away somewhat, but it was still there. I would caress it from time to time, to remind myself that I was still alive, to ground myself in times of disconnection. Touching it would always bring me back to the kitchen.

ж

I've been hanging around kitchens as long as I can remember; beginning with all the time I spent tagging around my mother while she cooked dinner for my family. I'm sure I was a real pest at first, but eventually she started giving me small tasks to perform, just to keep me busy. She was no gourmet chef or anything, but that's not really what I learned from her. What I remember as important was the time and the effort and the love she put into the food she made. I learned the secrets of the white, lower middle class kitchen; delicacies based on the time tested recipes of heartland America. Chicken and dumplings, black eyed peas, ham hocks and boiled greens; at the end of the month we'd have my father's favorite, chipped beef on toast. Her masterpiece was homemade chicken and vegetable soup. The aroma of celery, onions and chicken bones that formed the stock wafted through the house bringing tears to my lips and eyes. Bay leaves and thyme would be added later, igniting the senses with some kind of primal recognition. The rich, savory, slightly salty broth was clean, with undertones of sweet carrots and parsley. It was sublime. Dinner time was always the time of talking and arguing and catching up and getting to know my family. It all started in the kitchen, and that is where I most liked to be.

ୡ

In the movie *Tampopo* by the Japanese director Juzo Itami, there is a scene in which a woman is lying on her bed, surrounded by her children and husband, all of whom are crying. A doctor informs the family that the woman is dying. The distraught husband, desperate to return to some sort of normalcy urges his stricken wife to get up and prepare a meal. Near death, she manages to make her way to the kitchen where she hastily throws together a batch of fried rice, all while the husband and children are moaning and carrying on. The family then sits down together and the husband instructs his children to enjoy this meal for, as he tells them, it will be the last meal prepared by mother. Satisfied that her family is adequately fed, the woman dies.

ୡ

Dear Fuga, how are doing? What are wearing? Is today a sunny day or is it cloudy? Are you having fun right now? I just want to say something to you...

ୡ

My wife Eri and I frequently cook together. In fact it is one of the things we both most enjoy. It is time that we share creating and discovering, like explorers in a new land, stumbling sometimes, bumping into each other, and uncovering new secrets in a pot of boiling water. The sounds of chopping vegetables, hissing kettles, and Ella Fitzgerald singing "Cheek to Cheek" provide the soundtrack to our dance in the kitchen. In the mornings I'll wake up early to fix some pancakes the way she likes them, small and thick, but crispy around the edges. She just lies in bed smelling the toasty sweetness as it slices through the morning air, waiting for me to call her to breakfast. I have made pancakes for other women before, but I always made them the way that I like them.

ॐ

Though we eat little flesh and drink no wine, Yet let us be merry; we'll have tea and toast; Custards for supper and an endless host of syllabubs and jellies and mince pies, And other such ladylike luxuries   Percy Shelley

ॐ

The phone rang late that night, and the memory permanently remains dreamlike. I still have not woken from that dream, as a signpost forced its way onto my path.

My mother, her always steady voice now wobbling, tells me the news about my niece.

"JJJJennifer's dead!"

I rubbed my eyes trying to comprehend the meaning of her words. Jennifer is dead.

How could this be? I just finished developing a roll of film with pictures of my sister, her two daughters Jennifer and Stephanie, and my mother. I mean, I just saw her, staring up at me in the night, undulating in a tray of stop bath, arms folded, with a smirk on her face that only a fourteen-year-old girl with the world at her feet could deliver. It occurred to me that the sweatshirt she was wearing had the word "Esprit" silk-screened on the front.

My girlfriend Yuko, sensing my body tighten, then silently convulse, reached over to hold my hand.

"What's wrong?" she asked, after I clumsily hung up the phone.

"My niece died. That was my mother. She told me my niece died."

"What happened?"

"She had an asthma attack. She was camping with her family. She went hiking and had an attack. They tried to save her. My sister was there and saw it happen. They tried to save her but they couldn't. A helicopter came and took her to the hospital."

I felt numb and dizzy. Yuko squeezed my hand again and looked at me. I needed something to sustain me through the darkness until the dawn broke, when all hell would break loose.

We made love; sweet, desperate, aching, love. It was to be the last taste of the "before" time.

⁊⁊

Two weeks later, Yuko told me she was pregnant.

⁊⁊

I have seen many Japanese films. Akira Kurosawa is one of my favorite directors. He has a reputation for a kinetic style of filmmaking, and his use of motion and action propels the narrative along, particularly in his most famous movie *The Seven Samurai*, which is one of the classics of world cinema. There is one film by Kurosawa called *Ikiru*, however, that I have always found quietly compelling. It is the story of a man who finds out he is dying and realizes that his life up to this point has been purposeless. His job as a faceless government official has left him spiritually dry, and his wife and son have nothing but contempt for him. In his final act he summons up the courage to right a wrong and sets out to have a park built instead of a planned office building. In the dreamlike final scene he is sitting on a swing in the park, slowly rocking back and forth.

⁊⁊

Dear Fuga, I want to tell you a story. Get some cookies and a warm blanket...

ะะ

After Jenny died, I quit my job working for a furniture delivery company. I couldn't stand the routine anymore. I had no energy left to haul fifteen-foot sofas up spiral staircases in Rancho Santa Fe. My friend, Kitty, told me there was an opening at the vegetarian supermarket where she worked, so as soon as I finished up my final two weeks of wrestling ottomans, I started my new job in the service deli, where I've been now for the last seven years. I rubbed my fading callous. It had been several years since I worked as a cook but now I was back in the kitchen.

ะะ

I met Yuko through a mutual friend while visiting Maui. Our friend Yukie was living there with her daughter, after moving from New York. I had met Yukie several years before that when we both worked for a restaurant called Sushi Deli in the downtown area of San Diego. I noticed she was reading *Catcher in the Rye,* translating it into Japanese while she worked her way through the novel. During my breaks from the kitchen we crunched on tempura and laughed about the "phonies" we met at work and Holden Caulfield and New York; cautiously we became good friends. When I saw her in Maui eight years later, she had changed. Children and divorce will do that I suppose.

ะะ

When I was single I often cooked my own meals, spending time to ensure that I had healthy (and sometimes not so healthy) sustenance. After preparing my food I would sit down and quietly graze, reading a book, and more often than not, accompanied by some music or television.

ะะ

A sudden lightning gleam:
Off into the darkness goes
The night heron's scream
          Basho

❧

Yuko and I had a whirlwind six months of togetherness. We were both captivated by the intensity of our feelings. We thought we were soul mates, and told everyone about our new discovery.

It was so heavy and so beautiful.

After awhile though, our relationship just became too much; what with Jennifer dying and Yuko getting pregnant; me starting a new job, going to college; trying to heal and celebrate at the same time just tore us apart. Plus Yuko was getting a lot of flak from her parents, who vowed to disown her if she stayed in the United States. This rigidity is something about some Japanese people I have met that really bugs me; a rather overripe sense of honor and status. When it's a Samurai protecting some peasants it's great. In my case it meant there was little attempt to understand the situation Yuko I were facing. Before I knew what was happening Yuko was getting on a plane, returning to Japan. We hugged each other for an hour at the airport in LA until she had to leave, and then I felt her slip away from my arms, watched her drift down the corridor, turning once to look at me, drifting until she disappeared. I stared at the empty space silently screaming.

For the next nine months I truly believed she was coming back to San Diego with our child, to be with me, to be a family. This did not happen however. Yuko never came back.

❧

My son was born May fifteenth, in the year two thousand. I came home after closing up the kitchen to see his face beaming up at me from my computer. Two weeks later I was in Japan, surrounded by Yuko and her family, holding Fuga in my arms. I stared at him for hours, noticing his new skin, pink and tender, covered with peeling flakes that looked like snow. He smelled so fresh and warm and tiny. His little dimpled fingers clutched my clumsy calloused hands and held on for a moment, a breathtaking moment, before releasing his grip, allowing me to exhale and smile. Three weeks later I tore myself away from Fuga, leaving him behind to return to San Diego, feeling like someone had hit me in the face with a baseball bat; devastated and crying like a baby.

ॐ

She is a healer
My partner
She is a healer
My wife
She is a healer
My heart.

ॐ

I don't know what it is about Japan that attracts me. When I was nineteen I started working as a busboy at a Japanese steakhouse in Kearny Mesa called Kobe Misono. The chef there found out I had some kitchen experience and asked me if I wanted to take a position as a kitchen helper. I laughed to myself thinking about that title. What did that mean, kitchen helper? I thought it was quaint and amusing, like hamburger helper, or mother's little helper. I wanted to find out so I accepted his offer. I was going to be a kitchen helper. For the next eight years I worked in various Japanese restaurants around San Diego.

ॐ

My earliest memory of this strange appeal concerned a friend of mine named Jimmy that I knew in the first grade. I went to his house one day after school. I'll never forget having to take my shoes off before entering the small apartment that was part of the vast monotonous Navy housing project in Paradise Hills. Something smelled very strange, and it wasn't my feet. It was salty and vinegary, oily and most of all fishy. I followed Jimmy into the kitchen and saw his mother working at the stove, cooking something completely unknown to me. It was definitely not chicken soup. She said something to Jimmy in a different language, then smiled at me and said "hello." I remember seeing kitchen gadgets and tools that I had never seen at my house.

❦

I was at a party once when someone called me a rice king. A rice king is the hipster term for a guy who likes Asian women. It's also the name of a fast food restaurant. I don't like the restaurant, and I don't care too much for the term. It sounds vaguely racist and narrow-minded. I cannot deny that I have some mysterious attraction to Asian women, particularly Japanese women. And it is not just a look. If a woman is Asian American then the attraction is less powerful. If I'm having a conversation with a girl who was born in Los Angeles to Japanese parents it is no different than talking to any American girl. If I close my eyes I cannot tell what she looks like, especially if I start to hear the unmistakable whine of the dreaded Valley-speak.

"Ohmagod"

"Totally"

"I am so sure"

You see, it is not a look I am attracted to, it is a culture. It is something I can't really put my finger on to tell the truth. My friend Yukie used to tease me about always falling for Japanese girls. I had always had a thing for Yukie; but she knew that we were meant to be friends, although it took me awhile to figure that out. After I met Yuko I knew she was right.

❦

My friend Yukie believes in reincarnation. While visiting her in Maui we engaged in an exercise that would supposedly reveal something about our past lives. Sitting face to face in a dark room, we would stare at each other. After a few minutes the eyes would adjust to the darkness enough to sort of make out each other's face. We would continue staring until we started to see other faces emerge in place of our own. These other faces represented our past lives. As the images materialized, we wrote down what we were observing. After awhile we would turn the lights back on and compare notes. We both had several faces written down, like an old man or a young woman, even the image of an alien from outer space. One of the faces I saw was of a bleeding young man. She then told me about a dream she had about a previous life in which she was killed in some kind of war. We came to the conclusion that night that we were both soldiers in Japan in a past life, and that I was with her when she was killed in a battle.

꙳

After my son turned three I stopped receiving any communication from his mother. I sent, and continue to send, gifts and letters and photographs to him, but I hear nothing. Yukie occasionally tells me how he is doing, since she is still in touch with her friend. She tells me that Yuko thinks my son Fuga is the reincarnation of my dead niece Jennifer.

꙳

My hut, in spring:
true, there is nothing in it—
there is everything
                    Basho

꙳

I gave up on relationships in April 2003. Enough I said, rubbing the callous that had now grown to my heart. The callous that was the result of so much pressure and pain, now protected me from the same forces. Then one day—into the kitchen, into my life, into my soul came Eri. She had just arrived in the United States from Tokyo to study English and to pursue her interest in holistic living. One of the first places she came to was People's Co-Op in Ocean Beach, where I work. I was drawn to her immediately. There was no way to stop the feelings that started to blossom that day. I followed her around, watching her curiously explore the store. I felt like a stalker. I was a stalker that day. After about two hours she made her way up to the deli, and like a moth to the flame I was powerlessly drawn. I learned that first day that she was a massage therapist and a certified aroma therapist in Tokyo; that she came here to immerse herself in a new lifestyle that she desired. She was planning to stay for a year, and then return to Japan. She loves to cook.

⁂

We can no more give up on relationships that we can stop the sun from rising in the sky. We are inextricably linked to all the things we touch and are touched by. We are a stew of the multitude of ingredients that make up our personal recipe. And in the kitchen there is nothing that can protect me from getting burned or cut or bruised once in awhile. Kitchens are where we simmer, and bake, and stir the pot.

⁂

Dear Fuga, I will tell you a great story some day, when you are older. I think of you everyday my son. Always remember that your daddy loves you.

⁂

Eri and I are already planning our meal for this weekend. We will be having salmon, rice, and miso soup. We haven't decided what to have for dessert.

Olivia Chin
Meeting Over Coconut Drinks
Phnom Penh, Cambodia

Christine Huynh
On the Plate

Eating guava
Is your favorite past time
While ants in my bathtub
Sing a concerto   a long one in fact
You are still a firefighter/homosapien
Removing car wax from your ear
I waited for you
Like clowns in painted blue moo-moos
It's a damn sickness I have
Smelling cologne on necks and asses
That's not an obsession but I try
Passed out on linoleum-covered couches
Making sense is too easy
So I make love
Outside in small elevators
It's almost like you don't notice
Optical illusions on featherdusters
Makes the nose sneeze garter belts
Your boxers smelled like elephant wings
Last night I wrapped them around my legs
You found a new title for a book
Memoirs Of A Used Sex Bed
Know that the emergency exits
Will only sound when the alarm
Is stroked just right
Mi novio
These are the only two words I know
In Spanish
So let me start out with the obvious
And end up on an archipelago of dung
Only if it's easy   supereasy
And takes less time than cooking eggs

Michael Adams

Wild Apples

I'm leaning against my truck at the farmer's market in Louisville, Colorado eating an apple—a small, firm, very tart Jonathan. The market's just a tent and a refrigerated truck in the parking lot of a small shopping center. You know the kind of place, you find them everywhere these days—eight years ago it was alfalfa fields and pasture, now there are a couple of restaurants, a liquor store, doggie boutique, and a coffee shop. I stop here at least a couple of times a week and, if it's not busy, spend 10 or 15 minutes talking to the farmer. He's in his 30s and passionately dedicated to organic farming. You have to be, to make a living at it in the Boulder Valley, on the northern edge of Denver's rapidly growing metropolitan area of 3 million. Still, there's a strong demand for fresh organic produce here, and so he scrapes by, and for that I'm glad and give him as much business as I can.

The apple I'm eating is deep purple-red and small, the size of a large plum, but what does size matter? The right apple can give you the whole world—the tang, bite and zest of it, the strong sweet rot of an abandoned orchard in November, a May blizzard of apple blossoms, the salt and sweet of a girl's lips at a first kiss. And it's best enjoyed out-of-doors, with wind and sun or rain or the smell of sweat and wet leaves. In *Wild Apples*, written a few months before his untimely death in May of 1862, Henry Thoreau wrote,

"To appreciate the wild and sharp flavors of these October fruits, it is necessary that you be breathing the sharp October or November air."

Of wild apples, he said, "Some of these apples may be labeled, 'To be eaten in the wind."

I'm on my way home from work, I'm tired and I smell bad, not the honest odor of physical labor, but the kind of funky smell you get from too many meetings and sitting in front of a computer all day, never getting outdoors. It wasn't a bad day; it wasn't a good day, but it's over now, the work part. It's October and the mountains to the west — the Indian Peaks, Longs Peak, the Mummy Range — have a dusting of new snow that fell last night. It's warm and sunny now, but a solid bank of black clouds is moving down fast from the northwest, and when it gets here I know it will bring wind and cold. It looks like I have 5 or 10 minutes to enjoy the sun, no more. But I'm looking forward to the coming of the front and the change it will bring, the blast of wind coming from the west, moving through the trees like a breaking wave, the sharp clean smell of rain.

This apple is good, but the best ones are wild, from a tree long abandoned and forgotten by all but the deer and the wanderer, returned to its own true nature, what Thoreau called "the Saunterer's Apple — you must lose yourself before you can find the way to that." One of life's great gifts is to be offered such an apple when you're still young enough for that magic when the whole earth turns around a single moment and what comes after is different from what came before. For me it was the hills of western Pennsylvania, a late September afternoon in 1970, just shy of my 21st year. My girl and I had ridden down the Youghiogheny River, south of Pittsburgh, through the old coal mining district with the beehive coke ovens dug into the hillsides, through towns that had sunk into a long senescence years before — Dawson, Broadford, Connellsville — towns with narrow potholed streets, many of brick or cobblestone, quiet and nearly deserted downtowns, and modest frame houses sided in asphalt that crowd the street. South of Connellsville we left the river and rode up into the mountains, up Chestnut Ridge and into the Laurel Highlands, our ancient BMW motorcycle sputtering on the steep grades. The hills were ablaze with the red of maple trees and the gold of oaks. We chose the narrowest, least traveled roads we could find. The tree branches made a tunnel over our heads and the wheels of the bike kicked up leaves as we passed and swirled them around us, so that there was a continuous play of light and shadows and flashing golds and reds to mark our passage.

We had our sleeping bags, a block of white cheese, loaf of whole wheat bread, and a half gallon of cheap red wine, the screw-top variety—we were damn poor but always managed to scrape together enough cash for gas for the bike and wine for our souls—and we pulled off onto an overgrown lane. The sun was high and warm. At the end of the lane was an abandoned orchard. The apples were green and no larger than a baby's fist. We drank a couple of tin cups full of wine and started eating the apples. They were so tart they pulled the moisture right out of our mouths, and we had to screw our eyes shut and wrinkle our faces like prunes to eat them, but we had a nice buzz on and even with the tartness there was a touch of sweetness and a spice like nutmeg and cloves that I couldn't get enough of. Or maybe it was her, she was everything to me in those days. God, we had plans. We were going places, Karen and I. I was in my last year of college; she was a junior. We would both graduate with degrees in anthropology. Maybe there would be graduate school somewhere down the line, but for the immediate future I'd work for a year and then, after she graduated we'd buy a camper van, travel up to New Hampshire to pick apples for the harvest and then drive down the east coast and winter along the Gulf. After that, on to California. It didn't work out that way, and I haven't seen her in 30 years. I hope she's doing well. When I eat tart green apple I still taste the cool moist of her lips, the hint of cinnamon in her breath.

After we'd eaten one or two, she said, the seeds have cyanide, you know. I said, watch. That was when I learned how to eat an apple, the way I do it to this day. Make your first bite from the bottom, the small indentation where the blossom was, then eat all around the core until you reach the stem. Place the core in your mouth, suck the remaining flesh from it. Savor the tartness you find there. Then bite down. Enjoy the bitterness of the seeds, a little poison, along with the sweetness, to remind you of what life holds in store. And equally a reminder of the heart's innate resilience, that it can bear some poison and still beat strong.

The wind rises, the air fills with a blizzard of leaves, and the wall of dark clouds blocks the sun. Hard, cold drops of rain sting my face. I stay in the wind and rain while I finish the apple. I chew the last of the core into pulp, swallow it, then climb back into my truck. The taste stays with me all the way home.

Cheryl Klein

The Rocky Bottom of the Sea

1997

There must have been doctors and nurses there that night. It must have been as crowded as the dorms, where I'd lived for one week as of September, 1997. Someone must have brought me the styrofoam cup of tea that I held in my shaking hands for hours. But I don't remember any of them.

I remember my dad looking like his flesh was going to slide off his skeleton. He kept asking questions about morphine dosage. I knew morphine was the drug they gave you when it didn't really matter if you became an addict at that point, and I looked at my mom, gaunt beneath the nubby hospital blanket, and then at my brother Evan to see if he shared my alarm. His dark red hair was matted and his brown eyes darted around the room. It was all wrong. I started crying, partly because I was scared but also because I hoped it would make my dad and brother snap out of it.

My dad took my hand and Evan's, and Evan took my other hand.

"Doctor, uh, Ramaswamy, she, uh, said we should think about whether we want them to take heroic measures if, uh, her organs start shutting down." On "shutting down," my dad shut down too, a sob shaking his body like an earthquake.

"I can't believe they're using terms I've only heard on *ER*," Evan whispered, his half-sarcasm at a low, uneven pulse.

"I don't want her to suffer," my dad said. It sounded like a prayer the way he said it, and his fingers gripped mine so tightly my knuckles hurt. We were a prayer circle. A prayer triangle. And it seemed messed-up that my mom wasn't a part of it. Her eyes had been closed for hours now, her breathing ragged and steamy beneath the oxygen mask. She hadn't eaten real food for weeks, and even though nutrients were ostensibly cascading down one of the tubes that disappeared beneath the blanket, they didn't seem to have any effect. Not like the things she loved: crunchy egg rolls, Caesar salads dusted with parmesan cheese, Oreos dunked in milk.

"I want us all to make this decision together," my dad said.

Except we couldn't make it all together because All Together was my mom and my dad and Evan and me. No one else, no one less.

He looked at us, lost behind his splattered glasses, and someone had to say something, so I said the impossible: "Okay. If it comes to that, we'll let her...we'll let her go."

I went to her bed. I put my hands on her leg, felt her bones beneath the blanket. We were not one of those hugging families, but that night we couldn't stop touching each other. I would put one hand on my mom and loop my free arm over Evan's shoulders so that I could touch my dad's back. We would stay like that until someone had to pee or stretch, and then we'd reform in a different interlocking shape.

We were a we, all night long, as cars slow-danced in the parking lot below and doctors and nurses checked boxes and probably a million things happened in a million places. Then my mom's breathing got even and then something shifted. Before she got still, before the green line on the machine next to the bed took note, something shifted. Just the quietest leaving.

And then we were not a we.

Three weeks later, Evan left too. Our sad world had grown too small for him, and so he traded it for someone else's sadness, a big, exciting sadness, working with an aid organization in rural Mexico. My dad and I were left in the house my mom had decorated, eating microwaved food off her Southwest-style plates, reading letters from Evan.

People are hungry here, he wrote, *in a way you could never understand.*

2005

I woke up sweating in the dark. Where was I?

Kuching, I reminded myself, Eastern Malaysia. It had taken me two planes, 13 hours and, arguably, eight years to get here.

I groped my way to the light and then to the air conditioner and my hotel room slowly became real. I studied myself in the bathroom mirror, wondering how I looked in another country. My freckles seemed quieter than usual, and my eyes were Siamese-blue, big and afraid. And my stomach was growling.

The hotel restaurant, I learned, had stopped serving dinner at 9 p.m. It was just after 10.

I had been raised, like all girls with overprotective parents, not to go out by myself after dark in strange places. But Lawndale, the dingy L.A. suburb where my boyfriend Care and I lived, had softened us to hard places. We were left alone in a way we would not have been if we'd been young black or Latino boys. I could feel the neighborhood wanting things from them—allegiance, years of their lives—but from me the most it ever wanted was a few dollars.

And so I went out in Kuching. I felt like a cat sneaking into the night, my pupils expanding to make the most of what little light there was, my tail a periscope. I made my way down the hill, scanning doorways and alleys for people I should avoid. But the city seemed to have gone to bed. I saw an actual cat—skinny, gray, cropped tail—slink beneath a parked car, but other than that, there was nothing alive within view.

I let my gaze float upwards and took in the cityscape at night. I had seen pictures of Hong Kong—all lights and water for miles—and it was mesmerizing and terrifying. Kuching had lights and water in smaller doses. This made it seem manageable, somehow, and I tried to picture Evan here. It had been years since he'd written to my dad or me regularly. The last I knew, he was in China. When I'd tried to email him a few months ago, my message had bounced. I'd Googled him, which had led me to his blog, a restless diary of his life here that re-ignited a previously abandoned mission to fold him back into our unraveled family. The blog had contained just enough clues for me to be sure it was him without being able to narrow down his whereabouts. I'd left a comment at the bottom of his last entry, dated a few months ago, but he hadn't replied. Blogs were funny beasts, intimate yet rootless, and I'd closed my browser feeling closer to Evan and further away at the same time.

I flanked the river, taking quick steps, searching the small docked boats gently bumping the bank and the row of closed shops to my left. This must be what it's like to be a stray, I thought, always on the lookout for something that could hurt you or help you.

Towards the far end of the bank, I finally found a restaurant that was open. I smelled a steamy, fishy smell. Not the kind of scent that would have normally excited me, but my inner stray cat had taken over my vegetarian stomach. I pushed open the glass door and saw what amounted to a long, brightly-lit hallway lined with plastic tables and chairs. Clean, utilitarian, like a school cafeteria.

Two middle-aged men ate bowls of rice and meat at one table. They ate fast and didn't say much. I decided that, despite being on the waterfront, this must be one of those places where only locals ate. I imagined myself telling Care, "I skipped the touristy places. The local spots have the best food."

I didn't see a waiter, so I slid nervously into one of the plastic chairs and waited. Did the two men work here? Was I interrupting their end-of-the-day meal? Although my guidebook promised that most people in Malaysia spoke English ("Thanks, colonizers!" I could hear Evan say; I could see his bushy raised eyebrow too), I hadn't actually seen a sign that said "open" in English and I didn't know how to say "open" in Malay.

Finally, an older woman wearing an apron came out and stood in front of me, frowning. Her long black hair was streaked with gray and not hidden by a headscarf, so I decided she must be Chinese.

"I'm sorry," I said, "I, uh—are you open?"

She said something in what I think was Malay-as-a-second-language. The sounds were like beads rolling, not the pointy sounds of Chinese.

"I only speak English. I'm sorry." Why hadn't I bought a Malay phrase book? Or at least looked at the glossary in my guidebook? *Stupid egotisti-*

cal American, I admonished myself, while simultaneously hoping that she would say, "Ah, English!" and begin speaking fluently.

"English," she repeated in an accent that made it clear she did not speak much, and in a tone that suggested she did not approve of those who did.

"Do you have, um, menus?"

She shook her head. Did she mean no, she didn't have menus, or no, she didn't know what I was saying?

I pantomimed the act of opening a menu.

"You hungry?" she barked.

"Yes, very," I admitted.

"Okay. Okay, I bring you."

She left and didn't reappear for almost 20 minutes. In that time I became even more conscious of the circles of sweat expanding beneath my armpits and on my back. The night was hot and the restaurant was cooled only by ceiling fans and I was worried that the waitress — or owner or cook or whoever she was — had given up on me. Or, just as bad, that she would return with a roast chicken or something and I would have to decline it, rudely and confusingly.

Instead, she brought plates of whole small crabs, a whole large fish and a curly plant steamed bright green.

I cleared my throat. "I'm actually, uh — I am a vegetarian?"

It came out like a question, and she must have thought I'd asked what the food was. She pointed. "Crab. Rock cod. Vegetable." She pulled a pair of paper-wrapped chopsticks from the pocket of her apron, put it loudly down in front of me and walked away.

God, she must think I'm an idiot, I thought. Then I thought, *God, that food looks good.*

And all of it looked good — not just the fern-like vegetable, but the creepy crabs with their legs falling off and the fish staring at me with its fried, wrinkled eye. I was a predator now, someone who knew the dark truth about eating.

I studied the crabs, dark brown and freckled with pepper. The number of them on the plate was disgusting and fascinating. That was how I felt about meat in general—I wasn't squeamish because I didn't have to be. I had no stake in it. It could be burnt, bleeding, sinewy, fatty, abundant or presented on a plate with a sprig of parsley. It was all the same to me.

Except, suddenly it wasn't. Crabs were animals, but they were invertebrates. We didn't make it past the same kingdom. Was it really so wrong to eat a creature that didn't even share the same phylum as you? Feeling lightheaded, I tried to remember why I didn't eat meat, other than the fact that I *hadn't* eaten meat for 11 years. My mom had taken it personally at first, the first stand I ever took.

Did I not eat meat because it was so much like me? No, I reminded myself, it was the factory farming thing. I didn't eat meat because it was kept in tiny cages and fed its own ground-up relatives. It wasn't that meat led a short life—I figured the food chain itself was too big and ancient to question—but that it led a terrible one. These crabs had crawled the rocky bottom of the sea, doing their crab things, until they wandered into a fisherman's trap.

They were exempt, I thought hungrily.

Using my chopsticks, I slid a crab from the big plate onto my small one. Hot brown juice poured off of it. Two legs did not make the journey from plate to plate. I pried open the round body with my chopsticks. I thought of heart surgeries I'd seen on TV, the gruesome parting of the breastbone. I thought of my mom's surgery, the one that hadn't saved her.

And then I pulled out a sliver of crabmeat and put it in my mouth and it tasted perfectly fine. I didn't really remember what chicken tasted like, but it probably tasted like this.

I ate ravenously. Crabs, ferns and most of the fish. Crispy skin and delicate meat holding onto its toothpick-thin bones. If I could do this, I thought, I could do anything.

I made it to the lobby of the hotel before I threw up. It would have been infinitely better to get sick five minutes earlier or later. I'd stumbled up the hill, bargaining with my lurching stomach. Was it because I'd broken my vegetarian promise, or was this food poisoning?

I was only vaguely interested in the answer when I bent over a few feet from the lobby door and vomited into my hands, tasting fish. Barely digested, it spilled hotly onto my jeans and dripped onto the floor. For a minute, I was only my body. I felt too awful to be embarrassed. It was like how my mom had described childbirth: "You wouldn't care if it was being broadcast on national television. You just want that baby *out.*"

But as soon as I'd wiped my chin with the back of my wrist, I looked up to see who'd seen. The lobby was empty except for the front desk clerk, who was busy writing something in a notebook, and a white guy sitting in front of the computer the hotel made available to guests. If I could just get some paper towels, I could clean this up and sneak off to my room.

I was looking around for a bathroom when the white guy walked over.

"Food poisoning getcha?" he said. Kindly, I'll admit.

I squeezed my eyes shut and nodded. Maybe he would go away before I opened them.

"I'll be okay," I managed. "I just need some paper towels."

"Don't be foolish." He had an Australian accent. "There's people for that. You're sick—we better get you to bed." He looked about Care's age, but more sun-damaged. He had a stubbly brown beard and slightly dirty shorts.

By now we'd attracted the attention of the front desk clerk, who leaned into the speaker on his phone and said something in Malay. Soon a girl who did not look old enough to do any work besides babysitting appeared with a mop and bucket. *Oh my god, they're using child labor to clean up my barf,* I thought. Was it possible to wince so hard you imploded? I hoped so.

There was a lot of waving of hands and nodding of heads. Somehow all of us except the Australian were apologizing. Then the Australian shuffled me out of the lobby, assuring me, "It happens to everyone who's not used to travel, and a lot who are. New continent, new critters lurking in your food. You from the States?"

We were by the pool now, and the fresh air felt good. I tried not to think about my wet jeans.

"Yeah, from Los Angeles."

"Alright. I'm from Cairns myself. That's in Australia. I'm Grady, by the way." He cocked his head and crinkled his eyes. Their color—light green ringed with brown—made me think of safari gear.

"Eliza," I said. "I'd shake your hand, but I don't think you want to touch it right now."

"What brings you to Borneo, Eliza?" I could tell he was trying to put me at ease.

"I'm visiting my brother. He's, um, working here. For a while."

"Smart man. It's a beaut of an island."

"How about you? What brings you to Kuching?" I didn't feel like making small talk—I just wanted to change into pajamas and go to bed—but I didn't want to be rude.

"Oh, just making the rounds. You know, it's a shorter flight from my part of the world. I was in Thailand for a month before this."

"I heard Thailand's great," I said, thinking of the woman from West Virginia I'd met at the airport, who'd sold her truck and was on her way to Thailand to "live like a queen."

"Nah, it's just…used up. Everything there's geared toward tourists in one way or another. Here, I'm hoping to take a longboat and see a bit of the upriver tribes. They don't hunt heads these days, but they're still quite untouched as aboriginal peoples go."

No one—myself included, I realized—wanted to be a tourist. But we all were, and there seemed to be something more gross about denying it. Right now, a tour bus that expected me back at a certain hour and a guide explaining what to eat and what not to eat sounded like the most wonderful thing in the world.

"Well…g'night, Eliza." We were in front of the door to my room now. The hallway was quiet, but from somewhere faraway came what I can only describe as jungle noises. Squawks and cackles and hoots. The turquoise pool shined like a tropical bird over Grady's left shoulder.

"Thanks again," I said. "I guess I'll see you around."

"I'm in 19B if you need anything." This should have been the part where he waved and walked away, but he just stood there, like he was expecting a goodnight kiss.

Even though he could not possibly have wanted to kiss a mouth that had just thrown up all over the lobby, the thought made me nervous.

"Thanks," I said to Grady again. "Goodnight." I put my key in the door and pushed it open. I turned back to face him, trying to take up the entire space the door created.

"Maybe I should stick around a bit, make sure it's nothing worse than an upset stomach," he said.

"I'll be fine. I promise."

"You can't promise a thing like that."

For some reason, I thought of my mom promising she'd recover from cancer. "Okay, well I promise I'll call a doctor if I'm not." I had no idea how to call a doctor in Malaysia. Was there an equivalent of 911?

"That might not be so reliable. You could get a bad one or at least one who'd take all your money. In Thailand, I got what I thought was a mosquito bite, but it started looking bloody disgusting — "

"I really just need some rest," I said. "I'm sorry to interrupt — "

"Of course. Look at me going on like a fool. Well. Sleep well, Eliza. And if you're feeling better tomorrow, buzz my room."

I shut the door and fumbled for the power button, which you had to turn on before you could flip on any lights. I peeled off my jeans and went to the toilet and threw up some more, and then I started to feel better again. I hoped that this time it would last more than 15 minutes. The comforter on the bed had a cheesy tropical print, but it was fluffy and cotton and felt good against my skin.

I wasn't sure if I was afraid of Grady or attracted to him. Maybe both. I had been with Care for eight years, and only one person before him, a girl named Diana. We'd met at a play when we were both high school students, back when the world was constantly revealing itself. Now it was happening again in a country with steam-room air, crabs like boiled aliens, tourists with time to kill. I could do things here that had seemed impossible — maybe adulthood was as simple as that. But this world promised consequences. Food poisoning. Adultery. Disorientation at the least.

I lay as still as I could and studied the door. I wondered who else had keys, and if the lock was strong. You always hear how you're safer in a plane than you are on the freeway, and I was sure I was safer here than I was in Lawndale. But you always grip the armrests during takeoff anyway. You always think about how there's nothing but air beneath you.

Al Zolynas
The Siberian Journal

My father's cousin's husband, V.,
a man in his late seventies, long white hair, dignified
face, spent almost ten years in Siberia (nine years,
ten months, and twenty-six days, as he tells us).
Now, in his own backyard on the outskirts of Kaunas,
a free city once again, on a summer afternoon, he reads
to us from the pages of his Siberian journal.

The yard, like most in Lithuania, is eighty percent
vegetables and fruit trees—
tomatoes, cabbages, potatoes, apples, and plums.
The rest is taken up with V.'s experiments in
making his own building blocks out
of various materials: cement and pebbles, clay and
bark, cinders, ashes, and straw.
We, the American and the local relatives, sit
in chairs and benches hand-made by our host.
Not the least of what he learned in his long
exile was how to make almost
anything out of almost anything else.

He reads to us, his head bent forward, a swathe
of long white hair obscuring half his face, he reads
what I recognize as an old-fashioned Lithuanian prose—
dignified, resonant cadences, the tone reserved and ironic,
the irony of one who has suffered so much he
knows he can't possibly recreate it for us so
has to distance himself and bring us in by means
of indirection and understatement:

*A typical day's bounteous nourishment consisted of Mr. Stalin's
famous leaf and tree bark soup, occasionally supplemented with
a single delicious floating mushroom or, perhaps, a thoroughly
moisture-free slice of aged bread.*

On he reads, and it's fascinating, though the language
is sometimes obscure or difficult, but then I notice
my own father beside me—also of V.'s generation and
no slouch himself in the suffering department—
is nodding off! I give him a gentle elbow in the side and
he starts and smiles wryly and elbows me back as if
to say, "Yes, the man suffered, no doubt about it. But
so did we all. There can be only so much tolerance
for the story of another's sufferings. I'm an old
man, have seen and done much, and here
and now, in this pleasant yard under
the dappled shadows of
the apple tree, the droning of the bees and
the hum of this man's self-conscious prose—
it's simply too much, and sleep
tugs insistently at my sleeve."

V. continues in his ironic mode:

> *Food was in such abundance, that once we even had a special
> delicacy for our single work horse, a handsomely slim fellow who
> kept himself that way through the exercise of pleasant long hours
> of work each day. Yes, we were able to treat him once with a deli-
> cious straw broom, which he gratefully ate down to the wooden
> handle. He might have continued with the handle, but enough is
> enough; indulgence we can live with, over-indulgence—never!*

He has been reading now for fifteen minutes, still
about food, to an audience of some twelve people:
his relatives by marriage, his own son who holds
a two-year-old on his lap, his son's wife, his
own wife, cousins, and the nieces and nephews of
those cousins, post-independence pilgrims from America,
many met for the first and possibly only time, and
the truth is we are starting to get bored and restless;

the truth is we, sitting in this pleasant yard, stomachs
full after an abundant and truly memorable feast
(oh, the *kugelis*, the beet salad, the home-made plum wine!)
are suffering—of course, not the suffering of exile,
of hunger, of unspeakable privations, but
suffering nonetheless: the boards of the bench
are uncomfortable, the sun on the back of our necks
is too much, that fly pestering our ear,
the belt now too tight around our waist,
the little two-year-old starting to squirm and complain.
Finally, his own wife, A., a survivor
of three years of Siberian exile herself, speaks up,
"V., that's enough already. I think they get the idea."

With great dignity and with the economical movements
of a Zen master, V. closes his aged and worn note book and
tells us that he hopes he's been able to at least capture
for us a small part of what it was like
in Siberia as comrade Stalin's guest.
He has. I've been moved to tears, and
impressed by the indomitable human spirit,
and glad I've been so-far spared such trials—
though somehow envious, too,
I must confess, like any writer,
always with an eye out for material.

Lucille Lang Day
Reject JELL-O

The man I married twice—
at fourteen in Reno, again in Oakland
the month before I turned eighteen—
had a night maintenance job at General Foods.
He mopped the tiled floors and scrubbed
the wheels and teeth of the Jell-O machines.
I see him bending in green light,
a rag in one hand,
a pail of foamy solution at his feet.
He would come home at seven a.m.
with a box of damaged Jell-O packages,
including the day's first run,
routinely rejected, and go to sleep.
I made salad with that reject Jell-O—
lemon, lime, strawberry, orange, peach—
in a kitchen where I could almost touch
opposing walls at the same time
and kept a pie pan under the leaking sink.
We ate hamburgers and Jell-O
almost every night
and when the baby went to sleep,
we loved, snug in the darkness pierced
by passing headlights and a streetlamp's gleam,
listening to the Drifters and the Platters.
Their songs wrapped around me
like coats of fur, I hummed in the long shadows
while the man I married twice
dressed and left for work.

Gary R. Hoffman

Incident in Itawamba

I knew it weren't gonna be a good day for Oat, and bad days for Oat usually meant bad days for me. Orville Anderson Tilley was sheriff of Itawamba County Mississippi. Most folks didn't call him sheriff—they just used his initials and called him Oat. I'm a deputy for Oat, and they call me Range 'cause I'm tall and skinny. Today was also the first day for a new deputy, John Kelly. New deputies weren't all that uncommon, but this one had been forced on Oat, and he was a might upset about it.

Seems John was a nephew of County Commissioner Aaron Boyer. Mr. Boyer hired his nephew right under Oat's nose—never even asked him about it. Not only that, but this new guy was from New Jersey. Oat had been bouncin' around like a drop of water on a hot griddle ever since he heard the news. So here we was, ready to start trying to train this new guy, when we get a call from over at Mantachie that someone had been shot. So we takes off—Oat and John in one car, and me and Deputy Becky Mann in the other.

Turned out the guy lived in a dumpy little shack out in the country, closer to the Tenn-Tom Waterway than town itself. Oat said the victim's name was Jerry Butler, but I don't think I ever knowed his real name. We'd had a couple of minor run-ins with him, and I just always called him Catfish. Everyone else around did, too.

When we got to the house, Bobby Gene Winslow was sittin' on the front stoop. He was the one who made the call about Catfish. "What was you doin' out here anyway?" Oat asked Bobby Gene.

"I stopped by to see if Catfish had any .22 shells he could borrow me 'til next week."

"And just what were you gonna do with .22 shells?" Oat asked.

Bobby looked at the ground and made a circle in the dust with his foot. "Thought I'd see ifin I could get a couple squirrels fer dinner."

"Ain't even squirrel season, Bobby."

Bobby picked up a stick and threw it down. "I know! I thought you might give me some trouble 'bout that, but I knew I needed to call about Catfish. He was a good friend."

"You stay out here and keep an eye on him," Oat told Becky. "Let's see what we got inside."

Catfish was alayin' on his back right in front of his cook stove. There were a couple of small holes in his chest with blood tricklin' out. "What's that all over the floor?" John asked.

"Looks to me like he was frying up some catfish for breakfast," Oat said. "Just took the skillet off the stove and dropped it when he got shot."

"What's all that other stuff?" John asked pointing to a large puddle around the cast-iron skillet.

"Probably bacon grease. Looks like it got splattered all over the kitchen here."

"Bacon grease? He not only fried his food, but did it in bacon grease?" John said.

Oat pulled a toothpick from his hatband and stuck it in his mouth. "We got a sayin' down here, John. If it can't be fried in bacon grease, it ain't worth cookin', let alone eatin'!"

"My God! What's the average life expectancy down here, thirty-seven?" John said.

"Little shorter for northerners who come down here criticizin' us," Oat said. I wanted to laugh out loud, but figured it weren't the right time. Oat walked back to the porch.

"Let me see your rifle, Bobby Gene." Oat smelt the end of it. "Been fired recently."

"I told you, I was goin' squirrel huntin'. I shot at one on the way over here, but missed and then I was out of shells. That's why I come by to see Catfish."

Oat checked the chamber of the rifle and handed it back to Bobby Gene. He took a couple steps back and eyed him up and down. "Think you better come into Tupelo with us, Bobby."

"Why? I ain't done nothin' wrong."

"You want to tell me why you shot Catfish?" Oat said. Kind of took me by surprise as well as everyone else. "Tellin' us about it now will probably go easier on you later."

John started to say somethin', but Oat held up a hand to stop him. Bobby hung his head. "I didn't shoot him! I called you guys, didn't I?"

"Maybe just to make it look like you didn't do it," Oat said. "Range, you go in and get a sample of that bacon grease. I think we can get a DNA match to the bacon grease splattered on the bottom of Bobby Gene's pants."

Well, Oat's day turned out to be better than he thought it was gonna be. Bobby Gene confessed to the shooting—said it was over money Catfish owed him. We was sittin' around the office later, and John asked Oat about doin' a DNA test on the bacon grease. "We can't, yet," Oat said, "but folks down here watch a lot of television. I figured Bobby Gene watched a lot of CSI." Oat kicked back and put his feet up on his desk. "Course, now that he's confessed, a DNA test really doesn't matter, does it?"

I wanted to laugh out loud again, but thought better of it. Oat might think I was laughin' at him, and I wanted to keep him in a good mood and not ask me to work late, cause I got a date tonight to take Nellie Caldwell, from over at Sugar Creek, to the drive-in movies. Nellie told me she was goin' to bring some snacks for us, and I figured it was gonna be a big plate of chicken wings, fried in bacon grease. Sure hope she brings a butter-tub of that home-made dippin' sauce of hers, too.

Lou Fisher

Menu

Today Steve grabs a pizza slice at the mall, a few steps from the bargain shoe store where he works four afternoons a week. Not that he's supposed to get a lunch break. The shoe manager is already peering out the door.

"Eat at home," the manager says.

"I don't cook anymore," Steve tells him, but not why.

In his kitchen space, the front burner of the stove has been taken over by an ugly brown spider who is so quick and industrious that Steve can't bear to watch it for more than a minute.

Even if he would get rid of the spider and set up the little folding table that came with the apartment, he has nothing: not oatmeal, not eggs, not egg noodles, not broccoli ever again, not meat or mustard, not his favorite Progresso black bean soup, not a drop of milk, not bran flakes to keep him from getting cholesterol and constipated, not Oreos or other kind of cookies, not potato chips in any form or for that matter those snappy toasted sunflower seeds — in fact, not a single bag or jar or box or can of anything.

Well, all right, he does have Robin's unopened can of tennis balls. Though she claimed to play the game, she must have used the court time (and her cozy sky-blue warm up suit) to find a new boyfriend.

"Who is he?" Steve recalls asking at the very last moment.

"Just somebody," Robin said.

"Do I know him?"

Robin wrinkled her tiny nose. "He's not from the neighborhood."

That night when he couldn't sleep he tossed everything from the cupboards into the cans in the alley. He meant only to throw away her finicky foods, but he couldn't stop there. And he hasn't cooked since.

Now when he's home, before or after work or on his several days off, he might drink a glass of water, being sure to let the noisy pipes run for a while to clear the lead deposits. He leaves the glass on the counter near the sink (but upside down, remembering the spider) in case he wants a refill. He uses his own glass for two days. Then Robin's glass. Then he has to wash both glasses: six times washed since she went out the door. He decided recently, and once again at the sink this morning, that if he ever convinces his feet to traverse the full length of the mall to the discount drugstore he will exchange Robin's can of tennis balls for a package of paper cups that he can use for water.

"Got a receipt?" the lanky clerk wants to know.

"No. No, I don't." Steve twirls the clear plastic can until he comes to a tiny white sticker. "But here's the price tag."

The clerk looks. "That says Wal-Mart."

"Oh...right." Steve puts on a big smile. Shows his teeth. Inside, though, he's giving it some somber thought. Could there have been another can of balls, one that Robin really used? How and when did she get to Wal-Mart? Where exactly is she now?

Still, he won't cook.

He won't shop for groceries...

He won't slice, squeeze, mix, thaw...

He won't broil, boil, bake, fry...

Yet he'll admit, sometimes directly to the spider, that eating out can be chancy. A frequent test of his resolve. For example, the best he can do in the middle of a sleepless night is maybe force a Snickers bar from the Exxon vending machine, if he has the right change and the right smash of a fist.

Worse yet, in this gray January he has to trudge through snow and slush while the itchy blue stocking cap smashes his hair. Suppose at the diner he meets someone as cute as Robin. Sure, just his luck, with his hair like this, with dirty gloves and a frayed scarf. The wet snow worries him in yet another way. Won't he get hypothermia sitting at the table in sneakers that are soaked through to his socks—and aren't these the days when service seems the absolute slowest?

"I didn't get a check," he says at the register.

"That so?" inquires the old lady in her snide way. "Who's your wait-ress?"

He glances back. "I don't remember."

"We only have *two*," she tells him.

Despite eating in these cheap neighborhood diners and luncheonettes (Gracie's, Lucky Guys, Split Silver Café, and the one with the plastic cow in front), Steve has to worry about expenses. He dines on chili or spa-ghetti or a cheese omelet. Add in sales tax, fifty-cent tips… He makes so little money part-time at the mall. He thinks that's why Robin left him. That it wasn't really the snapped condom. Or the way he splashes sham-poo on the shower doors. Or even the view out the bedroom window of the boarded-up community center and the trash heap that used to be its parking lot. No, at the end he felt certain, as she left, as she departed, as she exited with a flip of her hip, that she'd found a guy with an ATM card and a microwave.

In desperation he takes the bus to the tennis club.

"She had a good backhand," remembers the guy at the desk.

In further desperation he takes the bus to the chiropractor's office where Robin works.

"Not anymore," says the full-faced woman who's in there now.

She's gone for sure. And if it's up to Steve he'll never cook again. Oh, he'll give in and get some peanut butter, some white bread to slap it on, some milk to drink right out of the carton. He's bound to buy sardines too, with the lid that peels open. For breakfast he'll return to bran flakes and also come to discover fruit tarts. And eventually the shoe store at the mall will promote him to full-time (with HMO insurance and a real lunch break), the weather will turn warm, and Robin will fade to a soft dreamy hunger.

"That's the way it is," he tells the spider still secure on the stove.

Jamie Asae FitzGerald
Poi

There's the bowl or the checked paper trough,
a spoon or a finger, sugar or salt,
then the gray paste, the stuff of babies
to grow them thick and strong,
the purple root, a spirit color, pounded,
mashed and mixed with water.

There's the mongrel wandering the streets
or the beach, panting, always hungry,
or tied in the yard, well-fed and sleeping
in the shade. She lifts a lazy eye to any passerby,
then goes back to her fragrant canine dream.

There's the ancient one, over-fed and retarded,
good enough to love or eat, throw a dog a bone,
then lick theirs clean.

Eat me or love me with a spoon or a finger.
Depending on if you roast me or stroke me,
I'll taste of sugar or salt.

NOTE:
Three definitions of the Hawaiian word *poi* are referenced in this poem:
    1. an edible paste made from taro root, eaten in the Pacific islands;
    2. an extinct breed of Hawaiian dog that lived with the tribes as pets, but
       were also eaten as a delicacy;
    3. Hawaii Pidgin English for mongrel dog.

Harold Jaffe

Salaam

When the Palestinian terrorist opened his shirt to display the explosives taped to his chest, the Israeli shop owner pointed to a large cast iron pot simmering on the stove. It contained cabbage, potatoes, green onions, and—unmistakably—a tiny human hand.

※

When the Palestinian opened his shirt to display the explosives taped to his chest, the Israeli shop owner on the crowded Jerusalem street pointed to the old pot simmering on the stove. Cabbage, potatoes, green onions, and a tiny human hand.

The Palestinian was young, slender, with black eyes and the tracings of a black mustache.

The shop owner was wiry with bloodshot eyes and a once black now grey and white mustache.

They glared into each other's eyes.

Then, as the young Palestinian raised his fist, the old man raised his arm with numbers tattooed on it.

The young man pronounced the word *Palestine* even as the old man uttered the word *Auschwitz*.

Each in his own tongue.

※

When the Palestinian opened his shirt to display the explosives taped to his chest the Israeli shop owner pointed to the large pot simmering on the stove. It contained cabbage, potatoes, green onions, and—conspic-uously—a tiny human hand.

Palestinian, —I know that hand. It is my sister's hand.

Israeli, —You are wrong. It is my sister's hand.

—The hand is tiny. You are an old man.

—I was young then as you. In another country.

≈

—So you are a suicide bomber.

—Freedom fighter.

—Murdering hundreds of anonymous Jews will provide this freedom?

—It is the only way left.

—You have heard of the word genocide?

—Every day of my life I hear this word.

≈

When the Palestinian opened his shirt displaying the explosives taped to his chest the Israeli shop owner on the crowded Jerusalem street pointed to the large pot simmering on the stove. Cabbage, potatoes, green onions, and a tiny human hand.

Glaring into each other's eyes.

—What is it that you want?

—The Jews to give us back our land. That we can live in peace.

—And if I tell you that this land in Jerusalem and beyond is not yours but ours. Historically ours.

—Let the United Nations decide.

—And the Jew-haters in the UN. What about them?

≈

—You are prepared to murder yourself and hundreds of ordinary people you do not know who happen to be Jews. Why? Because of a principle?

—If this principle means truth, then yes, God willing, I am prepared to join my martyred freedom-fighting brothers and sisters.

—There are many others who feel as you do?

—I cannot give numbers. But I have never met a Palestinian who was not prepared to die for freedom.

—And if you did meet one?

—I would refuse to shake his hand.

❧

When the Palestinian opened his shirt and displayed the explosives taped to his chest the Israeli shop owner pointed to the large pot simmering on the stove. It contained cabbage, potatoes, green onions, and—unmistakably—a tiny human hand.

—You Jews are cannibals.

—The opposite is true. We have been cannibalized.

—You are talking about Nazis. You cannot stop talking about your Nazis.

—No.

—That is the problem with you Jews. You live in the past.

—No. We live in the present under the weight of the past. There is no other way.

❧

—These Nazis that so obsess you. You have become them.

—What are you saying?

—Just that. You Israelis in your crisp uniforms with your advanced weapons slaughter us and degrade us as the Nazis did you.

—What you are parroting here I have heard before. It has become fashionable. It is an unspeakable slander. And coming from you with genocide taped and strapped across your body!

❧

When the Palestinian freedom fighter opened her blouse to display the explosives taped to her body the Israeli shop owner's daughter gestured to her breast then pointed to the Palestinian's breast.

They gazed long into each other's dark eyes.

Then the Palestinian jerked her head to the side, reached under her blouse, detonated.

That is one version. The other version follows.

After looking long at each other, the Palestinian freedom fighter nodded her head once, slowly.

Carefully, she disarmed the explosives.

Then she and the shop owner's daughter embraced and arm in arm stepped out into the turbulent Jerusalem street.

Elizabeth Tibbetts

Land of Everything

after reading The Crystal Frontier

Today while the sauce simmered on the stove
I read your chapter twice, Dionisio "Baco" Rangel—
your name's syllables nothing in my mouth
beside your creator's, Carlos Fuentes—and I'm made

dizzy by your disdain because you leave little
beneath me. I am, after all, living in a land
where history's been rewritten, as you know,
and where gadgets are as plentiful as fleas.

To make matters worse, I've nearly loved
my washing machine, an old Maytag
that sits on the porch waiting for a new home
the way an old dog pines inside the pound.

And though, perhaps, I'll love the new one too,
I understand what you say about greed
and bad manners in my country. You might find me impertinent writing to you this way,
but I have to say I'd like to be the gringa
who appeared with the sherbet, one of
the different women for each course granted you
by the genie who smoked out of the open neck
of the jalapeno sauce bottle at your table. Did you discuss food with
her as you admired her undisguised *imminent maturity*? You'd had a
quite good Texas meal, and she

was probably distracting you with her tongue,
though she'd have agreed there's lots of bad food here,

the landscape tied from border to border, coast to coast, with chains of
burger and taco joints.

The meal you go on to describe as *my* country's,
rubber chicken, boxed potato, and tasteless beans,
exists. But "Baco," let me tell you some gringas
know how to wash and dry a fat young hen

that's seen dirt and sun, rub it with rosemary,
and oil, then roast it until the air's so thick
with its smell that even you, from the page,
could taste it. Or pick string beans when they're

long and full of themselves, and squashes
that are crooked and textured like toads.
"Baco," such food's as satisfying as your words,
rolling slowly inside my mouth — the way

you describe my country, and yours, Mexico,
with its city of 800 (!) desserts. If you had
time, I could show you recipe after recipe:
brown-butter cake, my grandmother's lemon pie,

Indian, province, and rice puddings lightly
sweetened and soaked in cream, or gingerbread
with its dark bite, until you'd choose one
of my hundred desserts, sit at my table

(in my own small land of everything, or nothing)
and, perhaps, remember me as a woman
who has no cardboard pizzas in her freezer,
and who stops at McDonald's only to pee.

Jennifer Berney

Picnic

Before I set out on my own, Veronique explained how a picnic is properly arranged. Americans, she assumed, need training. A proper picnic requires two couples though they need not be married. On that day, she and I qualified, hostess and foreigner. One couple drives, the other prepares a lunch and packs it in a basket. Veronique baked two quiches with caramelized onions and thick chunks of bacon. We packed cloth napkins, glass plates, cutlery, and ate in a park near Switzerland, the mountains dipping into the overcast sky. Jean-Claude, a round man with thick fingers, teased me for not drinking enough, while his wife tried to keep him from sneaking more wine into my glass. When we were finished, we re-folded our napkins and stacked our plates, filling the basket with orderly mess. We squeezed back into the car, fingers cold from gray weather, insides warm from the wine. I was restless on that drive. The space of that *We* felt cavernous, all those crevices in W, bodies that were merely shapes and names. I craved the simple line of *I*.

This picnic begins in Lyon. It is May and the sky cradles blue. I've just trudged up two kilometers of sloping sidewalk and concrete steps to sit on the grassy side of the hill. When I take off my backpack, the back of my t-shirt is stuck to my skin. I unzip the sack and lay everything I will need on top of a flattened paper bag: a half-eaten round of cheap camembert, a hunk of cured ham, the stale end of a baguette, my Swiss army knife. Laid out on the grass, my lunch appears complete without me.

I have left a mess at home, an unsettled romance. She is nearly twice my age and nearly married. Here, she trails my thoughts, an imaginary friend on a leash.

Before I eat, I take off my shoes. The fuzz of my socks has left little dents in my skin and beneath the sun my feet look tiny and white. I unwrap the ham from its white paper package and cut a crooked morsel. It's salty and dry and takes a long time to chew, the fat spreading and warming. Small clouds hover over the horizon, but the curved bulk of the sky is empty.

Mornings in Grenoble, I sit at the café across the street from my hotel and drink coffee while I write rambling pages of words that struggle not to mention her. There is nothing special about this café. The building is new, bright, covered in speckled white linoleum. The owner stares at a TV that is mounted in the corner and after four days of arriving at the same time, no one begins to notice me or smile. My lungs are tight from the smoke that is in every building. The rest of my body too feels like it's shrinking, like I could fold myself neatly into the briefcase of the man drinking coffee at the bar. He wouldn't notice.

When my pen stops moving, the story replays itself again. Incident One (she takes off a yellow glove to shake my hand) sets off the entire list of filed memories (Incident Two: she sees me in a parking lot and calls my name) until I butt up against the final one, the moment of sitting in a parked car, listening to her tell me that I am one of a number of choices to be made. I have a phone call to make when I get back. I gulp my last cold sip of milky coffee and leave.

I decide to shop for a spoon. I find one in the sale bin with black handles with silver rivets. Upstairs in the grocery department, I buy a tub of rice pudding to celebrate. There is a *randonnée* that begins on the edge of town, a path marked by small yellow stripes (like minus signs) painted on rocks or trees, that winds around the green foot of the mountain. I walk, I eat, I brood, I walk some more, and by two o'clock, when the yellow stripes deposit me back in town, I have nothing left to do. The sun is still high. I want to go home. I want to call her right now

and ask her for an answer. If she told me, I could breathe again. I have a
calling card in my wallet and the slip of paper she wrote her number on,
folded in four and slipped behind my library card. It has been there this
whole time. I find a payphone at the *Maison du Tourisme*. I call my Dad
instead. He tells me about his walk to the library this morning. He saw a
nuthatch and three squirrels. His voice sounds like disaster averted.

My hotel room is slightly larger than the bed, the floor a worn wood
that stores the smells of cigar and lemon, and the single window opens
out to a neighboring roof where pigeons gather. In the evening, I sit on
the windowsill and eat yogurt out of a jar with my new spoon, the sky
softening with night. The way the room is dark, the window small, it
looks like the pigeons and the clay tiles of the roof are the whole world.
I lick my spoon as clean as I can before rinsing it in the sink and resting
it to dry behind the faucet.

I spend a week in Paris before coming home. I eat Chinese dumplings
in the Luxembourg Gardens, *tarte à poireaux* in *les Tuilleries*, a Nutella
crêpe by the Moulin Rouge. The day before I leave, on Isle St. Louis,
I wait outside in a long line for a chocolate cone from *Bertheleon*. It is
smooth and dark; it shines. As I lick the bottom edges, I walk down the
steps to the Seine and sit on the edge of the quay. The water is bright
green and still. There are teenage boys with skateboards and girlfriends
as accessories, everyone tan with unkempt hair. They speak in French too
fast for me to follow. The girls have bought sandwiches and they slice
them to share and the boys take bites between smokes. An open can of
Coke circulates.

In my dreams last night, she was in my apartment. She looked tired,
leaning from one chair into another. She was single, but she didn't want
me.

I notice that I'm staring when a cool dribble of chocolate runs down
my finger. At the same moment, one of the girls catches me watching.
She stares back and whispers to her friend. They steal drags while their
boyfriends chew. I feel permanently old. I was never a girlfriend as a
teenager; I never wore a bikini or cut school to drink vodka in plastic

bottles of orange juice. Suddenly I want to cut my hair and wear it messy, to get stoned in the park and kiss open-mouthed. I want to be a passenger in a car with broken seatbelts and a brand new stereo and I want to wear skirts that yield to the driver's fingers.

When I return from my trip I look gaunt in my clothes, slendered from aimless searching. In an effort to convince myself that she is not my life, I wait three days to call her. I can barely eat anything. In addition to new shoes and a bottle of wine, I've brought home a tube of *crème de marron*. I puncture the foil closure with the pointed end of the cap and squeeze a pea-size taste on my finger. I roll it between tongue and pallet and the sweetness leaves behind granules of chestnut that feel like sand. My view is a dirty carpet, a counter, a window that looks over a driveway. This will no longer do.

Karen Greenbaum-Maya
Bouchons de Fromage

Vivian Shipley

The Difference Between a Raw Onion and a Slow-Cooked One

I strip to skin hidden during the day, allow
sagging flesh I keep under sleeves to shine.
Habits of love have turned you into a fish

in Mammoth Cave that has no eyes. Wary
of fishhooks that can not glint without light,
I do not want the moon to cut through clouds,

dilute ink of the cove that scratches out years
annotated by stretch marks. Listening to waves,
I can't stop myself from timing the lapping,

loud breaks, imposing patterns, making rules
for the sea, for what I cannot control. Calling
out, you ask me to sit in full view of neighbors

on the Stony Creek pink granite, let high tide
lick my feet, take my edge. Molly O'Neill,
you'll teach me about hammock time, summer

cooking that breaks down walls, changes internal
sugars. Cooking this late in August, we need
to layer flavors and textures of the twenty-one years

we have spent together, learn to mix the fierce
with the mellow. You finger my spine, perhaps
to learn how I am connected, but I imagine

you as a vegetable chef breaking peapods open
at the vein, clean every time. No vegan, it does
not comfort me to hear raw carrots or peppers,

with cell walls firm as adolescent buttocks,
restrict the release of sweet tasting compounds,
or that baked, garlic sags as it loses its fire,

but gains a touch of soul. Without something
aggressive and dark below the surface, sweetness,
like youth, becomes cloying, is more fleeting

than lasting. Knowing I am afraid to reshape what
has cooled, with your thumb hooked around my wrist,
you lecture about chemical changes: rearranged

proteins can evaporate bitter tasting compounds.
Generated by a convection oven, or by emotion,
heat like passion changes everything, is able to
melt solids to liquid, even within the human heart.

Ilya Kaminsky
from Natalia

We fell in love and eight years passed.
Eight years. Carefully, I dissect this number:
we've lived with three cats in five cities,
learning how a man ages invisibly.
Eight years! Eight!—we chilled lemon vodka, and we kissed
on the floor, among the peels of lemons.
And each night, we stood up and saw ourselves:
a man and a woman kneel, whispering Lord,
one word the soul destroys to make clear.
How magical it is to live! it rained at the market
(just imagine: the water falling from the sky!)
And you sang, Sweet dollars,
why aren't you in my pockets?
With your fingers, she tapped out your iambics
on the back of our largest casserole.
and we sang, Sweet dollars,
why aren't you in my pocket?

Edward Espe Brown

The Sincerity of Battered Teapots

In the late sixties, when I was working so very hard and struggling to learn how to cook and how to direct the operations of a kitchen, the battered teapots were one of the things that kept me going. Dented and tarnished they sat on a shelf in the kitchen, ready to be used when called upon. My tired, despairing eyes would wander around the kitchen at all the jars and bowls, pots and utensils which were so much a part of my busy life and finally come to rest on those teapots. How did they do it?

Once they had been new, bright, perfect, a softly lustrous golden tone. Made of polished metal, probably aluminum, they were pleasingly round and plump, with a long perky spout and a graceful curving metal handle wrapped with bamboo stripping.

The teapots were used several times a day to serve hot water and tea. To see them filled and waiting was a cheery sight, not just because of the hot refreshing liquid stored inside, but because their shape greeted the eye with easy-going ampleness. Nothing pretentious, sleek, or stylish distinguished these teapots, which were always ready and always willing.

Zen offers a simple dictum for how to care for things, how to respect them: Carry one thing with two hands, rather than two things with one hand. The teapots rarely received this respect. Especially once they were empty, people would grab two handles in one hand and two handles in the other, and the teapots would clang their way back to the kitchen.

To practice respect or to care for something or someone intimately takes time, and even spiritually minded zen students are as much in a hurry as the next person. Instead of dashing to work or school, the zen student races for time off, a nap, or a hot bath. Teapots become an obstacle between here and rest, so grabbing two pots in each hand seems like a great time-saver.

After a while the teapots reflected the way they had been treated. Gazing at the teapots on the shelf, I would feel a certain camaraderie: I too am like that—dented, discolored, drained. Yet as I looked I would sense something else: quiet dignity…tremendous forgiveness…the willingness to go on. "Sweethearts," I would think, "if you can do it, I can too." Inspiration comes from the strangest places.

Please do not suppose that I am condoning abuse. It is just that we all get beaten down by life—with disappointments and frustrations, annoyances and fatigue. And somehow we find the strength to continue. And sometimes the courage to change.

Recently my sweetheart Patti asked me if I knew what sincere meant. She had been working endless hours on a figure sculpture, which was to be cast in bronze eventually.

"No," I replied, "tell me about the meaning of sincere." Her explanation was that the s-i-n was like sans in French, meaning "without," and that the c-e-r-e meant "wax." To be sincere is to be without wax, the wax which can be used to cover up all the dents and blemishes, the chips and cracks, all those places we think we need to hide.

To be sincere is to be of a piece—with the imperfections showing. The lines and grooves are part of the beauty. The faults and shortcomings are part of the sincerity. When it comes to cooking, I put my faith in sincere, honest effort. I am less interested in showy, dramatic results intended to impress and astound than in day in and day out cooking. According to an old Chinese saying, "The uses of cleverness are soon exhausted, while the apparently simple is infinitely interesting."

To be committed to covering up faults is to be continuously anxious that we could be unmasked or seen through. When the imperfections are pointed out, we can become angry or quite discouraged. Yet although we are "up-set," this removal of wax can also be a relief. Then we don't have to put all that effort into covering up anymore. The secret is out.

In one zen story the student asks the teacher, "How can I attain liberation?" and the teacher responds, "Who is binding you?" The student is said to have had an awakening.

I find that story revealing. I notice how I bind myself at times with demands for perfection and mastery. I tell myself endlessly, "Watch what you say. Watch what you do," until a kind of paralysis sets in. I withhold love and respect from someone who is dented and tarnished, and even find fault with his efforts to wax things over.

Then I look at the teapots. And I am released.

Lisa Gavin

Ceremony

Contributor Biographies

Michael Adams fell from grace years ago and came to rest just east of the Continental Divide in northern Colorado. He is the author of several books of poetry and essays. His most recent work, a collaboration with the poets James Taylor III and Phil Woods, is titled *Underground* (Longhand Press). These three poets write and perform as the Free Radical Railroad. Michael is the winner of the 2007 Mark Fischer Poetry Prize, awarded by the Telluride Writers Guild. He teaches in the Master of Arts program at Prescott College and loves to cook. Michael can be reached at firegiggler@earthlink.net.

Kim Addonizio is the author of four poetry collections, most recently *What Is This Thing Called Love* (W.W. Norton). *Lucifer at the Starlite* is forthcoming in 2009, along with a new book on writing, *Ordinary Genius: A Guide for the Poet Within*. Addonizio is also the author of two novels from Simon & Schuster: *Little Beauties* and *My Dreams Out in the Street*. She is online at www.kimaddonizio.com.

Pamela Annas teaches courses in working-class literature and twentieth-century poetry at the University of Massachusetts/Boston. She is a member of *The Radical Teacher* editorial collective, reviews for *Women's Review of Books,* and has published poems in *Chomo-Uri, The Harbor Review, Sojourner, Ibbetson Street,* and *The Northwoods Anthology*.

Teresa Barnett is the head of the UCLA Library's Center for Oral History Research. She writes essays on collecting, food, and various other engagements with the material world.

Chris Baron is passionate about the importance of art as a practical resource for discovering truth, and as a means of survival, in our every day lives. With an MFA in Creative Writing, Chris is currently on the executive board for the Border Voices Poetry Project. He is also a Professor of English at San Diego City College where he coordinates the English Center. Chris worked in restaurants for eleven years as a busboy, server, bartender, and manager. His work has appeared in a number of literary magazines and journals including, *Pearl, Aethlon: The Journal of Sports Literature, Sierra Club Press, Fahrenheit, San Diego Writer's Monthly, Vision*, and more.

Josh Baxt was once characterized as odd but affable, lives in La Mesa, California, with his wife and two kids and writes internal communications for a local non-profit.

Jennifer Berney lives in Olympia, Washington. Her work has appeared in *The Coe Review, Wheelhouse*, and *The Barn Owl Review*, among others. She teaches at South Puget Sound Community College.

Ronda Broatch is the author of *Shedding Our Skins*, (Finishing Line Press, 2008), and *Some Other Eden* (2005). Nominated for the Pushcart Prize and Best of the Web, Ronda is the recipient of a 2007 Artist Trust GAP Grant. Her poems appear in journals, both in print and online, as well *Verse Daily*.

Dan Brook teaches sociology and political science, takes photographs and writes poetry, fathers an amazing kid, and tends a tiny garden. He also maintains *Eco-Eating* at www.brook.com/veg.

Sydney Brown is the co-director of the Creative Writing Program at Grossmont College in El Cajon, California, where she also teaches poetry, literature, and composition. Her work has appeared in *Sunshine/Noir: Writing from San Diego and Tijuana, Inside English, Red, two girls review, The Southern Anthology, Zaum: The Literary Review of Sonoma State, Hawaii Pacific Review, San Diego Writer's Monthly*, and *How2: Contemporary Innovative Writing Practices by Women*. Additionally, Sydney works daily to achieve domestic bliss — and sometimes gets pretty close — with her two schnauzers, mean cat, and husband, Steve, in La Mesa.

Edward Espe Brown began cooking and practicing Zen in 1965 and was ordained as a priest by Shunryu Suzuki Roshi in 1971. He has been head resident teacher at each of the San Francisco Zen Centers: Tassajara, Green Gulch, and City Center, and has led meditation retreats and cooking classes throughout the United States, as well as Austria, Germany,

Spain, and England. He is the author of several cookbooks including the celebrated *Tassajara Bread Book* and most recently *Tomato Blessings and Radish Teachings*. (Also *Tassajara Cooking*, *Tassajara Recipe Book* and co-author of *The Greens Cookbook*.) His critically-acclaimed movie *How to Cook Your Life* premiered in October, 2007. He was the first head resident cook, Tenzo, at Tassajara Zen Mountain Center 1967-1970. From 1979-1983 he worked at the celebrated Greens Restaurant in San Francisco, serving as busboy, waiter, floor manager, wine buyer, cashier, host, and manager. He has been teaching vegetarian cooking classes since 1985 throughout the United States (well, California (San Francisco Bay Area, Sacramento, Los Angeles), Austin, Houston, Evanston, Cambridge, Spokane, NYC (the Natural Gourmet Cooking School), Vermont (the New England Culinary Academy), Toronto (Dish Cooking School), Nantucket, Long Island, et al. as well as England (Schumacher College), Spain, and Austria.

Jeanne Bryner was born in Appalachia. Her books in print are *Breathless*, *Blind Horse: Poems*, *Eclipse: Stories*, and *Tenderly Lift Me: Nurses Honored, Celebrated and Remembered*. She has received writing fellowships from Bucknell University, Kent State University's Wick Poetry Program and the Ohio Arts Council.

Sandra Carpenter retired as a social worker with Orange County Social Services and began writing poetry, submitting, and publishing in 1990. She became a Freedom Papers and Gannett newspaper columnist shortly after and traveled all over the world as a travel writer/columnist, while writing freelance for many magazines and papers over the next decade. Today her focus is mainly poetry, and she belongs to the major poetry groups of North County San Diego. She has published 4 chapbooks, an autobiography entitled *Sandy Paths*, and a 2001 romantic-suspense novel *Casa Verde* (Rubenesque Romances, publisher).

Sharon Carter has a medical degree from Cambridge University. Her visual art can be seen in *Spindrift*, *Raven Chronicles*, *Disquieting Muses*, and *Switched on Gutenberg*. A series of digital prints was shown at the Amy Burnett gallery in Bremerton, Washington in conjunction with The Second Sunday Reading Series. She was a co-editor of *Literary Salt*, an online journal featuring poetry, fiction, non-fiction, art and photography She was a recipient of a Hedgebrook residency in 2001 and a Jack Straw writer in 2003.

Mary Chang is co-editor of *Enduring Questions and Essential Practices: Reflections on Writing Based Teaching* to be published by SUNY Press. She has taught writing in various programs including the Bard Prison Initiative and the Young Writers Workshop at Simon's Rock College. She has an M.F.A. in creative writing from the University of Oregon.

Jennnifer Chapis is the author of the chapbook, *The Beekeeper's Departure* (Backwards City Press 2007) and a limited-edition broadside, *Poem as Tossed Salad* (Center for Book Arts 2002). She has published poems with *The Iowa Review, DIAGRAM, Hotel America, McSweeney's, Barrow Street, Quarterly West,* the *Best New Poets* anthology series, and others. Her work was recently recognized with the Florida Review Editor's Prize, the GSU Review Poetry Prize, and a Pushcart nomination. Jennifer is a founding editor with *Nightboat Books* (www.nightboat.org). She lives in Southern California, where she operates a Web site marketing company (www.webaha.com) with her husband, fiction writer Josh Goldfaden (www.joshgoldfaden.com).

Denise Chávez has her roots in New Mexico, Texas and México. She grew up in Las Cruces, NM with her father's family and in Far West Texas with her mother's family and learned to love art, literature and tacos in all places. Chávez is working on a book, *Río Grande Family*, about her Sephardic Jewish roots in Chihuahua and Delicias, México. A true child of La Frontera, Chávez is the author of the a memoir *A Taco Testimony: Meditations on Family, Food and Culture*, novels *Loving Pedro Infante, Face of An Angel* and a short story collection, *The Last of the Menu Girls*. She has published a children's book, *La Mujer Que Sabía El Idioma de Los Animales/The Woman Who Knew the Language of the Animals*. The author of over 45 plays, Chávez considers herself a performance writer. Currently Chávez is working on a novel, *The King and Queen of Comezón*, a border mystery/love story as well as a collection of Cuentitos, little stories called *El Inglés Tan Bonito*. She is the Director of The Border Book Festival, a major national and regional book festival in Mesilla, NM, as well as the Cultural Center de Mesilla, the festival's home base. www.borderbookfestival.org.

Marilyn Chin's books of poems include *Dwarf Bamboo, The Phoenix Gone, the Terrace Empty* and *Rhapsody in Plain Yellow*. She was born in Hong Kong and raised in Portland, Oregon. Her books have become Asian-American classics and are taught in classrooms internationally.

She has won numerous awards for her poetry, including a USA foundation grant, a Radcliffe Institute Fellowship at Harvard, the Rockefeller Foundation Fellowship at Bellagio, Italy, two NEAs, the Stegner Fellowship, the PEN/Josephine Miles Award, four Pushcart Prizes, the Paterson Prize, a Fulbright Fellowship to Taiwan, residencies at Yaddo, the MacDowell Colony, the Lannan Residency, the Djerassi Foundation and others. She is featured in a variety of anthologies, including *The Norton Anthology of Modern and Contemporary Poetry*, *The Norton Anthology of Literature by Women*, *The Norton Introduction to Poetry*, *The Oxford Anthology of Modern American Poetry*, *Unsettling America*, *The Open Boat*, and *The Best American Poetry of 1996*. She was featured in Bill Moyers' PBS series *The Language of Life*. She has read and taught workshops all over the world. Recently, she taught at the Iowa Writer's Workshop and was guest poet at universities in Singapore, Hong Kong, Manchester, Sydney and Berlin and elsewhere. In addition to writing poetry, she has translated poems by the modern Chinese poet Ai Qing and co-translated poems by the Japanese poet Gozo Yoshimasu. She teaches in the MFA program at San Diego State University. Presently, she is working on a book of tales.

Olivia Chin migrated to San Diego from Long Island, NY, in 2003. She is an amateur artist who explores her creative side by dabbling in photography, mixed media art, ceramics, cooking, and jewelry making. Through her photography, she seeks to capture the extraordinarily ordinary beauty found in everyday life. The photographs included in this anthology were taken on a trip to Cambodia with her church in 2005.

Jennifer Cost has an M.A. in American Literature from San Diego State University. She is an Associate Professor of English and Humanities at Mesa College and the American Federation of Teachers Vice-President for Mesa College. She also co-coordinates the Honors Program at Mesa College. Her photographs have appeared in *City Works* in 2000 and at *Dos Mil Espacios* at San Diego City College in the spring of 2000.

June Cressy is a Brooklyn native living and writing in San Diego for the past twenty-five years and studying Zen for the past nine. She has been a writer, editor and photographer published locally and nationally in newspapers, anthologies and magazines.

Jeff Crouch is an internet artist in Grand Prairie, Texas. Google "Jeff Crouch" to see where he's been on the internet.

Lucille Lang Day has published a children's book and seven poetry collections and chapbooks, most recently *The Book of Answers* (Finishing Line, 2006) and *God of the Jellyfish* (Cervena Barva, 2007). Her first poetry collection, *Self-Portrait with Hand Microscope*, was selected by Robert Pinsky for the Joseph Henry Jackson Award. She received her M.A. in English and M.F.A. in creative writing at San Francisco State University, and her M.A. in zoology and Ph.D. in science and mathematics education at the University of California at Berkeley. She is currently director of the Hall of Health, an interactive children's museum in Berkeley.

Brandel France de Bravo's poetry has appeared in *Fugue, The Kenyon Review, Black Warrior Review,* and *The American Voice.* She has been nominated for a Pushcart Prize in poetry and her first collection, *Provenance*, will be published in the fall of 2008 by Washington Writers' Publishing House.

Sharon DeBusk has been a writer, editor and photographer for newspapers, magazines and journals around the Pacific Northwest for more than 25 years. She lives in Portland, Oregon, with her husband and two daughters.

Ella deCastro Baron is a full-time wife and mother of two little ones, a part-time English and Creative Writing instructor at San Diego City College, and an 'other'-times published writer in publications such as *Fiction International, Sunshine Noir,* and *City Works.* She is currently working on publishing her first book of creative nonfiction—a witness to her Filipino-American, once chronically ill, charismatic Christian identity—all while trying to get back onto a longboard and into dance classes at the gym.

Mark Dery is a cultural critic, freelance journalist, and the author, most recently, of *The Pyrotechnic Insanitarium: American Culture on the Brink* (Grove/Atlantic). A San Diego homeboy living in New York, he is writing a book about the cultural psyche of the Southern California borderlands.

Vi Dutcher, Ph.D. is a professor of Rhetoric and Composition and teaches writing courses at Eastern Mennonite University where she is chair of the Language & Literature Department and Writing Program Director. Her research interest is community literacy practices, in particular, Amish and Mennonite female literacy practices.

Heather Eudy holds an M.F.A. in Creative Writing from San Diego State University and a BA in English from San Francisco State University. She has taught in Chiapas, Mexico and in a number of schools in San Diego, her native city. She currently teaches English composition, creative writing and literature at Southwestern College in Chula Vista, California. Her work has been published in *Sunshine/Noir: Writing from San Diego and Tijuana* from City Works Press.

Corie Feiner, poet and performer, is the author of *Radishes into Roses* (Linear Arts Press). The winner of the 2007 "Vent Your Inspirations" Poetry Contest, she publishes her work regularly in journals, anthologies, and literary magazines. She performs her work internationally and has been featured in *The New York Times, Backstage Magazine, Metro News* and on NY1 and NBC. She is the Poetry Editor of the *Bellevue Literary Review.*

Michael S. Ferrill was born in Wisconsin and raised in California. He makes money as a cook, drinks wine, and listens to Otis Redding very loud on Saturday night. Sometimes he writes stuff.

Lou Fisher is the recipient of the *New Letters* Literary Award for Fiction. His stories have also appeared in two prize issues of *Mississippi Review* and in other journals and magazines including *Other Voices, The Crescent Review, The Florida Review* and in several anthologies including the recent *Bar Stories* (Dog Bottom Press, 2007) and *The Way We Work* (Vanderbilt University Press, 2008). He lives with his adorable wife in downstate New York and limits his cooking to their scrambled eggs each morning.

Jamie Asae FitzGerald's poetry has appeared in both print and web journals, and on public buses. She earned degrees from the University of Southern California—where she was the recipient of an Academy of American Poets College Prize and the Edward G. Moses Poetry Prize—and San Diego State University's M.F.A. writing program. She has taught writing and literature, and has a background in copywriting. Originally from Hawaii, she now works for *Poets & Writers* in Los Angeles.

Lisa Gavin has a passion for learning about and experiencing life in different parts of the world. She loves building relationships with the people she meets and has a heart for capturing the beauty of their lives on film as a means to share their stories with others. She has been deeply impacted by her travels, especially her trips to Cambodia and Ethiopia, where her photographs included in this anthology were taken.

Heather Grange left school at 16 and has been an air stewardess, secretary at the OECD in Paris and a mature student at university, earning a BA and MA. She has published poems in The Imperial War Museum, London, women's magazines, small presses, and has had two stories broadcast by BBC Radio. She works backstage as tour guide at the Theatre Royal.

Karen Greenbaum-Maya is a clinical psychologist in private practice in Claremont, California. She earned her B.A. at Reed College in German Language and Literature, and her Ph. D. in Psychology at the California School of Professional Psychology. She has reviewed restaurants for the *Claremont Courier*, sometimes in verse. Her poems have appeared in *Spring Harvest*, and will appear in *Untamed Ink*. More photos appear in www.fotolog.com/pieplate.

Stephen D. Gutierrez is the author of *Elements*, a short-story collection that was award the Nilon Excellence in Minority Fiction Award, and of the chapbook *The Barbershop*. He is Director of Creative Writing at California State University, East Bay.

Lauren Guza grew up in a suburb of Los Angeles, writing and eating with enthusiasm. She received her B.A. from Middlebury College and taught high school English and ESL with Teach for America. She currently lives in Berkeley and is pursuing her interests in literature, public education, and blueberry pancakes.

Gary R. Hoffman taught English and Speech/Drama for 22 years. He quit teaching over 20 years ago to go into business for himself. He now lives in a motor home and says, "Home is where you park it!" He travels the North American continent, with Sandy and their cat, Callie, and attempts to stay in moderate climates. He has over two hundred short stories published in anthologies, e-zines, and magazines. He has also won many awards for his short stories.

Sonya Huber is an assistant professor of creative writing at Georgia Southern University. Her book, *Opa Nobody* (University of Nebraska Press, 2008), is a family memoir and multi-genre exploration of German and

American activism. Her work has appeared in many literary journals and anthologies. More information is available at www.sonyahuber.com.

Christine Huynh graduated from San Diego State University with an MFA in Creative Writing. Her poems have been published in *Border Voices Anthology, City Works Anthology, Lake Effect, LA Miscellany,* and other publications. She can be found in Los Angeles writing, perusing used bookstores, and singing karaoke badly.

Sara Irene's dreams of a writing career began when her grandfather bought the first (and only) copy of a "book" she wrote at the age of 7. Since that time she has published fiction, poetry, and creative nonfiction essays in both print and web-based literary journals. She will complete her B.A. in English at SDSU in August 2008. She currently resides in San Diego, CA, with her boyfriend and two turtles.

Donna Isaac has taught high school English for 30 years. She holds an M.F.A. from Hamline University, where her thesis won Outstanding Poetry Thesis for 2007.

Harold Jaffe is the author of nine fiction (or "docufiction") collections, four novels, and a collection of creative nonfiction. Titles include: *Beasts, Dos Indios, Eros Anti-Eros, Terror-dot-Gov, Straight Razor, Madonna and Other Spectacles, Sex for the Millennium, 15 Serial Killers, Mourning Crazy Horse, Beyond the Techno-Cave: A Guerrilla Writer's Guide to Post-Millennial Fiction. Jesus Coyote.* His fiction and creative nonfiction have been anthologized in *Pushcart Prize, Best American Stories, Best of American Humor, Storming the Reality Studio, American Made, Avant Pop: Fiction for a Daydreaming Nation, After Yesterday's Crash,* and elsewhere. His writings have been translated into German, Japanese, Spanish, Italian, French, Polish, and Czech. He has won two National Endowment awards in fiction, a California Arts Council grant in fiction, a New York State CAPS grant in fiction, and two Fulbright grants: to India and to Prague. Jaffe is editor-in-chief of the literary/cultural journal *Fiction International* and Professor of Literature and Creative Writing at San Diego State University.

Kim Jensen's first novel, *The Woman I Left Behind,* was published in 2006 by Curbstone Press. In 2001, Jensen (www.kimjensen.org) won the Raymond Carver Prize for Short Fiction, and her writings have appeared or are forthcoming in *Liberation Literature, Coe Review, Poetic Voices without Borders 2; Rain Taxi Review;* and *Left Curve* among many others. Jensen currently teaches writing and literature in Baltimore, and is an editor for the *Baltimore Review*.

Ilya Kaminsky is the author of *Dancing in Odessa* (Tupelo Press) which won the Whiting Writers Award, the Dorset Prize, American Academy of Arts & Letters Metcalf Award, and was named the "Best Poetry Book of 2005" by *ForeWord Magazine*.

K. Nadine Kavanaugh received her Master of Fine Arts in Fiction Writing from Columbia University in October 2003, and has taught composition, literature, and creative writing courses at Columbia University, Yeshiva University, Ursinus College, University of the Arts and the Delaware College of Art and Design. She is currently working as a Staff Writer at the University of Pennsylvania. Her undergraduate degree is from the University of Chicago, where she received special honors for her collection of short stories. During the summer of 2003, she was a resident at the Woodstock Guild's Byrdcliffe Arts Colony. She has published stories on www.NYCBigCityLit.com and www.slackfaith.com, and her story "The Way Maria Moved" appeared in the April 2005 issue of *Ellipsis*.

Barbara Kingsolver's twelve books of fiction, poetry, and creative nonfiction include the novels *The Bean Trees* and *The Poisonwood Bible*. Translated into more than 20 languages, her work has won a devoted worldwide readership and many awards, including the National Humanities Medal. Her most recent book is *Animal, Vegetable, Miracle: A Year of Food Life*, co-written with her husband, Steven L. Hopp, and daughter, Camille Kingsolver. Before becoming a full-time writer she received a graduate degree in biology. She lives with her family on a farm in Southwest Virginia.

Janet R. Kirchheimer's book of poems about the Holocaust, *How to Spot One of Us*, was published by CLAL, (Fall 2007). Her work has appeared in *Atlanta Review, Potomac Review, Kalliope, Lilith, Natural Bridge, PoetryNZ, Main Street Rag, Alimentum*, Beliefnet.com and babelfruit.com. Janet was nominated for a Pushcart Poetry Prize in 2007. She teaches adults and teens about Judaism using poetry and creative writing, and leads a "Poetry Shmooze" for seniors.

Cheryl Klein's first book *The Commuters: A Novel of Intersections* won City Works Press' Ben Reitman Award and was published in 2006. Her fiction has appeared in journals including *other*, *CrossConnect* and *The Absinthe Literary Review*. An alumna of UCLA and Cal Arts, she works in the California office of Poets & Writers, Inc., lives in Los Angeles and has been a guilty pescatarian for many years.

Steve Kowit was an animal rights activist for several years. His latest books are *The Gods of Rapture* (City Works Press) and *The First Noble Truth* (U Tampa Press). He lives with his wife Mary, seven cats and one dog in the back country hills near the Mexican border.

Kathryn Law has been painting professionally since 2003. After receiving a Masters in French with an emphasis in art history from UC Berkeley, she completed a BFA at Oregon State University, where she received a full merit scholarship for painting. Her work has appeared in many shows and juried exhibitions, as well as private and corporate collections. She currently lives and paints in San Diego and can be reached through http://kathrynlaw.blogspot.com.

Li-Young Lee is the author of three critically acclaimed books of poetry, his most recent being *Book of My Nights* (BOA Editions, 2001). His earlier collections are *Rose* (BOA, 1986), winner of the Delmore Schwartz Memorial Award from New York University; *The City in Which I Love You* (BOA, 1991), the 1990 Lamont Poetry Selection; and a memoir entitled *The Winged Seed: A Remembrance* (Simon and Schuster, 1995), which received an American Book Award from the Before Columbus Foundation. A new volume, *Behind My Eyes*, is forthcoming by W.W. Norton in January 2008. He lives in Chicago with his wife Donna and their two sons.

Sylvia Levinson's publishing credits include *Snowy Egret, Blue Arc West, City Works, San Diego Writers Ink, Poetic Matrix, Christian Science Monitor,* and *Magee Park*. Writing awards: City Works, 2007, American Society on Aging, San Diego African-American Writers and Artists, Inc. Her book, *Gateways: Poems of Nature, Meditation and Renewal,* was published by Caernarvon Press. www.sylvialevinson.com.

Bethellen Levitan is an interdisciplinary artist working with words, paint, and clay. She is the author of two chapbooks, *Scenic Route* (1996), and *Through the Glass* (2001), and her writing has appeared in numerous small press publications. She lives and works San Francisco and Willits, California.

Janice Levy is author of eleven children's books, winner of Writer's Digest Competition for Best Literary Short Story three times, and her work has appeared in *Glimmer Train*, *Alaska Quarterly*, *Iowa Review*, and *Story Quarterly*, among others.

Cali Linfor is a native Californian and has been the poetry editor of *Epicenter*, a literary magazine based in Southern California, since 1994. She is a graduate of San Diego State University's MFA in Creative Writing. She has been published in *The Beloit Poetry Journal*.

Luciana Lopez is the pop music critic at the *Oregonian* in Portland, Ore. She's lived in Japan and Brazil, and hopes to live abroad again someday. Her journalism, creative non-fiction and fiction have appeared in a number of journals. She loves takoyaki.

Susan Luzzaro has published two books of poetry *Complicity* and *Flesh Envelope*. Her essays have appeared in *Crab Orchard Review*, *Healing Muse*, *Puerto del Sol*, *Under the Sun* and *The San Diego Reader*. She lives in Chula Vista with her family.

Katharyn Howd Machan, professor in the Department of Writing at Ithaca College, is the author of 28 published collections, most recently *The Professor Poems* (Main Street Rag Publishing Company, 2008) and *Flags* (Pudding House Publications, 2007). Despite Ithaca's excellent Farmers' Market, she does indeed detest beets. "The Beets Poem" first appeared in *HANGING LOOSE* magazine.

Krista Madsen is the author of two novels (*Degas Must Have Loved a Dancer* and *Four Corners*, both out by Livingston Press), a writing instructor at NYU and Gotham Writers' Workshop, and the sole proprietor of Stain arts/wine lounge in her neighborhood of Williamsburg, Brooklyn.

Mary Makofske is the author of *The Disappearance of Gargoyles* (Thorntree) and *Eating Nasturtiums*, winner of a Flume Press chapbook competition. Her poems have appeared in *Poetry*, *Zone 3*, *Mississippi Review*, *Flint Hills Review*, *Quadrant*, *Calyx*, and other magazines and in the anthologies *In a Fine Frenzy: Poets Respond to Shakespeare* (Iowa), *Proposing on the Brooklyn Bridge* (Grayson), and *Tangled Vines*, 2nd ed. (Harcourt Brace).

Nadia Mandilawi has lived in San Diego since 2000. She has an MFA in Creative Writing from San Diego State University and is an Assistant Professor of English at San Diego City College.

Alys Masek is a public interest attorney living in San Diego. Previous publications include *Noe Valley Review* and *City Works*. She has a collection of over 500 hundred cookbooks and when she is not reading them, she enjoys haunting farmers' markets (especially free-sample booths).

Rochelle Mass is Canadian born and has lived in Israel since 1973, most of the time in Kibbutz Beit HaShita. She now lives in a small community crawling up the western flank of the Gilboa Mountains. She has three poetry collections including *The Startled Land*, by Wind River Press.

Trissy McGhee lives in San Diego. Her work has appeared in *Sunshine/Noir: Writings from San Diego and Tijuana* (City Works Press) and *Parting Gifts*.

Mimi Moriarty is the producer and host of "Write Stuff," a cable access TV program in the Albany, NY, area. Her short fiction, poems, essays and articles have been published in many journals, magazines and newspapers, including *Margie, Alehouse, SLAB, Thema, Rockhurst Review, Connecticut Review, Peregrine* and *Irish America*. She holds an MFA in Creative Writing from Goddard College and teaches creative writing to adults and teens. Her chapbook of 23 poems about the aftermath of war, *War Psalm*, was published by Finishing Line Press in 2007.

Sue Parman is an anthropologist (http://anthro.fullerton.edu/sparman/) who loves to travel, and whose goal is to publish in as many different genres as possible, from poetry, crime, and science fiction to historical literary fiction and playwrighting. She has a beloved husband and daughter, a wok, and no cats.

Amy Paul is a San Diego native who studied at the University of San Diego, receiving a degree in Humanities and later her MA in Art History. She is currently a resident of North Park, where she contributes to a thriving art community. Learn more about her work at www.artbyamypaul.com.

Andrea Potos is the author of two poetry collections: *Yaya's Cloth* (Iris Press) and *The Perfect Day* (Parallel Press). Her poems appear widely in journals and anthologies. She lives in Madison, Wisconsin, with her husband and daughter.

Terrie Leigh Relf and her daughter Willow Katsumi Relf-Discartin recently received a Rhysling nomination for their poem, "Space Envelopes," which originally appeared in *Sporty Spec*. Recent releases from Sam's Dot Publishing include *The Poet's Workshop — and Beyond* (March 2008), *Blood Journey* (April 2008), a vampire novel co-authored with Henry Lewis Sanders, and *My Friend, the Poet, and other poems about people I think I know* (May 2008).

Carlos Reyes is a noted poet and translator whose latest poetry book is *At the Edge of the Western Wave* (Lost Horse Press, 2004). At present he is fine-tuning his *New and Selected Poems*. His most recent translation: *La Señal del Cuervo / The Sign of the Crow* by Mexican poet Ignacio Ruiz-Pérez is due out from Eastern Washington University Press in 2009.

Susan Rich is author of *Cures Include Travel* (White Pine Press, 2006) and *The Cartographer's Tongue / Poems of the World*, winner of the PEN USA Award for Poetry, and the Peace Corps Writers Award for Best Poetry Book. She has been a staff person for Amnesty International, an electoral supervisor in Bosnia, and a human rights trainer in Gaza. Her poems have been translated into Slovenian.

Karen Rigby received a 2007 literature fellowship from the National Endowment for the Arts. Her second chapbook, *Savage Machinery*, has been accepted by Finishing Line Press. *Festival Bone* is available from Adastra Press.

Susan Richardson is a writer and tutor of writing based in Wales. Her collection of poetry, *Creatures of the Intertidal Zone*, inspired by her journey through Iceland, Greenland and Newfoundland in the footsteps of an intrepid tenth century female Viking, has just been published by Cinnamon Press.

Elizabeth Schott has a doctorate in Art History from UC Berkeley and taught art history and writing for 12 years at Berkeley, USC, and UCSB. Her work has been nominated for the Pushcart prize and has appeared or is forthcoming in numerous literary journals including *North American Review, South Carolina Review, California Quarterly, Illuminations* and several anthologies. She currently works as a Poet in the Schools and writes for the *Santa Barbara Independent*.

Barry Seiler has published four books of poetry. His most recent book *Frozen Falls* was a finalist for the Paterson Poetry Prize. He lives in a very small town in the Catskills with his wife, three cats, and a cockatiel.

Vivian Shipley is the Connecticut State University Distinguished Professor and the Editor of *Connecticut Review* from Southern Connecticut State University. She has published five chapbooks and her seventh book of poems *Hardboot: Poems New & Old* (Southeastern Louisiana University Press, 2005) won the 2006 Paterson Prize for Sustained Literary Achievement and the 2006 Connecticut Press Club Prize for Best Creative Writing. In 2007, she was inducted into the University of Kentucky Distinguished Alumni Hall of Fame and won the Hackney Literary Award for Poetry from Birmingham-Southern University in Alabama and the *New Millennium* Poetry Prize. A new book of poetry *All of Your Message Have Been Erased* is forthcoming from Southeastern Louisiana University Press.

Leon Stokesbury teaches in the graduate writing program at Georgia State University in Atlanta. His first book *Often in Different Landscapes* was a co-winner of the first AWP Poetry Competition in 1975 and was published the following year by the University of Texas Press. His *Autumn Rhythm: New & Selected Poems* (University of Arkansas Press) was awarded The Poets' Prize for the best book of poems published by an American in 1996.

Alison Stone's poems have appeared in *The Paris Review, Poetry, Ploughshares*, and a variety of other journals and anthologies. She has been awarded *Poetry's* Frederick Bock Prize and *New York Quarterly's* Madeline Sadin award. Her first book *They Sing at Midnight* won the 2003 Many Mountains Moving Poetry Award and was published by Many Mountains Moving Press. She is also a visual artist and the creator of The Stone Tarot.

Flavia Tamayo earned her MFA from California State University at Long Beach. Her poetry has appeared in *Nerve Cowboy, Puerto del Sol, CRATE, RipRap*, and in the anthology *Sunshine Noir: Writings from San Diego and Tijuana* (City Works Press). She is also an English instructor at Los

Angeles City College where she teaches creative writing, composition, and literature. She is married to photographer Mario Romero.

Elizabeth Tibbetts' book *In the Well* (2003) won the Bluestem Poetry Award. Her work has appeared in journals such as: *The American Scholar, Prairie Schooner, Green Mountains Review, and Northwest Review.*

Ray Trautman is a Chemistry Professor at San Francisco State University and enjoys cooking, especially on a backpacking stove. His photographs have been shown at Other Avenues in San Francisco, where his salsa made him famous.

Ivy Warwick was born in Poland and came to this country when she was 17. Her publications include *Poetry, Ploughshares, Best American Poetry 1992, Nimrod, The Iowa Review, Texas Review, Wisconsin Review, Southern Poetry Review*, and many other journals and anthologies. She has worked as a college instructor and a journalist. Currently she is a private instructor. She lives in Chula Vista.

Donna J. Watson teaches writing and literature at San Diego City College and is a founding member and editor of *City Works Press*. She was honored at the 2008 KUUMBA fest for community service as an artist/ educator. Publications include *Nommogeneity* and *Sunshine Noir*. Performance work includes *Lavanderia, F-Stop,* and *Uncommon Grounds*. When not teaching she spends time on her farm in Bucks County, PA, planting and cultivating food for her family and community. *Makin' Groceries* is part of that harvest.

Alia Yunis is a PEN Emerging Voices fellow who has just completed her first novel *The Night Counter*. A screenplay version of her award-winning short story "A Minnesota Christmas" was a 2008 Top Ten finalist in Francis Ford Coppola's American Zoetrope screenplay competition. Alia's work has appeared in several publications, including the *Los Angeles Times, Angeleno* and *Saveur*.

Joseph Zaccardi is a Fairfax, CA, poet whose poems "float like a flotilla of dragonflies" over the hard situations of life. His language is like a river: malleable and ever changing. His poetry has most recently appeared in *The Southern Poetry Review* and *Runes: A Review of Poetry*. His book *Vents* was published in 2005.

Al Zolynas' books include *The New Physics* (Wesleyan University Press, 1979), *Under Ideal Conditions* (Laterthanever Press, 1994), winner of the San Diego Book Award, Best Poetry, 1994, and *The Same Air* (Intercultural Studies Forum, 1997). Six poems were recently featured in the movie, *Fighting Words* (Indican Pictures, Los Angeles, 2006). A longtime Zen practitioner, he teaches at Alliant International University, San Diego, and lives with his wife in Escondido.

Credits

The editors would like to thank all those who gave us permission for their written material to appear in this book. We made every effort to research and contact copyright holders. If an omission or error has occurred, we apologize.

We would especially like to thank those writers we originally thought to invite to be contributors as the idea for this book took shape: Kim Addonizio, Edward Espe Brown, Denise Chávez, Marilyn Chin, Mark Dery, Harold Jaffe, Ilya Kaminsky, Barbara Kingsolver, Cheryl Klein, Steve Kowit, Li-Young Lee, and Al Zolynas.

Eat, Memory

"Chocolate Hearts" by Ivy Warwick. First published in *Wisconsin Review*. © 1989 by Ivy Warwick. Reprinted by permission of the author.

"Eating Together," "Eating Alone," and "The Cleaving" by Li-Young Lee, from *Rose*. ©1986 by Li-Young Lee. Reprinted with the permission of BOA Editions, Ltd., www.boaeditions.org.

"Pear Tree," by Sharon DeBusk. Reprinted by permission of the artist.

"Manteca Vieja" by Denise Chávez . From *A Taco Testimony*. © 2006 by Denise Chavez. Reprinted with permission of the publisher Rio Nuevo Publishers.

"The God of Hunger" by Sonya Huber. Adapted from *Opa Nobody* by Sonya Huber by permission of the University of Nebraska Press. © 2008 by the Board of Regents of the University of Nebraska.

"Bread and Gratitude" by Al Zolynas. Reprinted by permission of the author.

At the Kitchen Table

The Blessings of Dirty Work

"Gardening with My Father" by Janet Kirchheimer. First published in *Potomac Review, issue 40*. Reprinted by permission of the author.

"The Harvest" by Dan Brook. Reprinted by permission of the artist.

"Burdock" by Corie Feiner. Reprinted by permission of the author.

"Delivery" by Mary Chang. Reprinted by permission of the author.

"The Weird Vegetarian Poem" by Elizabeth Schott. Reprinted by permission of the author.

"Children, Growing in a Vacant Lot" by Mary Makofske. Reprinted by permission of the author.

"The Blessings of Dirty Work" by Barbara Kingsolver. © 2007 Barbara Kingsolver. First published in the *Washington Post*. Reprinted by permission of the author.

"A Day at the Market" by Olivia Chin. Reprinted by permission of the artist.

"Served" by Kim Addonizio. First published in *Nightsun*. Reprinted by permission of the author.

"Thursday Dinner" by Donna Isaac. Reprinted by permission of the author.

"Long Shelf Life" by Kim Jensen. Reprinted by permission of the author.

"Makin' Groceries" by Donna Watson. Reprinted by permission of the author.

"Borrowing Breath" by Terrie Relf. Reprinted by permission of the author.

"The Lesson" by Flavia Tamayo. Reprinted by permission of the author.

"Bringing Home Dinner" by Lisa Gavin. Reprinted by permission of the artist.

"The Last Table: an Entry from a Waiter's Journal" by Chris Baron. Reprinted by permission of the author.

Song

"After Enlightenment, There is Yam Gruel" by Marilyn Chin. First published in *The Harvard Review*. Reprinted by permission of the author.

"*from* Musica Humana" by Ilya Kaminsky. See earlier credit under **Eat, Memory**.

"Song for the Onion" by Karen Rigby will appear in forthcoming *Savage Machinery*. © 2008 Finishing Line Press. Reprinted by permission of the author.

"Piute" by Carlos Reyes. From *A Suitcase Full of Crows*. © 1995 by Carlos Reyes. *Bluestem Press*. Reprinted by permission of the author.

"Air Wasn't Air" by Krista Madsen. From *Urban Folk* and *Driftwood*. Reprinted by permission of the author.

"Sacred Fruit" by Amy Paul. Reprinted by permission of the artist.

"Lace" by Brandel France de Bravo will appear in *Provenance*. © 2008 Washington Writers' Publishing House. Reprinted by permission of the author.

"Celebrating Humus" by Rochelle Mass. From *The Startled Land*. © 2003 by Rochelle Mass. Wind River Press. Reprinted by permission of the author.

"A Political Poem" by Al Zolynas. *The New Physics*. Reprinted by permission of the author.

"The Legacy" by Leon Stokesbury. From *Autumn Rhythm: New & Selected Poems* © 1996 by Leon Stokesbury. University of Arkansas Press. Reprinted by permission of the author.

"Spoon" by Sylvia Levinson. Reprinted by permission of the author.

"Cookery Book" by Heather Grange. Reprinted by permission of the author.

"To the Coffee Shop" by Andrea Potos. From *Yaya's Cloth* © 2007 Iris Press. Reprinted by permission of the author.

My Body Knows

"My Body Knows the Four Colors of Corn" by Cali Linfor. Reprinted by permission of the author.

"Bertie Stiles Searches for Answers: Winter the Cow Died, Crossroads, West Virginia, 1918" by Jeanne Bryner. Reprinted by permission of the author.

"Pumpkins and Squash en Clair et en Obscur" by Karen Greenbaum-Maya. Reprinted by permission of the artist.

"The Difference between a Horror Film and a Scary Movie" by Sydney Brown. Reprinted by permission of the author.

"First Christmas Single" by Jennifer Chapis. First published in *Thin Air,* Northern Arizona University. Reprinted by permission of the author.

"Pear Able Less" by Jeff Crouch. Reprinted by permission of the artist.

"The Cleaving" by Li-Young Lee. See earlier credit under **Eat, Memory**.

"Wendigo" by Susan Richardson. Reprinted by permission of the author.

"Hunger" by Ronda Broatch. Previously published in *Pontoon #7*. Floating Bridge Press. © 2004. Reprinted by permission of the author.

A Little Poison, Along with the Sweetness

"Vons" by Josh Baxt. Reprinted by permission of the author.

"The Promise of Trout" by Nancy Cary. Reprinted by permission of the author.

"Cooking For Life" by Mike Ferrill. First published in *City Works Literary Anthology* © 2007. Reprinted by permission of author.

"Meeting Over Coconut Drinks" by Olivia Chin. Reprinted by permission of the artist.

"On the Plate" by Christine Huynh. Reprinted by permission of the author.

Editor Nancy Cary

Nancy Cary's feature stories have appeared in *San Diego CityBeat* and *San Diego Magazine*. She's published articles, reviews, and columns in *The San Diego Reader, Rattle,* and *Let's Talk Plants* as well as poetry, fiction, and personal essays in other publications. She is especially proud of her *CityBeat* cover story "MMMMM...Cruelty" and is grateful to *CB's* editors for trusting in her writing. She continues to be inspired by the founders of the Animal Protection Rescue League, who have fought to end the production and serving of foie gras. An alumna of the University of Oregon and San Diego State University's MFA program, Nancy teaches Creative Nonfiction and other English courses at San Diego City College. She lives in Ocean Beach with her family.

Co-editors

Left to right: **Alys Masek** is a practicing attorney, eclectic gourmet, and poet; **Trissy McGhee** is a fiction writer, teacher, and world hiker; **Ella deCastro Baron**, poet and fiction writer, mothers, teaches, and surfs with her husband Chris; and **June Cressy**, personal essayist and poet, practices Zen meditation at the Zen Center of San Diego, pets her 20-year-old cat Cactus, and sits at the ocean when she's not practicing counter-culture — her next book — at San Diego City College.